From One Leader to Another

Command Sergeant Major Joe B. Parson
General Editor

Carl W. Fischer
Combat Studies Institute Editor

Combat Studies Institute Press
US Army Combined Arms Center
Fort Leavenworth, Kansas

If your actions inspire others to dream more, learn more, do more and become more, you are a leader.

                                          -John Quincy Adams

Foreword

The Combat Studies Institute along with Command Sergeant Major Joe B. Parson of the Combined Arms Center (Leader Development & Education) at Fort Leavenworth is pleased to present "From One Leader to Another."

This work is a collection of observations, insights, and advice from over 50 serving and retired Senior Non-Commissioned Officers. These experienced Army leaders have provided for the reader, outstanding mentorship on leadership skills, tasks, and responsibilities relevant to our Army today. There is much wisdom and advice "from one leader to another" in the following pages.

CSI - The Past is Prologue!

Roderick M. Cox
Colonel, US Army
Director, Combat Studies Institute

Table of Contents

Foreword iii
Contributors v
Introduction vii
Section 1: Skills 1
Section 2: Tasks 197
Section 3: Responsibilities 343
Closing Thoughts 383

Contributors

SGM Dave Abbott
CSM Erik Arne
CSM Robert Austin
SGM Stanley J. Balcer
CSM Kevin Bryan
CSM Carlos Medina Castellano
CSM Sheldon Chandler
CSM Brunk W. Conley
CSM Joanne Cox
CSM John Crenshaw
CSM Roger Daigle
CSM(R) Robert Dare
CSM David Davenport
CSM Dennis Eger
CSM Allen Fritzsching
CSM Christopher K. Greca
MSG (P) Garrick Griffin
CSM Naamon Grimmett
CSM Blaine Harvey
CSM Frederick Heard
MSG Kevin Henderson
CSM Jeremiah Inman
CSM Joseph Jacobs
CSM Clifton Johnson
CSM(R) David J. Litteral

SGM Craig T. Lott
CSM Marc L. Maynard
CSM Norman McAfee
CSM Christopher J. Menton
CSM Chip E. Mezzaline
CSM Dwight Morrisey
CSM John L. Murray
CSM James Norman
SGM Sam S. Oak
CSM Mark H. Oldroyd
CSM Ronald Orosz
CSM Joe B. Parson
SGM(R) Dennis W. Paxton
CSM Ronald Riling
SGM Tony A. G. Romero
SGM Don Rose
SGM(R) Toni Gagnon Ross
CSM Charles V. Sasser Jr.
CSM Fritz U. Smith
SGM Dave Stewart
CSM Richard D. Stidley
CSM Kevin B. Stuart
CSM John Wayne Troxell
CSM James VanSciver
CSM Michael Williamson
CSM Shelton R. Williamson
CSM Sam Young
SGM Alma L. Zeladaparedes

From One Leader to Another
SMA Raymond F. Chandler III

Our Army is in the midst of considerable change, and over the next few years we must be prepared for a smaller force and a smaller budget. As Non-Commissioned officers, that means our roles will become more important, and that the Soldiers we lead will have to be more disciplined and take on more responsibility. Some may see these reductions as bleak, but I prefer to see it as an exciting and challenging time to be an Army NCO and leader.

As you know, these changes mean our units will have to become more self-sufficient, relying on the eight-step training model and leaders must know how to plan, resource and evaluate. This will also require us to be wise stewards of everything provided by the American public, including our budgets, equipment, facilities, and most importantly, their sons and daughters.

The Chief of Staff of the Army's "Marching Orders-Waypoint #1" lists leader expectations that include being a moral and ethical compass and the ability to adapt and develop high-performing teams — all expectations that are embodied by the NCO Creed.

Each of us must take those words and internalize them. This is who we are, and this is what we must aspire to be -- the example, the role model, the mentor, the leader that our creed describes and that the American public expects. Even if you don't seek it, those stripes on your shoulder mean others will look to you for advice, guidance, mentorship and support.

The NCO Creed says no one is more professional than a noncommissioned officer. As the Army moves toward 2020, that means NCOs will have to remain broadly skilled and be prepared to take on more responsibility. The Army is going to ask us to be that critical and creative thinker, that adaptive and agile leader. Most importantly we will need to be grounded in the traditional role of the NCO, and that's about accomplishing missions and taking care of Soldiers.

I often talk about "engaged leadership" which allows us to learn more about those Soldiers we lead. This interaction allows us to find out what events are happening in their lives. A long time ago a retired Command Sergeant Major told me something that has always stuck with me: "Every Soldier should have an NCO checking on him or her every day." That's engaged leadership, and that's the leadership we'll need to fix these problems.

Are you engaged with the Soldiers who look to you for guidance? Do you have a leader book? Do you provide good sponsorship when they arrive and timely counseling when needed and required? Do you create opportunities for your Soldiers to come together and develop esprit de corps? Do you encourage your Soldiers to seek help when you see their resilience is challenged? Do you leave your office and meetings to interact with your Soldiers regularly? These are some of the hallmarks of an engaged leader.

But, we cannot only look to the past for "best practices". We must also use today's tools and information to make our leadership efforts more effective and efficient. For instance, do you use a printed leader book like I had when I was a squad leader, or is yours an app on your smartphone? Do you see every Soldier in our formation for the talent they can bring to your unit and the Army, or do you see them only as males or females? The bottom line is that you have to consider all options to best support everyone on your team, the mission and the future for our Army.

Part of that caretaker role is leading by example and ensuring that the principles of the Warrior Ethos are upheld at all times. Do you take your APFT with your Soldiers, make the tough decisions that our Army Values require, and enforce standards and discipline when you see problems? Sometimes you will make mistakes, but that should not stop you from doing what is expected of a leader.

Being a leader does not mean being zero-defect. In fact, making mistakes should be expected and seen as an opportunity to learn. But don't stop there; we need to share what we have learned with others, including those we lead. Our example will encourage others to do the same.

This same approach is the reason the Army created its Multi-Source Assessment and Feedback website, sometimes referred to as a "360 evaluation." These evaluations provide both surveys and assessments to assist us in leadership self-development by asking peers, superiors and subordinates to evaluate us. It can be a humbling and surprising experience for many leaders to read what others say about us, but it is necessary since many of us are sometimes blinded by our misperceptions or fears to see our own weaknesses and strengths. Our willingness to overcome those fears and learn from others will likely inspire those we lead.

Your efforts to develop tomorrow's leaders will be supported by our ongoing Army Profession campaign. I expect all NCO leaders will incorporate the tools and resources provided at the Center for Army Profession and Ethic website (cape.army.mil/aaop) into their NCO development training. This campaign includes quarterly themes and five essential characteristics that define us as professionals.

Here's one example of that professionalism that I experienced last year when I traveled to a small combat outpost in Afghanistan called Bari Alai. This remote, platoon-sized camp sits high atop a mountain, and the only way to get on or off this outpost is by helicopter. On top of this mountain, I met the 3rd Platoon, Company A, 1st Battalion, 12th Infantry Regiment, 4th Brigade Combat Team, 4th Infantry Division. During the visit, I had the privilege of awarding them the brigade's first Combat Infantry and Combat Action Badges. These eight young men—five infantry Soldiers, two generator mechanics and one cook—had never deployed before. Most were under 21, yet they decisively engaged the enemy less than 24 hours after arriving at the outpost. The enemy knew that the platoons were rotating and decided to test their defenses, but 3rd Platoon was ready. They repelled the attack and, just as important, sustained no injuries during the firefight. It's a testament to that young platoon leader, who had been with the platoon less than a month before deploying and ensured his Soldiers were ready for combat. It's a testament to that platoon sergeant, who ensured his Soldiers, regardless of military occupational specialty, were trained in their Warrior Tasks and Battle Drills. And of course, it's a testament to the young men who comprise 3rd Platoon. Each had given the same oath: to support and defend the Constitution. Each lives the Army Values: Loyalty, Duty, Respect, Selfless Service, Honor, Integrity and Personal Courage. Each lives the Warrior Ethos: I will always place the mission first, I will never quit, I will never accept defeat and I will never leave a fallen comrade. This platoon is just one example of the type of professionals who make up our Army today, and who will become the leaders of our Army tomorrow.

I thank the Combined Arms Center for producing this document and thank the authors of the numerous papers for initiating a discussion of leadership among our NCO Corps. I encourage every enlisted leader to take lessons learned here and put them in your kit bag.

Section 1

Skills

From One Leader to Another
The Army Values
Command Sergeant Major John Crenshaw

"The Army Values are the basic building blocks of an Army professional's character. They help us judge what is right or wrong in any situation. The Army Values form the very identity of the Army, the solid rock on which everything else stands, especially in combat. They are the glue that binds together the members of a noble profession."

— (*ADRP* 1)

Values tell us what we need to be every day, in every action we take. Army Values form the identity of America's Army, the solid rock on which everything else stands. They are the glue that binds us together as members of a noble profession. The following definitions can help you understand Army Values, but understanding is only the first step. As a Soldier, you must not only understand them; you must believe in them, model them in your own actions and teach others to accept and live by them.

LOYALTY: To bear true faith and allegiance to the US Constitution, the Army, your unit, and other Soldiers. Loyalty is the big thing, the greatest battle asset of all. But no man ever wins the loyalty of troops by preaching loyalty. It is given to him as he proves his possession of the other virtues. Loyalty is a two-way street: you should not expect loyalty without being prepared to give it as well. You can neither demand loyalty nor win it from other people by talking about it. The loyalty of your peers is a gift they give you when, and only when, you deserve it—when you show your competence, treat people fairly, and live by the concepts you talk about. Soldiers who are loyal to their peers and the unit never let them down. Soldiers fight for each other—loyalty is commitment. The most important way of earning this loyalty is performing well in combat. There's no loyalty fiercer than that of Soldiers who trust each other to make it through the dangers of combat as a team. However, loyalty extends to all members of our profession—to your superiors and subordinates, as well as your peers.

DUTY: Fulfill your obligations. The essence of duty is acting in the absence of orders or direction from others, based on an inner sense of what is morally and professionally right. Duty begins with everything required of you by law, regulation, and orders; but it includes much more than that. Professionals do their work not just to the minimum standard, but to the very best of their ability. Soldiers commit to excellence in all aspects of their professional responsibility so that when the job is done they can look back and say, "I couldn't have given any more." Soldiers should always take the initiative, figuring out what needs to be done before being told what to do. What's more, they take full responsibility for their actions and those of their subordinates. Soldiers should never shade the truth to make the unit look good—or even to make their teammates feel good. Instead, they follow their higher duty to the Army and the nation.

RESPECT: Treat people as they should be treated. This discipline is what makes the Soldiers of a free country reliable in battle. He who feels the respect which is due to others cannot fail to inspire in them regard for himself. Conversely, he who feels, and hence, manifests disrespect toward others, especially his subordinates, cannot fail to inspire hatred against himself. Respect for the individual forms the basis for the rule of law, the very essence of what makes America. In the Army, respect means recognizing and appreciating the inherent dignity and worth of all people. This value reminds you that people are the Army's greatest resource. Soldiers should always honor everyone's individual worth by treating all people with dignity and respect. Everyone who serves with this profession deserves respect no matter their uniform or dress.

SELFLESS SERVICE: Place the welfare of the nation, the Army and subordinates before your own. The nation today needs men and women who think in terms of service to their country and not in terms of their country's debt to them. You have often heard the military referred to as "the service." As a member of the Army, you serve the United States. Selfless service means doing what's right for the nation, the Army, your organization and your teammates—and putting these responsibilities above your own interests. The needs of the Army and the nation come first. This doesn't mean that you neglect your Family or yourself; in fact, such neglect weakens a Soldier and can cause the Army more harm than good. Selfless service doesn't mean that you can't have a strong ego, high self-esteem or even healthy ambition. Rather, selfless service means that you don't make decisions or take actions that help your image or your career but hurt others or sabotage the mission. We must function as a team and for a team to work the individual must surrender their self-interest for the greater good of the whole.

HONOR: Live up to all of the Army Values. What is life without honor? Degradation is worse than death. Honor provides the "moral compass" for character and personal conduct in the Army. Though many people struggle to define the term, most recognize instinctively those with a keen sense of right and wrong, those who live such that their words and deeds are above reproach. The expression "honorable person," therefore, refers to both the character traits an individual actually possesses and the fact that the community recognizes and respects them. Honor holds Army Values together while at the same time being a value in and of itself. Honor means demonstrating an understanding of what's right and taking pride in the community's acknowledgment of that reputation.

INTEGRITY: Do what's right—legally and morally. The American people rightly look to their military leaders not only to be skilled in the technical aspects of the profession of arms, but also to be men and women of integrity. People of integrity consistently act according to principles—not just what might work at the moment. Soldiers with integrity make their principles known and consistently act in accordance with them. The Army requires leaders of integrity who possess high moral standards and are honest in word and deed. Being honest means being truthful and upright all the time, despite pressures to do otherwise. Having integrity means being both morally complete and true to oneself. As a Soldier, you are honest to yourself by committing to and consistently living the Army Values; you're honest to others by not presenting yourself or your actions as anything other than what they are. Soldiers should always say what they mean and do what they say. If you can't accomplish a mission, inform your chain of command. If you inadvertently pass on bad information, correct it as soon as you find out it's wrong. People of integrity do the right thing not because it's convenient or because they have no choice. They choose the right thing because their character permits nothing less. Conducting yourself with integrity has three parts:

- Separating what's right from what's wrong.

- Always acting according to what you know to be right, even at a personal cost.

- Saying openly that you're acting on your understanding of right versus wrong.

PERSONAL COURAGE: Face fear, danger, or adversity (physical or moral). Personal courage isn't the absence of fear; rather, it's the ability to put fear aside and do what's necessary. It takes two forms, physical and moral. Good Soldiers demonstrate both. Physical courage means overcoming fears of bodily harm and doing your duty. It's the bravery that allows a Soldier to take risks in combat in spite of the fear of wounds or death. In contrast, moral courage is the willingness to stand firm on your values, principles, and convictions—even when threatened. It enables Soldiers to stand up for what they believe is right, regardless of the consequences. Soldiers, who take responsibility for their decisions and actions, even when things go wrong, display moral courage. Courageous Soldiers are willing to look critically inside themselves, consider new ideas, and change what needs changing.

> "Our professional responsibility is to strengthen our honorable service by living the Army Values daily. These values are the basic moral building blocks of our profession." "The Army Values are more than mere words we recite. The Army Values understood but not acted upon are meaningless."
>
> - (*ADRP* 1)

CSM John Crenshaw
2d BN, 3d SFG (A)

From One Leader to Another
The Army Values
Sergeant Major Tony A. G. Romero

It was not long ago that the Army officially adopted what we today call the Army Values of Loyalty, Duty, Respect, Selfless Service, Honor, Integrity and Personal Courage. Indeed, during the exploration of these United States, men like Washington, and Lewis and Clark sought men who stood up for principles that went beyond their own desires and dreams. These were men who promoted the well-being of others before themselves. To do this, they sought the company of men who would stand ready and live what they believed without compromising their principles.

Therefore, I would argue that long before the written format of the seven Army Values, men and women in service to the United States of America, responded to something deep inside them. Something that moved them to exude the very best of humanity in defense of this nation. It provoked them to treat their fellow human beings fairly and to reach out in defense of not only America, but also the world to preserve democracy. To do this, people had to die, giving the very best of their years, and in many cases, their lives in order to preserve our way of life.

Looking back, one can readily identify that *loyalty* to the cause of our freedom and the willingness to carry out the responsibility of *duty* to humankind so that freedom may continue to blossom. It is the need to fulfill our obligation to this generation so the next generation will not have to carry our load. Consequently, by fulfilling our obligation, we give the next generation a benchmark to strive for as they carry the torch of freedom. R*espect* for their fellow man and the ability to transplant themselves into the shoes of those who are poor, needy, hungry, cold, and abused allowed them the capacity to become champions - champions that created a way of life and influenced those who will follow to become champions too.

However, none of this was possible or is possible without the stamina it takes to overcome insurmountable odds as we have seen in the tapestry left by our brothers in arms from the wars America has engaged in as well as innumerable conflicts over the last 237 years. The ability to give up self and the preciousness of life so that others may live in freedom and peace is an ability that defies common sense except for those who do so. The act of *selfless service* brings out the true character of a man – those who will work together for the group applying the balm of justice and fairness even when everyone else objects.

Paradoxically, living the values is something that we do in the absence of orders or standing authority. It is the determination to go on and to do what one is trained to do without supervision. It is the ability, not to impress others, but to do a duty the best way one can and whenever one can – to travel the difficult path of justice when given the opportunity to defect. It also requires *personal courage* especially when many, even best friends, will forsake you and when one is called to try new territories of the heart when threatened by the wickedness about them.

Additionally, it calls for a spirit of *integrity* forged by the baptism of combat and in the leadership of men/women who have dedicated their lives to secure this great land called America. There is no greater *honor* than witnessing one man/woman giving all of their being to preserve the life of another. As Soldiers, we do that every day and in all corners of the world.

We have forsaken all, even the presence of Family and friends, to assist other nations and people we do not even know. That requires a different and unique human being. It is no wonder that less than 1% of our population serve the other 99%. It is no wonder the world looks to America in times of great tragedy, injustice, and human loss for help.

The Army Values, for me, are something that has developed and matured over my 52-year journey. It did not start with the Army nor will it end with the Army. I have learned that is it necessary to pause when making decisions, especially when it affects others around me. Hasty decisions often incorporate loopholes that can easily violate any one of the values. Also, I have learned that the values depend upon each other and if violated will trigger a domino effect within your life. Violation of one value will ultimately affect the other six. I have noticed though that if one lives the values, he/she will tend to act according to those values and your friends will be limited to those who encapsulate the true essence of friendship. That is, adhering to a way of life conducive to positive development, not only in self, but in society as well. If one does not live the values, he/she will tend to seek compromise to attain goals in life. Goals realized in this way are built upon the sands of ignorance and inconsideration, which will succumb to the terrible storms that life offers us.

The shallowness of humanity is revealed when these storms beat upon the shores of our hearts and minds to test our resolve and mettle as human beings. Practicing and living the seven Army Values allow us to steel our character and temperament. It demands from us positive actions and holds our conscience responsible when we violate its domain. As Soldiers, this becomes an issue during training and especially on the battlefield which can lead to terrible consequences.

To avoid this, the development of the seven Army Values must be nourished daily because neglect of them can lead to destruction of our mental and spiritual dimensions. Failure to give heed to what we do and how we do it in light of our values can harden our decision-making process. Failure to adhere to the summons issued within our hearts when we attempt to engage in activities that run contrary to what we say, believe, and live will make us victims of our own ignorance. It undermines one's character, pollutes their reputation, and erodes trust in those we lead.

The Army Values therefore are a barometer, set within us by a higher being, to help us keep our equilibrium as humans living among other humans. It helps us become tolerant of others' ignorance as we educate them to another way of life, another way of thinking. It helps us stand up for justice for those who cannot defend themselves. It makes us stalwart sentinels to preserve our God-given rights to freedom and humility. It gives us strength to endure the silent neglect when we choose to do the right thing, especially when everyone is reveling in those activities that are wrong. It is the ability to go it alone, when necessary, to influence others, and lead them back when they have strayed from the essence of the Army Values.

The Army Values are my compass and my rudder when travelling upon unchartered waters such as a new assignment, dealing with a Soldier who was sexually assaulted, or giving counsel to an old student who is having problems with his new supervisor. It is my anchor when making decisions that affect not only the Soldier but also the Family and friends of that Soldier. It is a requirement, especially in the life of a Soldier. We must remember, our actions or inactions impact generations even after we leave the profession of arms.

In conclusion, the following publications can be used to support the tenets of the Army Values as well as provide meaningful application.

AR 600-100. *Army Leadership.* 17 Sep 1993; *DA PAM* 600-25. *US Army Non-Commissioned Officer Professional Development Guide.* 30 Apr 1987; *FM* 1 (100-1). *The Army.* 14 Jun 1994; FM 1-04.10 (27-10). *The Law of Land Warfare.* 15 Jul 1976; FM 6-22 (22-100). *Army Leadership.* 31 August 1999; *US Army Center of Military History*, dated 13 September 2011; Lewis & Clark Expedition: *Teaching with Documents* - National Archives and Records Administration, dated 27 June 2011; and Lewis & Clark and the *Revealing of America* - Library of Congress, dated 27 June 2011.

SGM Tony A. G. Romero
Equal Opportunity Proponent SGM

From One Leader to Another
Army Values
Sergeant Major Alma L. Zeladaparedes

"Our Army Values are American Values," they are instilled within each Soldier and in each Civilian. They exist in the U.S Constitution, in the Soldier's Creed, the Warrior Ethos and in the Army Civilian Creed. The Army Values have held each Soldier and leader together and led them to defeating their enemy even when the odds were against them. Army Chief of Staff, General Odierno went on to state, "They are the essence of who we are."

For the past 237 years our Soldiers have won wars during boots on-the-ground, face-to-face conflicts and struggles. Despite the conditions, they have successfully dominated, seized and secured every objective. Their obligation and loyalty to our nation has made the United States of America the most superior of nations. The Army's transition had no affect because each leader carried out his or her duties as a professional. Our leaders lead and our Soldiers serve with a common trust, loyalty, honorable service, esprit de corps and stewardship. There can be no question that our values have been instrumental in our Soldier's actions. These values remind our leaders to make choices with both honor and integrity. They encourage loyalty, duty and respect for one's nation and inspire our force to always act with professionalism. Only one percent of our citizens join the military forces, therefore we are unique and we should always be a proud and honorable community.

To uphold the Army Values is the responsibility of every leader and we must see it in our Soldiers. Make it routine by including our values in every training exercise. To do so will be to guarantee an increase in your team's morale, esprit de corps, discipline and motivation while also significantly increasing the quality of life of every Soldier and their Family. Consistently empower each junior leader through the Army Values. Take a few minutes to discuss why we pay respect to our "First Call" and "Reveille" and why we remain loyal to the team not allowing our minds to quit. "Pain is temporary but honor is eternal." As a leader you have the responsibility to develop the character of your Soldiers. "Train as you fight," test their personal courage and selfless service. Assess their integrity, honor and duty with unannounced and/or scheduled inspections to ensure that they are living up to the Soldier's Creed in maintaining their equipment. Inspections measure a team's discipline and the leader's ability to lead.

Always ask your NCOs which of the Army Values drives their leadership style and why? The answer is usually, "Loyalty." However the Army Values are held together and mutually supported by one another. A leader might think that his or her leadership style is based on one value rather than the rest but that simply is not so. When you use a single piece of 550 parachute cord, aren't you really relying on the seven white smaller ropes that are inside? For example, a Staff Sergeant said that his leadership style was based on loyalty to his Soldiers and he reasoned that, "my Soldiers are always welcome at my door, they know where I live and they know my wife and my kid's names. If they don't have somewhere to go for the holidays and they aren't making any friends than they are invited to my home. I make sure they know the limits of our relationship that they maintain a professional conduct, and I always brief them of the consequences if they cross that line of respect." You see the value "Loyalty" was his external motivation but deep inside he acted on all of the values; Loyalty, Duty, Respect, Honor, Integrity, Selfless Service and Personal Courage.

As a Battalion Command Sergeant Major, I created a training event for all of my squad leaders; I called it, "The Rubber Meets the Road." My intent which I shared with my Battalion Commander (BN CDR), who assisted me in the training, was to ensure that our leaders fulfill their obligations by empowering them. Garrison leadership is the hardest because most NCOs don't feel the same passion, desire, confidence, character, commitment and motivation as they might while deployed. I knew that I had to train them in the skills needed for garrison; legal/administrative processes, medical readiness, non-judicial action, counseling, how to properly conduct physical readiness training and how to inspect their Soldier's organizational clothing and individual equipment. We enlisted the assistance of our battalion staff (S1, S4, Legal NCO, and the Battalion Aid Station OIC). They taught our leaders how to handle these processes, how each program works and how the staff forwards the requisite administrative data and supports them and the unit's leadership. The BN CDR and I taught them about the negative impacts the negative impacts of toxic leadership and about our Battalion History and Battalion Motto. We discussed our expectations for the leaders and we asked them to assist us in the mentoring, training and development of our junior leaders. As a result, our leaders experienced a greater sense of confidence and gained a new perspective of the unit and its leadership.

I had previously read, "The Tao of Leadership" by Lao Tzu. In it he wrote, "I have heard my master say that nurturing life is like keeping a flock of sheep, you lash the last sheep, and the rest will move." I didn't take this literally of course, I know how the organization's leadership structure works but we have all witnessed units in which those in charge or in leadership positions are not always the ones to which Soldiers migrate. In a Battalion, a Sergeant First Class or sometimes a Staff Sergeant is appointed to lead a platoon. Unknowingly the Soldiers may choose to follow another self-appointed leader. If the new Platoon Sergeant doesn't validate his role to the platoon, he or she may quickly lose his or her influence. This can and will lead to a decrease in the unit's readiness. A weakness in leadership in a battalion or in any team for that matter will create a vacuum which may allow self-appointed leaders to reign free. When Soldiers don't live according to the Army Values they are easy to control. Toxic leaders can be located anywhere within a Chain of Command or NCO Support Channel. As leaders we must remain loyal to our Army's code of conduct, professionalism and the Army Values. This implies that each of us have a responsibility to report on those leaders who take advantage of their Soldiers. You should never believe that as an NCO you have now joined the elite. Our NCO Creed guides our Army Values in three perfect paragraphs but not all leaders adhere to it. Don't be that type of leader and don't allow them to exist in your organization. Your loyalty is first to the nation, set the example, be the leader others inspire to be, know yourself and strengthen your weakness. Always do what is right. "If you want to improve the team, improve yourself." Know your Soldiers and know their goals and what they strive to be. Conduct realistic training that will build their resiliency, cohesiveness and communication. Evaluate their ability to win and fight together. A team must consistently train, fight and win to maintain its cohesiveness, competence and commitment to one another. Regardless of the Army's technical advances, continue to lead with

The Creed of the Non-Commissioned Officer and our Army Values.

All members of an organization must have mutual respect for each other; every individual brings a unique capability to the team. A team is more efficient, creative and can achieve more when everyone participates. Collaboration of every Soldier is needed in order to complete each task on time and successfully. John C. Maxwell authored, "The 17 Essential Qualities of a Team Player." In it he stated, "To a collaborative team member, completing one another is more important than competing with one another." Abraham Lincoln said, "I would not be a slave, so I would not be a master." Treat others as you want to be treated, yes even those Soldiers you might view as performing at a substandard level. Correct their behavior but don't strip them of their dignity and respect. As a new 1SG, I remembered cursing at a Soldier, using profanity and abusing my power. I embarrassed the Soldier and I placed fear on the faces of the remainder of the Soldiers in the formation. I didn't think I was wrong until the BN CSM called me into his office and calmly said, "the days of cursing a Soldier out are over, don't lose your military bearing, you are a professional, use other means to correct your Soldiers, I won't allow you to be disrespectful." He reminded me that I wasn't above anyone and that I had to lead as a professional. I became aware of my actions; I shared my experience with my Platoon Sergeants and Squad leaders. I apologized to all of my Soldiers and I adopted other means for correction. But I didn't stop correcting substandard behavior. A few months later my BN CSM started the School of Standards, it was held every weekend, and I was the primary trainer and supporter. "Real leadership is being the person others will gladly and confidently follow."

As a leader your actions are consistently being analyzed, magnified and judged. You are held to a higher standard of conduct. Live the Army Values and don't disregard their effectiveness.

If you would like to learn more about this topic, I recommend that you read *Army Doctrine Publication 1, "The Army", Army Doctrine Reference Publication 1, "The Army Profession"*, "The Tao of Leadership" by Lao Tzu, "The 17 Essential Qualities of a Team Player," by John C. Maxwell, *Army Doctrine Publication 6-22, "Army Leadership"* and *Army Doctrine Publication 7-0, "Training Units and Developing Leaders"*.

SGM Alma L. Zeladaparedes
1st Infantry Division CBRNE SGM

From One Leader to Another
Comprehensive Soldier and Family Fitness
Command Sergeant Major Blaine Harvey

The US Army Comprehensive Soldier and Family Fitness (CSF2) Program, as the title indicates, is a comprehensive program used to assess and develop a Soldier and Family's resiliency to stress. "The Army established CSF2 on October 1, 2008, as a directorate within the Army's G-3/5/7. (US Army) The Comprehensive Soldier and Family Fitness Program focuses on five domains; emotional, physical, spiritual, social and Family. Each of these domains is an essential part of a Soldier and his or her Family. In times of strife and hardship, it is these areas that a Soldier will draw upon to help cope with the stress that accompanies these hardships. Comprehensive Fitness begins when a Soldier first enters the military with an initial assessment and continues throughout his career with periodic assessments that are "linked to a customized menu of training modules and services for areas that need strengthening". (US Army) The Army has developed numerous tools and programs to assist in assessing and building comprehensive Soldier fitness, such as the Global Assessment Tool (GAT), the US Army Soldier and Leader Risk Reduction Tool (USA SLRRT), the Master Resilience Trainer Program and the Strong Bonds Program, to name just a few. "Enhanced resilience, achieved by a combination of specific training and improved fitness in the five domains of health, can decrease post-traumatic stress, decrease the incidence of undesirable and destructive behaviors, and lead to greater likelihood for post-adversity growth and success." (US Army) The Comprehensive Soldier and Family Fitness Program is essential to the well-being of the force and the Families that support their Soldier and must be a dedicated line of effort in every organization from the squad-level all the way to the major command headquarters.

Comprehensive Soldier and Family Fitness was developed in response to a rise in suicides, acts of indiscipline (drug use, alcohol abuse, domestic violence, etc.), and failed marriages within the military as a whole, but particularly in the United States Army. In 2008, when the Comprehensive Soldier and Family Fitness Program was instituted in the Army, we were heavily engaged in an asymmetric war in both Afghanistan and Iraq with Soldiers often spending only a year or less at home before they were called upon to deploy back into theater. The pace at which our Soldiers were deploying and the ferocity of the fighting in each theater was taking a toll on our Soldiers and their Families. The stress of combat and the stress of separation from Family and loved ones did not end when the Soldier came home and often left Soldiers wondering what was wrong with them or their Families and seeking answers or relief through a variety of self-destructive behaviors. It was clear that the Army needed to provide leaders and Soldiers the tools needed to develop resilience or we would lose our all-volunteer force from within.

Even today, we struggle with identifying and helping our Soldiers on active duty and those veterans who have left active service. A recent report from the US military "acknowledged that suicides hit a record in 2012, outpacing combat deaths, with 349 active duty suicides, almost one a day" according to the Huffington Post in 2013. I believe the answer to this dilemma is educated, engaged and compassionate leaders who develop resilience in themselves so that they may help others.

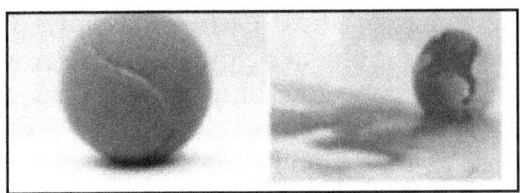

As leaders in our Army, if we are going to develop resiliency in our Soldiers, we must first demonstrate resiliency in our lives, both personally and professionally. One of the best pictures which depict resilience is that of a tennis ball and a cracked egg; the goal is to be the tennis ball that will bounce back versus the egg that will crack under pressure.

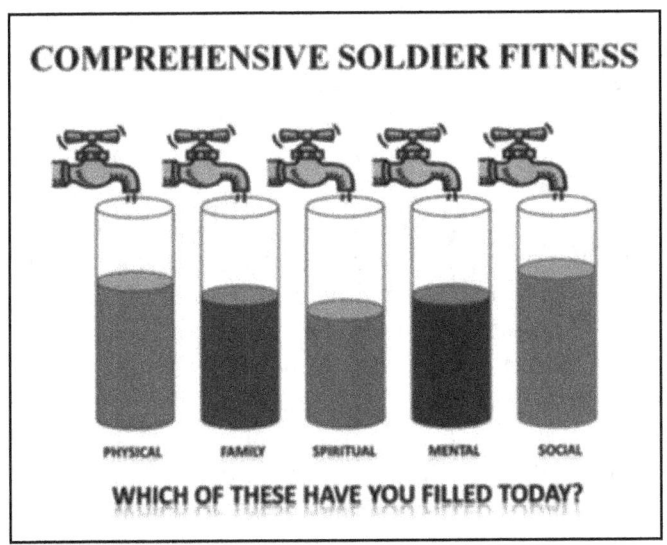

The old adage, "that which does not kill us, only makes us stronger" is really the intent of resiliency. Just as we build physical strength by putting our muscles under stress, we can build up our resiliency during times of stress so that we will be better prepared for future periods of stress. The first time I heard of the five domains a picture came to mind which I have attempted to illustrate in the picture above.

During times of stress each of us draws from one of these reservoirs to help us cope, but we are all designed to draw from different areas based on where our strengths lie. Some people have a strong Family base to draw from through close Family ties; while others look to the close friendships they have cultivated to be their source of strength during times of trouble. Some Soldiers use their faith, spirituality or purpose to help them cope while others use their intellect or mental agility to deal with adversity. Probably one of the consistent sources of strength for Soldiers is physical due to our need to be physically fit and our daily routine of physical fitness training. It is essential that we, as leaders, develop balance in these domains and create a routine of daily investment in each one of these areas because there will be times when we may not have one of these areas to draw from. For instance, when recovering from a physical injury, the physical domain may not be available to draw from and actually could be a source of stress. Or when you are faced with difficulties in your marriage or separation caused by deployment, your Family may not be available to lean on. One thing that is consistent in every one of our lives is that we will face times of trouble and that we must build up a reservoir in each one of these domains from which we might draw. I challenge each leader to deliberately and methodically develop and execute a daily plan to invest in each of these areas in their life. Your Soldiers will look to you as a source of strength and stability during times of stress and your behavior could mean the difference between success and failure for you and your unit.

Army Doctrine and Doctrine Reference Publications 6-22, *Army Leadership*, asks each of as leaders to be leaders of presence, leaders of intellect, and leaders of character. As a leader, we must be present with our Soldiers in order to influence them to accomplish the mission. Leader presence is not merely physical, but it is also the culture that we cultivate in our organization. As a leader, ask yourself, "Have I created an environment where my Soldiers can come to me in times of need without fear of ridicule or reprisal?" Do you see Soldiers who are reaching out for help as being weak for needing help or strong for identifying a need for assistance and having the courage to act upon that need? Are you utilizing all the resources available to you: Master Resilience Trainers, Resilience Training Assistants, your local Wellness-Fusion Campus, Military Family Life Consultants or your Chaplain to provide both training and counseling to your Soldiers in order to develop resilience in your Soldiers and their Families? Leader engagement starts before a Soldier ever arrives at your unit through your sponsorship program, continues when your Soldier arrives and you sit down and do his or her initial counseling and fill out their personal data sheet and never really stops as long as that Soldiers sees you as a source of help long after he or she has left your unit. As a senior leader in the Army today, I can look back over my career and identify those leaders that I chose to be my mentors and have often called upon for advice or counsel. The people that I chose as mentors were those who demonstrated competence and genuine concern for me and my Family. If you know your Soldier, you should be able to identify the warning signs when your Soldier is under duress and also know where your Soldier draws his strength from in order to assist him in getting the help he needs. It is not the programs and training that are keys to developing resilience; it is the leader who is engaged with his Soldiers and demonstrates to them how to be resilient in the face of adversity. It is the leader who deliberately develops a training strategy to train his Soldiers in comprehensive fitness and creates opportunities to build their resilience that will have an impact on the health of the unit. I cannot overstate your role, as a leader, in building a healthy unit that can sustain the stresses of deploying and winning our nation's wars.

Just as aggressive, realistic training is imperative to developing a combat-ready force, Comprehensive Soldier and Family Fitness is imperative to developing a combat-ready Soldier. The Army and its Soldiers are in a constant state of change as they move through the Army Force Generation Model in preparation for deployment or in preparation to respond to an unknown threat to our country both at home and abroad. During times of change our units and our Soldiers are more susceptible to stress caused by the demands of service to our nation; therefore, we must prepare them to identify these stressors and learn to appropriately cope with these demands. As leaders, we must demonstrate resiliency and use the myriad of resources available to us to develop resiliency in our Soldiers through the Comprehensive Soldier and Family Fitness Program.

If you would like to learn more about this topic please take the time to read the following: "Military Suicides: One US Veteran Dies Every 65 Minutes" from the February 9th, 2013 edition of Huffington Post, "The Army Posture Statement" from the US Army website, and *Army Doctrine and Doctrine Reference Publications* 6-22, Army Leadership. In addition to these references, please take the time to visit the Comprehensive Soldier and Family Fitness website at http://csf2.Army.mil/.

CSM Blaine Harvey
2 HBCT, 1AD

From One Leader to Another
Customs and Courtesies
Command Sergeant Major Fritz U. Smith

Customs and courtesies have been a part of our Army lifestyle since the beginning of its existence. Like the changing of the guard or staff duty, each generation has added a bit of flavor to an event or custom to make it a little different and relevant for the current time/operating environment, while upholding the customs and courtesies that keep our Army and our NCO Corps strong. For example, the tradition of commemorating the promotion of a Soldier to the rank of Non-Commissioned Officer, can be traced back to the Army of Fredrick the Great in the 17th Century.

Before one could be recognized in the full status of a Non-Commissioned Officer, he or she was required to stand four watches, one every four days. At the first watch, the junior Soldiers of the organization appeared and claimed a gift of bread and brandy from the aspiring NCO. The company NCOs then followed and on the second watch came to claim their gift of beer and tobacco and the First Sergeant reserved his visit for the third watch, when he was presented with a glass of wine and a piece of tobacco on a tin plate. It was during the fourth watch that the NCO figuratively crossed the time-honored line and joined the NCO corps. Today, we commemorate this rite of passage as a celebration of the newly promoted joining the ranks of a professional Non-Commissioned Officer Corps and emphasize and build on the pride we all share as members of such an elite corps. We also serve to honor the memory of those men and women of the NCO corps who have served with pride and distinction.

In ceremonies of the present, all of those items previously described have been replaced so as to reflect the current times but the customs and tradition of the induction remain intact. The induction is of significant importance because it is the transition from being the led to becoming the leader. However, with the rapid OPTEMPO of our forces over the last twelve years, these types of ceremonies are not as prevalent as they once were and not given the type of attention as it was in the past. Therefore, the promotion is not given, it's just due. It is up to us, the Non-Commissioned Officers, to keep this and other pertinent types of customs and courtesies in front of our Soldiers in order to demonstrate what right looks like.

Another custom is that of the greeting of the day, Army Regulation 600-25 outlines the proper procedures all Soldiers should execute. The senior is acknowledged by the junior Soldier with the greeting of the day or the unit's motto. The greeting is accompanied by the hand salute if it is an Officer to which that junior Soldier is addressing. Many Soldiers have a tendency to look the other way or choose to pretend they did not recognize the senior person. Many do not familiarize themselves with the regulation or they simply believe it is an option if the Soldier is having a bad day. This failure to conform displays a lack of discipline and often tells a lot about an organization without even visiting the unit. Moreover, the little things such as these are what we need to refocus on; doing so will help to ensure that the big things will fall in line and help to ensure their success.

Customs and Courtesies are important to our NCO Corps as well as the rest of the Army to ensure we remain a professional, self-disciplined, strong, relevant and ready force; full of pride, resourceful and out of the box thinkers. Soldiers must understand that if we are to remain the dominant fighting force, which we are today, that we cannot afford to forget the lessons of yesterday. It is not just the combat situations that bond us as Soldiers, but those customs and courtesies, values and beliefs we all share. We must not forget or dismiss any of it, as we contribute our part to this great and powerful Army. This is evident from the successes and shortcomings we have experienced in Iraq and Afghanistan. Many of our young NCOs are not exposed to many of our customs and courtesies and as a result often pay the price for that ignorance. Some are informal norms (customs that are rules not written in any books) that accompany the position or grade for which they hold.

Informal norms come in many forms, like being present for NCO Professional Development sessions, and ensuring it is the focus when on the training schedule at any level. Another is attendance at Dinning Ins/Outs, again a location where you get an opportunity to see what customs and traditions look like before it is your turn to execute one. It is important to support the ceremonies of your sister unit through your mere presence. This is a great opportunity to see how others execute ceremonies, traditions, and customs. By doing so, you often find that there is something you can incorporate into the programs within your unit. Informal norms were once explained in older field manuals. Most of our older doctrinal publications have been updated and some terms we once used have been dropped or renamed; however, the responsibilities of the customs live on through the continuity of our more senior leaders.

My advice is for you to start by educating yourself through reading and getting involved in some of our elite organizations such as the Sergeant Audie Murphy or Morales Club and by doing, not waiting for the schoolhouse or the NCOES system to introduce our history to you. Once you have been educated, share what you have learned. Volunteer to execute some of the events you discover in your unit. Not only do you expose others to our heritage, but you also instill a sense of pride in those around you. You spark curiosity in others and it becomes infectious. Young Soldiers get interested in areas where there was little prior involvement and then we all get better. I have listed just a few areas where you should take the time to educate yourself in some of the more common customs and courtesies that may be alive and well within your organization.

Lastly find a good mentor. There are plenty of senior leaders across our Army who are willing to take the time to coach, teach and mentor good Sergeants looking to make a difference in our Army. To preserve what so many have fought to create for us, their knowledge must be passed on. It is incumbent upon you to make the initial step and seek them out. It is the responsibility of each and everyone one of us to preserve the history of our Army.

The following is a list of documents and websites that I recommend you take the time to research on this topic.

Army Regulation 600-25, *Salutes, Honors and Visits of Courtesy, Field Manual* 7-22.7, *The NCO Guide, Army Doctrine Publication* 6-22, *Army Leadership,*
The Army Publication Directorate at
http://www.apd.Army.mil/ProductMap.asp
A History of the NCO at
http://www.ncohistory.com/files/NCO_History.pdf
History of the United States Army NCO Sword at
http://ncosword.com/
History of Enlisted Ranks at
http://www.tioh.hqda.pentagon.mil/

UniformedServices/Insignia_Rank/enlisted_hisotry.aspx
and The Year of the Non-Commissioned Officer at http://www.Army.mil/yearofthenco/history1.html

CSM Fritz U. Smith
57th Expeditionary Signal Battalion

From One Leader to Another
Emotional Intelligence and Leadership
Sergeant Major Sam S. Oak

Specialist Jones hurriedly arrives at the morning physical training formation, falling in late – about five minutes after the NCO in charge of PT that morning has received the accountability reports from each squad-leader. Lingering behind the formation is First Sergeant Smith. He sees SPC Jones and immediately grabs him and pulls him to a corner and starts yelling – without asking why he is late to the formation. "This is the third time you've been late to the formation SPC Jones," 1SG Smith said. "You can't seem to do anything right, you're a messed up Soldier, you need a lesson. Drop! Drop! Now!" SPC Jones is momentarily frozen and motionless. Then, in a desperate attempt he mutters something, but the 1SG is so irritated that he doesn't allow the Soldier a chance to explain. SPC Jones drops and stays in front-leaning rest position for a while until the 1SG orders him to get back to the formation. As Jones is moving slowly toward the formation, he fleetingly gives the 1SG a look of contempt then grudgingly joins the formation. Later, the 1SG learns that unlike the previous two times when he was late to the formation because of his negligence in setting his alarm clock the night before, this time Jones was late to the formation because his three year old son had a high fever.

With a well-built physique and an obvious temper, a battalion commander clearly intimidates those who work for him, especially his subordinate company commanders. The monthly Unit Status Report briefing has become an event that the company commanders want to avoid at all costs. During the monthly USR briefings, the battalion commander is quick to jump on any minor mistake. "What about this assessment?" he would say sarcastically. "This is ridiculous. Maybe you don't have any skills with this." With this abrupt criticism, the company commander in his crosshairs is usually so stunned and so fearful of the battalion commander's wrath that he says nothing and is dispirited and reduced to silence. After each USR briefing all of the company commanders and their first sergeants gather at a restaurant and commiserate among themselves about how miserable the USR briefing was and how angry they are when they were accused of seemingly trivial mistakes.

Everyone probably has a personal story of how irritated they have been when they felt they were emotionally mistreated. Everyone can tell how their mental clarity gets hazed when rage is aroused inside them. When a Soldier, or anyone, is emotionally troubled the cascades of hostile thoughts are what come first to mind. Getting obviously distracted from whatever they are doing and swamped by the feeling of hopelessness, their duty performance is plainly challenged since the only thing they are mulling about at the moment of rage is either how to get out of the situation or seek revenge.

Emotion, although little is it taught or explained in the core curricula of NCO education, has a subtle yet enormous impact not only on a Soldier's performance but on the overall health and readiness of a unit. A leader, who lacks control of emotion during a heated moment, loses their reputation as a leader quickly and almost always never fully recovers from it. The Soldier, who experienced emotional rattling caused by the leader, remembers that moment for as long as they stay in the unit and never forgets – not because they want to remember it continually, but because the leader often acts similarly in other situation.

Those who are seemingly incompetent in emotional intelligence create more trouble than harmony when coaching and mentoring Soldiers. The worst way to teach a Soldier is to use criticism as a teaching technique – voiced as personal attack with disgust, sarcasm, and contempt. The Soldier receiving the criticism can become defensive and dodge responsibility, stonewall or become embittered with passive resistance. One of the common forms of destructive criticism is a blanket, generalized statement like, "You are screwing up." "You did not even try." "You can't seem to do anything right." These are often delivered in a harsh, sarcastic, angry tone, providing neither a chance to respond nor any suggestion of how to do things better. This kind of criticism leaves a Soldier with the feelings of helplessness and anger and has a devastating effect on motivation, energy, and confidence in doing work.

What do the accused people do, instead? Experts find that they become defensive, make excuses, and evade responsibilities. They become demoralized, refuse to cooperate and no longer try as hard at work as before. "Most problems in an employee's performance are not sudden; they develop slowly over time (J.R. Larson, University of Illinois). Frequent improper criticism gradually sinks a Soldier's spirit like silt and makes him retreat, causing problems in a Soldier's performance which we often complain about.

What is emotion then? As a downright expert on Emotional Intelligence, Daniel Goleman, the author of Emotional Intelligence, defines emotion as a feeling and its distinctive thoughts, psychological and biological states, and range of propensities to act.[*]

There are so many different types of emotions we feel every day – from anger to enjoyment, from sadness to happiness, from fear to love, from disgust to shame. Though there is no clear answer as to how to categorize those scientifically as Goleman correctly points out, emotions nevertheless have inestimable impact on how Soldiers perform and act each moment of daily life as a Soldier, parent, or companion of someone. Leading Soldiers without acknowledging the effect of and impact of emotion on them would be like trying to clear a field of weeds by removing everything on the surface of the ground but leaving the roots intact; they will always grow back up within a few days. Emotion, for it is always there, alive and responsive to any outside stimuli, cannot be ignored.

In the first example that I've witnessed as a member of the unit, the first sergeant was swamped by frustration about why SPC Jones was late again and instantly generalizes him as a malingering Soldier. This preoccupied, yet instant thought leads him to act in such a way of releasing damaging words without thinking of possible consequences. Later, reduced to a corner, the formerly motivated and amiable Solder then proceeds to do what he is asked to do but hardly goes the extra mile. Some may argue that it is the Soldier who needs to be blamed for not being resilient, for the Soldier must confront the situation, spring up again and carry on without dwelling on the incident. What about the First Sergeant? Is it alright for him to release his frustration anytime as long as it is related to keeping a Soldier straight and disciplined? What we overlook is the way emotion is exchanged.

How do we exchange emotion? Emotional exchange is typically at a subtle and almost imperceptible level.* In every moment of meeting or talking with someone we send emotional signals, and those signals, either covertly or overtly, affect the emotions of those we are with. People imitate emotion but there is a flow of emotion. When two people interact, the direction of mood transfer is from the one who is more powerful in expressing feeling to the one who is more passive.* Emotion is contagious, as Goleman says succinctly.

In the military, the direction of emotion is typically from a senior to a subordinate: First Sergeant to Specialists, a BN Commander to Company Commanders, and Sergeant Major to First Sergeant. This tellingly indicates why equipping emotional intelligence among leaders is such an important matter. The direction of emotional exchange also explains why a team spirit is quickly lifted or reduced depending on who the leader of the team or unit is. Soldiers are keen in reading a leader's emotional competence and acting accordingly; it is one of the basic survival instincts of a human being.

A leader who is emotionally clumsy in controlling his emotion or believing that showing his temper is a way of demonstrating that he is a fearless leader is certainly mistaken. It is not to say that leaders have to be soft and nice at all times to Soldiers, but to say that leaders must have empathy toward Soldiers. Empathy is the ability to know how another feels. Showing empathy toward Soldiers is one of the key ingredients of leadership - an emotionally conscious leader.

Rather than putting emotions into words, people far more often express them through another cue: tone of voice, gestures, facial expression and the like. Reading those non-verbal communication cues effectively is an important skill. Every great and effective leader has shown those traits. Leaders who are able to detect a Soldier's emotional cues at any given moment are much more effective leaders. The better tuned emotionally, the easier and the more effectively leaders are able to lead the team. The First Sergeant was emotionally tone-deaf; his absence of emotional understanding between him and SPC Jones caused a rather expensive emotional toll in that unit.

Leaders should scan their Soldiers' emotional landscape and continually adjust frequency and guide their frequencies as well. The emotional toll that an emotionally inadequate leader may have to pay is far greater than the toll of missing training requirements. Lacking the reality check of the destructive effects of miserable morale, intimidated leaders, or arrogant bosses can go largely unnoticed by those outside the immediate chain of command. The toll is more subtle and has a greater underlying impact on the unit's mission readiness than what appears on surface.

We utter every day the importance of open communication, teamwork, cooperation, and speaking one's mind, in the presence of a leader whose emotional response is erratic and unpredictable, who sometimes appears to be approachable when they feel good or uplifted, but let go of the unfiltered feelings when facing a distressing event, Soldiers are afraid of speaking their mind and always try to appease the leader and hardly tell them anything negative. Often simmering in a Soldier's mind is the feeling of disgust. One of the most destructive effects of this incompetency is a mindset among Soldiers that within two years they or the leader will PCS out, so they lay flat and do the minimum while trying not to be noticed.

We all believe that handling disagreement properly is one of key leader's must-have capabilities. How to handle disagreement fairly and effectively? That is where the emotional intelligence finds its place. Leadership is not domination, but the art of persuading people to work toward a common goal. According to *ADRP* 6-22, Army leadership is defined as the process of influencing people by providing purpose, direction, and motivation. Influencing is not something leaders can demand Soldiers to have nor something you can give to them. It is something that Soldiers voluntarily feel and want to have. Leaders have a very limited option in this regard. Long research in what makes a good leader reveals that open sharing of emotions in a positive way is one hallmark of an effective leadership style.

Leaders need to think about their thoughts as they arise and challenge them before putting their raw thoughts into words and actions. Leaders should be more conscious about the state of their emotional landscape and remember – leaders are made, not born.

If you would like to learn more about this topic it is recommended that you take time to read:

*"Emotional Intelligence: Why It Can Matter More Than IQ", 978-0-553-38371-3, Daniel Goleman, Bantam Books, 2005-09-27

"Primal Leadership-Learning to lead with Emotional Intelligence"

Army Doctrine and Doctrine Reference Publications 6-22, Army Leadership.

SGM Sam S. Oak
Munson Army Health Center

From One Leader to Another
Engaged Leadership
Command Sergeant Major Joanne Cox

Engaged leadership is simply being personally involved in and taking responsibility for the professional development and well-being of our Soldiers. Engaged leaders have a presence, which entails "the projection of military and professional bearing, holistic fitness, confidence and resilience" (*ADP 6-22, Army Leadership*). Engaged leaders are connected with their Soldiers, Families and their organization and when they participate in a discussion, event, etc. they are completely present "in that moment." When leaders aren't engaged, the second and third order effects can be far-reaching.

When we are not effectively engaged in NCO leadership responsibilities at our level, a common result is that leaders at echelons above us become involved and start micro-managing those responsibilities for us. A prime example of this at the Army level is the Semi-Centralized Promotion's, Automatic List Integration (ALI) for promotions to Sergeant and Staff Sergeant that was implemented 1 January 2006; now called Command List Integration (CLI). It is well known that Sergeants are among the most critical leaders in an organization and they can have the greatest impact on mission and readiness. They operate at the point of closest contact with the Soldiers, executing day to day activities of our Army accomplishing the unit's mission. For years Commanders reported shortages of the Sergeants they needed to train and lead their Soldiers. As Human Resources Command (HRC) and Enlisted Personnel Management Division tried to fill the recognized vacancies, they quickly identified that there was an Army-wide shortage of Sergeants. There weren't enough in the inventory to support unit manning requirements. There was, however, an abundance of Specialists in the primary zone of eligibility for promotion, who were not promotable. Here in, lies the issue. What were commands doing to help fix their own problem? We can't have Sergeants to lead and train our Soldiers unless we help produce them. HRC and the Department of the Army do not produce NCOs; leaders produce NCOs. We just weren't doing our part. For various reasons, unit leaders were not sending Soldiers to the board and recommending them for promotion.

While Commanders continued demanding their authorization of Sergeants, direct and organizational leaders continued to assert that their Specialists just were not ready to become NCOs and "Big Army" kept telling us to do our part. Instead of fulfilling our responsibility of training, teaching, coaching and mentoring our junior Soldiers and ensuring they were prepared to assume the role of leader, we just kept taking cover behind excuses such as "Soldiers are different now", "they just don't have the motivation", "they don't want to go to the board" and the hollow, "they just aren't ready."

No matter how many times we were told to fix this leadership deficit, we just didn't do it. We were not effectively engaged. So the senior Army leaders at HRC and the Department of the Army engaged. They developed a course of action to eliminate the shortage of Sergeants using the proper source, the Soldiers eligible for promotion on the basis of time in service and time in grade. They couldn't come down and teach them how to be leaders for us, but they could impose measures to force us to do it. Automatic List Integration was a forcing mechanism. It was designed to force unit leaders to fix the problem of not having Soldiers who were trained, developed and prepared to be leaders before getting promoted.

The system created a choice; develop them before or after their promotion. Either way, Commanders were going to get their Sergeants. Yet we still did not fully engage.

For the most part we grumbled in protest, mourned the loss of our power to control enlisted promotions and seemed to take on the attitude "Oh well, there's nothing I can do about it now." The truth is, it did not take away our control over enlisted promotions, all we had to do was start doing what we should have been doing all along, such as conducting meaningful counseling with our Soldiers, and make sure we understood all of the rules of the ALI policy. Instead of acknowledging that we had become weak in the area of NCO development, learning from it and coming back strong, we used it as a reason to further distance ourselves from our responsibility. We have been paying the price ever since and the longer we take to get it right, the harder it will become.

As we scale back the manic pace we have operated under for the last decade, the fact that we have not maintained some of the essential leadership skills of our Corps will become increasingly clear. If we do not acknowledge these shortfalls and get back on track, we will not succeed in our part of the mission to shape the Army of 2020 and beyond. Engaged leadership is the solution.

Tens of thousands of combat proven leaders were forged in Iraq and Afghanistan. However, they are a generation of leaders who have spent their whole developmental career in an Army fighting its way through persistent armed conflict. They have been trained to lead Soldiers through the Army Force Generation (ARFORGEN) cycle and deployments. Their ability to lead decisively, at combat speed, is nothing short of remarkable. Day after day, deployment after deployment, they led from the front and demonstrated the Warrior Ethos in its truest form. Unfortunately, many of them do not understand or practice engaged leadership. Throughout this period when we were forced to prioritize the leadership knowledge, skills and attributes on which to focus our professional military education and professional development we sidelined some of the core competencies that made our NCO Corps the "Backbone of the Army" in the first place.

We've been moving so fast that we have failed to adequately teach subordinate leaders some of their responsibilities and how to effectively manage them. Two of the most obvious areas are professional development and accountability. We have to ensure all leaders know and understand their role in the development and well-being of their Soldiers and Families so that they can become fully engaged leaders.

Leaders must be proactive and engaged in order to manage the training and proficiency of their units. Direct leadership responsibility includes ensuring Soldiers and subordinate leaders participate in training and are proficient in their individual and collective mission essential and supporting critical tasks. Every leader with Soldiers in their charge is responsible for managing their Soldiers' training requirements and completion status; their team, squad or platoon's level of proficiency; ensuring that training standards are achieved; planning and conducting additional training when needed and conducting effective after action reviews. Commanders rely on the training readiness information, reported by first line leaders through the chain of command, to conduct accurate assessments of their units.

The Primary Leadership Development Course (PLDC) transformed into the Warrior Leader Course (WLC) as a result of our recognition that the tactical leadership skills required of the Soldiers graduating that level of NCOES had changed dramatically. The majority of these young NCOs would be responsible for leading teams or squads in a combat zone.

Our operational tempo could not support extending the course length to add combat leader training, so we had to reevaluate the curriculum and modify the Program of Instruction (POI) in order to achieve this new focus in training objective. Unit deployment cycles and the consequent NCOES backlog made it necessary to shorten the length of the course and remove some of the basic leadership modules. We chose this course of action to avoid compromising the effectiveness of our junior leaders' training. Leader development has always been the responsibility of the operational Army, accomplished through engaged leadership. I clearly remember NCOs teaching and testing me on the subjects covered in, then, PLDC before my selection to attend. WLC was never meant to serve as the stand alone leader development mechanism that some have come to view it as. In fact, the proponent of the NCO Education System, the United States Army Sergeants Major Academy, designed it to compliment, reinforce and confirm the common core leadership attributes and competency development processes of the operational Army. They never intended for WLC to fully indoctrinate them in a matter weeks. The overall impact of the POI changes should have been minimal.

Preparing Soldiers for successful attendance at NCOES courses requires significantly more involvement than just telling them that they need to have the items on a packing list, be ready to take an APFT and be at this place, at this time to report for school. Soldiers on an NCOES order of merit list should not find out that they are expected to attend a course when they get the ATRRS notice or the schools NCO calls and tells them. When a Soldier becomes eligible, leaders must counsel them on their responsibility to stand ready to attend as soon as they receive a class date and provide the Soldier with guidance on how to be fully prepared. That includes maintaining their physical readiness and completing Structured Self Development (SSD) requirements. When Soldiers are selected for attendance, the platoon sergeants and first sergeants need to ensure they are able to meet course entry standards and that they are counseled to ensure they understand all of the actions they must take prior to reporting, and monitor completion of SSD modules. Leaders must follow-up. Before it is sent for battalion Command Sergeant Major review and approval, 1SGs need to review the information being reported on the OML to ensure it accurately reflects their Soldiers' eligibility and availability status. Complimenting this effort we need competent operation NCOs within each company and schools NCOs at battalions to manage the unit schools programs, but the unit leaders must be involved. We have to be able to rely on our staff NCOs and delegate the management of programs to them. However, we cannot abdicate our responsibility to ensure the accuracy and effectiveness of unit programs, or our responsibility to ensure Soldiers properly plan, prepare and execute their requisite NCOES course.

Engaged leaders develop their Soldiers by knowing their strengths and weaknesses, helping them set goals and develop plans to achieve their goals while monitoring their progress and completion of Structured Self Development. They also conduct effective performance, developmental, promotion and event-oriented counseling. We cannot develop our Soldiers by mechanically churning out required counseling sessions as mandated by regulation in order to simply meet the requirement for an inspection. The mandatory counseling requirements specified in regulation and unit policies are the minimum standard and can be one of the best tools in our kitbag, but if we fulfill the requirement just to check the block in order to meet the minimum we are willfully neglecting our responsibilities.

As we develop our leaders, we need to ensure that we teach true leader accountability. I don't mean to "maintain 100 percent accountability of all assigned equipment". We must instill genuine leadership accountability. It starts with first line leaders maintaining accurate daily accountability of their Soldiers. This includes duty status, appointments, training requirements and completion of assigned tasks and details. Leaders must be involved ensuring Soldiers maintain their individual fitness, medical readiness, uniforms, equipment and quarters. Leaders cannot ensure that standards of conduct and discipline are maintained and their Soldiers are living in a safe, healthy environment if they are not engaged. Positive leadership presence does not mean conducting strict, basic training style room inspections or walking up and down their halls like prison guards. Leaders conducting routine barracks checks will quickly figure out which Soldiers need more leadership involvement and which ones might need less. Walking through the barracks after duty hours and on weekends, talking to Soldiers in such a way that shows you are genuinely interested in their morale and well-being can go a long way toward developing the trust and respect that builds strong teams. Leaders can pick up on indicators of at-risk Soldiers, illegal activities or safety concerns when they conduct leader walk-throughs at varying times of the day, night, weekends and training holidays. *FM 7-22.7*, Chapter 2 Duties, Responsibilities and Authority of the NCO states "First line leaders should inspect their Soldiers daily and should regularly check

Soldiers' rooms in the barracks. First line leaders should also make arrangements with Soldiers who live in quarters (on or off post) to ensure the Soldier maintains a healthy and safe environment for himself and his Family." Engaged leaders, who genuinely care for the well-being and personal readiness of their Soldiers and Families, conduct routine leader visits to all quarters, including barracks, BEQ/BOQ, as well as on and off post housing.

Leaders must dedicate their own time and possess genuine concern for their Soldiers in order to be effectively engaged in ways that help Soldiers develop and take responsibility for their own actions, professional growth and competence. We must know our Soldiers - their goals, experiences, capabilities, Families, challenges, strengths and weaknesses to properly lead them and foster in them the commitment to become the best leader and professional Soldier they can be.

Author's note:

My use of the term "we" throughout this paper, refers to the NCO Corps in general. I am not saying that every single NCO personally did or did not do or say the things mentioned here. These points are generalizations and I acknowledge that there are many great NCOs digging in, getting after leader development and providing effective engaged leadership.

If you would like to learn more about this topic it is recommended that you read the following publications: *ADP 6-22 Army Leadership*, 1 August 2012; *AR 600-100 Army Leadership*, 8 March 2007; *FM 6-22 (FM 22-100) Army Leadership - Competent, Confident, and Agile*, 12 October 2006; *FM 7-22.7 (TC 22-6) The Army Non-Commissioned Officer Guide*, December 2002, *AR 350-1 Army Training and Leader Development*, 4 August 2011; *ADRP*

7-0 *Training Units and Developing Leaders*, August 2012; AR 600-20 *Army Command Policy*, 8 March 2008; ADP 6-0 *Mission Command*, 17 May 2012

CSM Joanne Cox
US Army NATO BDE

From One Leader to Another
Engaged Leadership

Command Sergeant Major (Retired) Robert Dare

If one studies the turbulent times the Army has experienced, the almost continuous state of change, and the occasions of less than exemplary performance, one can see that the Army's ability to continue to accomplish any mission assigned can be attributed to the application of professional and consistent leadership. The Army's brand of leadership has been constantly engaged in providing direction, mentoring, coaching and decision making, with the profession of arms as the guiding principle. At the center of these activities stands the Non-Commissioned Officer (NCO) providing unit continuity and predictable daily performance of Soldiers.

Technology, doctrine, equipment, personnel, policy and regulations continue to evolve and impact the daily life of everyone in uniform. It has been said that the only constant in our life is change. Adapting technology, enforcing standards that are prescribed in policies and regulations, training Soldiers to be current, relevant and competent are the responsibilities of the NCO. Going forward the Army's NCOs will continue to perform these tasks. If the Army is to continue to enjoy its position as the most professional Army in the world, the Non-Commissioned Officer's role will not diminish. Every NCO will need to be "engaged" with the profession and Soldiers. What does it mean to be "engaged?" The following is offered not as an all-inclusive guide, but a selection of concepts and thoughts for consideration as the reader contemplates their definition of engaged leadership. The characteristics below can be found in many publications and are consistently present in the personalities and behaviors of successful leaders.

First, engaged leaders are always seeking knowledge that aids them in the execution of their duties. They use formal and informal educational opportunities to grow as a person and as a professional. They are positively relentless in increasing their competencies and circle of knowledge. They accept that there is always something that they do not know and that each experience brings growth. They do not fear failure as they embrace failure as an opportunity to learn and improve. Engaged leaders never conclude that they have fully matured professionally, intellectually or personally.

Engaged leaders are selfless and think of others. They reap a much greater reward by witnessing the success of subordinates rather than being personally recognized. They awake each day and put on their rucksack packed with the awesome responsibility as stewards of their organization's most precious resource, its people. They exude caring, compassion, and concern for others.

Successful leaders are positive. To be engaged is to be optimistic, choosing to spend one's time and thoughts on the glass "half-full." Engaged leaders do not carp or complain in less than ideal conditions and they do not allow their subordinates to do so. They focus on their circle of influence and do not waste their energies in their circle of interest. Their energy is contagious and sets an example for everyone in the organization. And because they choose to be positive in their approach to life, they handle challenges and disappointments positively, finding solutions and answers and always moving forward. John Wooden's statement, "Never let what you cannot do interfere with what you can do" is an axiom for them.

Engaged leaders believe in others. They trust and operate with a belief that most people do the right thing, are committed to the objectives, values and tenets of the organization and are determined to be part of a winning team. Leaders who care create a climate for growth and opportunity, an environment that provides motivation and purpose. The positive energy that engaged leaders possess is, in part, drawn from the people around them. They do not accept poor performance or failure but understand that a human being is not perfect, error is inevitable but correction is possible. Part of an engaged leader's job is providing constructive direction and a chance to atone.

Balance and predictability mark engaged leaders. There are no question marks concerning their behavior. Subordinates, superiors and peers understand what they get and what they can expect. Candid, honest feedback is delivered personally and professionally and is expected in return. They are willing to work as a member of the team and welcome ideas and recommendations. They build consensus whenever they can and they make everyone feel that they are contributing. When it's called for, engaged leaders are capable of making and announcing a decision. Once done, engaged leaders do not waiver or weaken. Everyone knows that a decision is final and was made with consideration of all facts and input.

Lastly but not inclusively, engaged leaders understand that leading is a mission, not a job or an assignment. Leading, and all that it entails, is a noble cause and purpose that starts with the heart, travels through the mind, and appears in the form of caring and commitment, love of Soldiers and a dedication to a higher calling. Engaged leaders know that their job is to do the right thing and choose the harder right over the easier wrong. These leaders clearly understand that their decisions, choices and actions affect others and as such are critical thinkers and truly lead by example. They live the golden rule and never ask, "What's in it for me?" They awake each day realizing that others are depending on them and relying on them to set a course for success. Engaged leaders conclude each day reflecting on the coaching, mentoring, and inspiring they have done and the affect it has had on the lives of others.

If you would like to learn more about this topic it is recommended that you read *Army Doctrine and Army Doctrine Reference Publications 6-22, "Army Leadership"*, "General of the Army, George C. Marshall, Soldier and Statesman" by Ed Gray, Leaders, "The Strategies For Taking Charge" by Bennis and Nanus, "The Leadership Challenge" by Kouzes and Posner and "Principle-Centered Leadership" by Stephen Covey.

CSM(R) Robert Dare
Former FORSCOM CSM

From One Leader to Another
Genuine Leadership, the Little Things Matter

Command Sergeant Major Sheldon Chandler

Over the last eleven years the Army has experienced significant challenges in the health of the force. These challenges include ill-discipline, increased suicide rates, behavioral health issues, escalated divorce rates and high risk behavior. As an NCO Corps, we must do our part to assist our senior leadership in solving some of the most significant challenges our Army has ever faced. We can do so by applying genuine leadership and making the little things matter. As an NCO Corps we have a responsibility to foster an environment where each Soldier is respected and can have trust and confidence in their leadership. It is our job to make a difference. By applying genuine leadership we can set the conditions for Soldiers to openly discuss the challenges they face in their lives. Your genuine leadership and wise counsel can and will make a difference.

Genuine leadership by itself is not the solution; however, it's a method NCOs can utilize to move us forward. Each of the problem sets discussed above, require engaged leaders at all levels to identify and resolve the issues within our ranks today. Whether you view these challenges as an individual or collective problem, a leader who is genuine and knows their Soldiers and their Families extremely well will notice when something isn't quite right. When Soldiers know you genuinely care about them, it fosters a climate of trust and open dialogue within your organization. Experience has shown that when

Soldiers face a difficult situation in their life they turn to the people they trust and count on the most. As an NCO Corps if we insert genuine leadership in our day-to-day business, we can make a positive impact on our Soldiers, their Families, and our Army. With a collective effort, the NCO Corps can begin to solve some of the most significant challenges in our Army. The challenges we face in our Army today can and often do have an adverse impact on the mission, unit readiness, organizational climate, and the trust relationship between our Army and the American people. It is critical that NCOs across the force do their part so our Army is ready, disciplined, healthy and postured to face the next operational mission.

Over the next few paragraphs, I will share personal experiences which I believe have made a difference. There are many philosophies, techniques, and "tricks of the trade" applied across our Army; I will not attempt to convince you that mine are better than another. However, I will share how I have applied genuine leadership and made the little things matter which resulted in a positive impact on Soldiers, their Families, and the organization.

In Army Doctrine Publication, *ADP 6-22*, the Army defines leadership as, "the process of influencing people by providing purpose, direction, and motivation to accomplish the mission and improve the organization". When you integrate genuine leadership, you have an impact on shaping a positive command climate, building trust with your subordinates and their Families, and showing the American people how we value the service of those we lead. Genuine leadership is nothing magical and can be accomplished by doing three things. First, know your Soldiers and their Families and take time to go the extra step. Second, always place their needs above your own. Finally, you must develop a professional relationship built on trust and proven action; where the Soldier knows unequivocally you will always be there for them no matter how difficult the situation.

I have always viewed leadership from the lens of a parent. Am I treating the young men and women who serve in our formation as I would want my children treated? As NCOs, each one of us assumes a level of parental-like responsibility. We nurture and protect our Soldiers from the things that might cause them harm; we apply discipline when needed to correct behavior; and we possess extreme pride when our Soldiers succeed. Leadership is the lifeblood of our Army and has been an essential element of our success as an institution for the past 237 years. From the formation of the Continental Army to the Global War on Terrorism, NCOs across our formations have led our nation's sons and daughters in peace and in war. In my professional opinion, it is direct leadership at the team and squad level which allows for the greatest opportunity to apply genuine leadership. The young Corporal or Sergeant who has the privilege of spending quality time with their Soldiers each and every day can have the biggest impact. This is where leadership happens in our Army, as many leaders have stated, "Where the rubber meets the road". This is where our NCOs know Soldiers and Families so intimately that they can quickly identify when something may be wrong.

An essential piece of my leadership philosophy has always been "Nobody cares how much you know, until they know how much you care". As an NCO, some may simply bark commands and demand that their Soldiers perform; however, at the end of the day they will likely only achieve minimal results with their subordinates. The NCO which demonstrates to a Soldier they have their best interest at heart and genuinely cares for their well-being will achieve far greater results; their Soldiers will exceed their greatest expectations. Caring and knowing is one of the most crucial things you can do and it is not a simple task. In order to make a difference, you must know your Soldiers and earn their trust and confidence. You must dedicate your time and educate yourself on everything about them…your knowledge base cannot be leader's book deep. You must know their life story, their spouse, their children, mother, father, siblings, birthdays, anniversaries, motivations, likes, dislikes, strengths and weaknesses and much, much more.

So why should you know these things about your Soldiers? First of all, it shows you care enough to take the time to know them and their Families. Secondly, Soldiers do not have expectations that their leader will know about a special event in their life; but when an NCO recognizes that special day it means the world to them. Finally, you have the ability to give a Soldier a memory of a special leader who cared enough and they will carry those moments with them forever. Taking the time to know and care for your subordinates and their Family leverages the human dynamic of leadership and it will earn their respect and admiration.

Throughout my career, I have gathered many stories on how I have made the little things count.

I will share two brief experiences where I applied genuine leadership and made the little things matter. As a First Sergeant, I experienced the unexpected death of a Soldier. I never realized how much I had personally touched this Soldier and his Family until returning to his hometown for his funeral. In the last few months leading up to his death, this Soldier had experienced the loss of many Family members and friends. One morning before PT, I learned he had experienced yet another loss in his Family; this time it was his grandfather... a decorated combat veteran and paratrooper in WWII. Prior to the Soldier's departure on emergency leave, his NCOs and I gave him a small memento to carry back for his grandfather's funeral. This gift cost us only $3.50 and mere moments of our time to prepare, yet it was quite meaningful to the Soldier and had a tremendous impact on him. Why did it have such impact? It demonstrated to the Soldier that his NCOs were genuine, empathetic and cared for him both as a person and as a Soldier. So what was this gift? It was a simple 8x10 framed copy of the paratrooper's creed dedicated to his grandfather with a set of airborne wings. Our words were simple and brief, "We're sorry for your loss, please pin these on your grandfather's chest, Once a Paratrooper always a Paratrooper". These simple words and genuine gesture from his NCOs who took that extra step had convinced him that he served in the best organization in our Army.

The second example I will share is a technique I have used and encouraged my NCOs to use throughout their career. I have routinely requested Soldier/Family contact information during a Soldier's integration to the unit. I inform them that with their consent, I will periodically send correspondence to their parents and loved ones about the great things they are doing for our Army. I would personally strive to correspond with five to ten different Families per month. With other key leaders in the unit also participating, we were able to dramatically expand our sphere of influence. The only resources required were stationary, an envelope, a postage stamp and our time. In less than one page, we would summarize how well their son or daughter was performing. Imagine the pride of a parent when they learn that their son or daughter briefed the Commanding General and received accolades. You would be extremely surprised at the positive impact it can have on a Soldier and their performance when their parents compliment them on the great things they have achieved. From the Soldier's view, you have gone well beyond what they expected from their NCO. Once again, by simply giving a little bit of your time, Soldiers quickly realize how important they are to you and the organization. A great time to craft these notes is during "Pay-Day Activities". Most units in our Army set aside time for their subordinate leaders to counsel their Soldiers during that particular day's events. This is a great time as a key leader to step away for an hour and take the time to write a few words to one of your Soldier's mother and father.

In the first example mentioned above, I stated I never realized how much I had personally touched my Soldier and his Family until after he had passed away. The Soldier's Platoon Sergeant and I had arrived at the home of our deceased Soldier, not knowing what to expect and we were greeted at the door by the Soldier's mother…a tremendous woman who was coping with the unexpected and tragic loss of her son. Surrounded by a mass of Family and friends, we were obviously anxious about meeting the Family for the first time. We quickly realized that the Family did not consider this as our first time meeting. Over a six month period, his parents had received eight letters from his NCO leadership keeping them abreast of how well their son was doing as a Soldier and those letters had clearly made a difference. We spent the next several hours talking about their son and the great Soldier he had become before his passing. Throughout our conversation their other Family members continually referenced letters written by their son and encouraged their mother to read them. She eventually mustered the courage to pick up a stack of those letters written by her son. It was not until she started reading the words on those pages that we realized how genuine leadership had influenced this Soldier. Teary-eyed and broken-hearted, she read letter after letter from her son who boasted about his NCOs and how they had become influential leaders in his life; how he desired to emulate their actions; and how they had such a genuine concern for each of their Soldiers. What we had not realized was that throughout his time in the unit, NCOs had consistently applied the genuine leadership that our great Soldiers deserve each and every day. We had simply treated him and his fellow Soldiers in the company as we would have wanted our own children to be treated.

Throughout the night, details were discussed about the funeral services scheduled for the following day. One such detail was that during the ceremony there would only be one speaker to deliver remarks. The Family had asked me to eulogize their son on behalf of our NCOs, so I graciously accepted, humbled by the opportunity to represent a great group of leaders. The pastor however seemed to be extremely anxious and troubled by their decision. Inquiring why he was troubled, we learned that the Soldier's church was not extremely fond of our current conflicts or the military; however, they were very supportive of the troops themselves. The pastor informed us that since the Church's existence, a Soldier in uniform had never walked into their church and most certainly had not addressed the congregation. He was troubled by what he thought would be a max exodus during the service.

Over the course of the evening in order to prepare my remarks, the Platoon Sergeant and I made a few phone calls back to his NCOs to capture their thoughts. What we realized that night was that the words flowed effortlessly onto the paper. They did so not because of our writing ability but because his NCO leadership had known him as both a Soldier and as a man. We knew his likes, dislikes, sad times, funny times, and what motivated him to excel. That next day I walked to the lectern and addressed the congregation fully anticipating a mass exodus; however, there was none. The words delivered on behalf of the NCOs were genuine and came from our experiences with the Soldier; every person in attendance was attentive, touched, and emotional at the words conveyed. After the funeral, the Platoon Sergeant and I were asked by the pastor and key congregation members to walk outside for a private discussion. The congregation was not aware leaders in the Army knew their Soldiers in such personal detail and cared for them in such a genuine manner. They had not known that leaders were emotionally attached to their Soldiers and took the time to know them individually. What came next demonstrated the impact that genuine leadership can have on a Family, a community, and the American people. The congregation had voted to change 150 years of their church's belief thereby welcoming any Soldier in uniform and allowing them to address the congregation at anytime. This impact had nothing to do with the Platoon Sergeant or I, our individual personalities, or an ability to address a crowd…it had everything to do with a group of NCOs which knew their Soldiers, genuinely cared for them, and who spoke proudly about their Soldier.

There are numerous ways you can apply genuine leadership. These are but two brief examples of things that can be done which can have a positive impact well beyond an organization's climate. Soldiers will remember the little things because they matter; rest assured that they will treasure those small experiences and carry it with them forever. Throughout the years, many of my former Soldiers have become NCOs and take great pride in sharing the little things they have done for their Soldiers. I was fortunate enough to leave an image in their mind of how little things matter to a Soldier and when applied consistently how they can make a difference.

In conclusion, I have shared a few of my own experiences which may help to not only explain what genuine leadership is but may also help my fellow NCOs become a more genuine and caring leader. Although these examples have taken place in my career, there are countless others where genuine NCOs across our Army have made an impact on their Soldiers, their Family and their organization. My intent was to share information which may help to shape your leadership skills and benefit the Soldiers, their Families and formations you help lead. When NCOs effectively apply genuine leadership we do our part in combating some of the most significant challenges we face in our Army. When a Soldier knows unequivocally that leaders genuinely care for them they are far less likely to have discipline issues and they will serve to make everyone around them proud. They will come to you in their time of need, potentially at that critical point when the Soldier is contemplating taking his or her own life. They will confide in you for your counsel when confronted with tough challenges. They will be far less likely to engage in high risk behavior and will think twice about how their actions will negatively reflect on you, the unit and our Army. Your genuine leadership and wise counsel can and will make a difference to a Soldier. Always remember, "Nobody cares how much you know, until they know how much you care".

CSM Sheldon Chandler
502d Military Intelligence Battalion

From One Leader to Another
Genuine Leadership
Getting back to the Basics
Command Sergeant Major Ronald Riling

While the Army has made significant changes over its 237 year history, some things never change. The fundamentals of a good leader have remained steadfast over the past few centuries. As Non-Commissioned Officers, we owe it to our peers and our subordinates to be the best leaders we can be.

I believe these are four primary tenets to maintain the strength of the NCO Corps: go back to the basics, maintain discipline, enforce the standards, and communicate. An NCO who is able to practice those four crafts will have a unit that can accomplish any mission it sets out to accomplish.

Back to the Basics

We've been a nation at war for more than a decade. The events of 9/11/2001 came as a surprise to all of us, but we've met the challenge head on. However, as a result of spending rotation after rotation in a combat environment, we've lost our focus on training and equipping the force. In order for the Army to succeed, we must be manned, equipped, trained and ready for combat. Our Army and our Soldiers – particularly our NCOs - must be ready for the unknown. We don't know when it's happening, or what it will be, but it is going to happen. We can't let our guard down. Only one percent of our population makes the choice to defend America. We've got to make sure we do it right.

When I talk about getting back to the basics, I'm talking about falling back to what we know works – about reestablishing the foundation that Soldiers need to be successful.

An NCO who gets back to the basics makes sure to make time to do some "housekeeping" – are you taking care of those garrison duties? Are you and your Soldiers doing maintenance on your personal and organization equipment? Are you conducting counseling? Holding inspections? Checking on the barracks? This is "NCO 101". We all learned how to perform these duties, we just need to get back to actually doing it.

While you're in garrison, work off your Professional Military Education back log. Send your Soldiers and NCOs to school. We must develop our future leaders because one day they will replace us. How about you? Are you working toward a degree? If not, you should be. One day you will retire, and that degree will serve you well.

A formal education isn't the only thing you should be focusing on – you need to make sure you are conducting Officer and NCO Professional Development. Sometimes you need to combine them. Make sure your Officers and your NCOs spend some good training time together. Remember your bearing, but don't try to make all of those sessions formal.

Physical training is also important. There's a new training circular out, *TC* 3-22.20. Get familiar with it. This is what is being taught in basic training. Don't go backwards in your unit. While you're looking at physical training, take a look at your height and weight standards. What are you doing as a leader to teach your Soldiers good eating habits and good PT habits? Lead by example here – if your Soldiers see you doing PT, and picking a healthy meal over a high fat, fast food meal, they'll understand how it works. Our Army has to get back in shape. We have to educate our Soldiers on the choices they make and then enforce the standards.

While we're getting back to the basics, don't forget the importance of counseling. Our Soldiers deserve to know what the standards are, and how well they are doing at meeting those standards. You can't expect a Soldier to meet the standards if you've never established the standards. Counseling doesn't have to always be negative. If your Soldiers are doing well, you should tell them as much. We all like a little encouragement and acknowledgment from our senior leaders. Don't wait to do counseling until it is too late. If you see something going in the wrong direction, see if you can steer it back on track.

Another basic area we must return to is maintenance. We've got Soldiers who have never had to take care of their own vehicles. That's going to change. The contracts we have in place now might not continue. We must train our Soldiers to do maintenance. Get in your motor pools and see what your Soldiers know. You will be surprised.

It's not just about vehicles; we've got to sustain our equipment. Do you know what your Sustainment Brigades are capable of? How about your AFSBs? Get them to help you out. Start thinking about motor stables. It's important that you start thinking about how to sustain your own equipment - as many of us did in the past. Dollars are dwindling. You're going to end up doing your own sustainment and maintenance.

Maintain discipline

We all know our equipment is only as good as our operators. What are we doing to maintain discipline in our operators – our Soldiers? What are we doing to make sure our Soldiers are good representatives of the uniform and the nation?

Let's clean up alcohol and drug issues. When was your last urinalysis test? Do you have a good screening program in place? If folks have a problem, it's your responsibility to get them help before it's too late. If you send a Soldier to rehab, give them a chance to do better. Why would you waste the funds if you don't give them a chance?

Drugs, alcohol and other discipline issues in senior NCOs and Officers will get you thrown out. We don't have time for bad leaders. We don't need to tolerate bad leaders. Bad leaders create toxic work environments, and we simply don't need to tolerate it. Hazing? Not in our Army.

Everyone complains about the young Soldiers who come in our Army. Instead of complaining, make it your responsibility to work with them. Basic training only has them for nine weeks. Take ownership of them and help them become a good Soldier. Show them what right looks like. If you've got a bad Soldier, take a long look at how you've helped mentor and train them. You might be part of the issue if you haven't taken time to be a good leader, a good NCO.

Enforce the Standards

A good NCO always enforces the standard. Salute. Give the greeting of the day to Officers. Be polite and professional. Are we calling "attention" and "at ease" for Officers and NCOs? Are we saluting? Are we standing at "parade rest" for NCOs? These are things that make our Army better than the rest. Let's not lose that tradition or that standard.

A great way to make sure standards are established and met is to use the Non-Commissioned Officer Evaluation Reporting System the way it was designed. NCOERs are changing to better align with the current doctrine on leadership. Use that NCOER to reduce inflated evaluations. Use that NCOER to provide greater separation between marginal, average and outstanding performers. Enforcing the standards in the evaluation process will ensure we have a disciplined system in place that paints a clear and accurate picture of our NCO Corps.

Communicate, communicate, and communicate

As is the case in so many things, communication is the key. As a leader and as an NCO, people are watching you. And they are listening to you. Our Army policies are changing constantly. Agree or disagree, you need to watch how you voice your opinion on contentious topics. It's your job to understand, explain, and enforce new policies and processes. It's not your job to spout off about how much you disagree or agree with the policies. Doing so can create a toxic leadership environment, and we don't need that in our formations. Try to keep in mind that leaders take care of Soldiers, and Soldiers take care of Soldiers. Don't make remarks about your personal feelings. You're there to communicate the standards and to enforce them.

I cannot overstate how important communication is. The number one reason for suicide is relationship issues. Does your Soldier trust you enough to talk to you if he or she has a problem? Do they feel like you will listen? We've got to be engaged and help prevent these suicides from happening.

Leaders care 24/7 – not just in combat, but also in garrison. You've got to know your people. You have to talk to your formations. Leaders and Soldiers are tired and we need to watch out for each other. Take leave and rest when the opportunity is given. If you need help, ask for it and make sure your Soldiers know they can ask you for help as well.

Our Army is changing. But it's nothing new – it's nothing we haven't been through before. As we change, we will find ways to grow stronger. One thing that will never change is the need for NCOs to serve as the best possible example to junior Soldiers. NCOs serve as the "go to" work force for senior leaders. As long as we continue to focus on the basics, maintain discipline, enforce the standards, and communicate – up and down the chain - NCOs will remain the "Backbone of the Army".

CSM Ronald Riling
US Army Materiel Command

From One Leader to Another
History and Traditions

Sergeant Major (Retired) Toni Gagnon Ross

"To be a successful Soldier, you must know history."

- George S. Patton Jr.

This quote is the basis for why military history continues to be studied at all levels of the Army. Recognizing and analyzing events, tactics, successes and failures contributes to developing a better fighting force, weapons and equipment. Over time, historians have studied famous, and not-so-famous, battles the United States has fought as well as those of our enemies.

We have learned from all of the men and women who have gone before us from the fight for liberty in our own backyard to the desert sands of the Middle East. Similarly, in the past ten years we have continued to develop combat techniques designed to address the asymmetric operating environment, urban sprawl, and jagged mountain terrain of Afghanistan and Iraq. Demonstrating we can learn from recent history, the first Army & Marine Corps *Counterinsurgency Field Manual* was published in 2006 while simultaneously fighting in Afghanistan and Iraq. Now, six years later, as we maintain a large presence in Southwest Asia and other regions, the first revision of this same manual as well as all of our doctrinal references are under revision.

Our documented history has also captured events in the Army's past that could have been easily overlooked. All of which were events that had a significant impact on both our Army and our Nation. Until President Truman signed Executive Order 9981 in 1946, segregation was openly practiced in the military. The US Army Air Corps' Tuskegee Airmen, the 555th Parachute Infantry Battalion and the 6888th Postal Unit are all well-known African-American units from World War II. Over time there were other smaller ethnic groups such as Asian-Americans (Philippine Scouts) and Native Americans (Navaho Code Talkers) who also proudly served our Nation. Up to 1942, women were not allowed to serve in the military but with the establishment of the Women's Army Auxiliary Corps that quickly changed. In 1943, the WAAC were re-designated as the Women's Army Corps and during World War II over 150,000 women served on both fronts. Later they would serve in Korea and Vietnam until the WAC was deactivated in 1978 and women were fully assimilated into the US Army. Why are these seemingly minor references to our history mentioned, because they had a significant impact on both our Army and our Nation's culture and climate?

Equally as important as our Army history but on a completely different level, smaller units possess their own histories known as a lineage. The lineage and honors of a unit include its origin, battles, awards, distinctive unit patches and insignias. The latter two articles mentioned are known as heraldic items. Army history books and websites always include a description of a unit's heraldic items "as they reflect the history, tradition, ideals, mission, and accomplishments." These practices stem from the Middle Ages where color and symbols reflected the heraldry, often Family lineage associated with a particular unit. Generally speaking it helped determine friend from foe. Today the US Army maintains The Institute of Heraldry (TIOH) that supports the offices of the Presidency, the Department of Defense and other federal agencies with its coats of arms, official seals, flags and streamers. These items possess significant value as they help to form an organization's identity which is foundational to the larger culture and climate.

Army uniforms also have a linkage to our organizational history and tradition. A Soldier's uniform represents many facets of Army history from the shoulder insignias, rank insignias, distinctive unit crests and special branch items such as the Infantry blue cord. Many wonder why the light blue trousers of the Army Service Uniform are a different shade of blue than that of the jacket. The difference recognizes the history of Army life out West on the Great Plains during the later part of the 19th century. The trousers faded because Soldiers packed away their coats while riding their horse or working in the hot sun. Another uniform item often misunderstood is that of the First Sergeant's rank. Few First Sergeants know that the geometric shape in the center of their rank insignia is a pierced lozenge centered between chevrons and arcs; not a diamond, stripes and rockers as they are traditionally referred to. Another example is that many like to say enlisted Soldiers wear their rank on their sleeves because they do the "heavy lifting" while Officers wear their rank on their shoulders because that is where they bear the responsibility of their position.

Traditions often go unseen but reside just about everywhere in our daily activities. We honor our Fallen Warriors in many ways; we say our farewells during unit memorial ceremonies where the fallen are represented by their helmet, boots, ID tags and rifle, they are buried in traditional military fashion with the US Flag after being folded and presented according to our tradition and history. There are also symbols such as the playing of "Taps", firing details, expended rounds/casings placed inside of the flag, and often in many circumstances, full military honors provided at such places as Arlington National Cemetery led by members of the 3d Infantry Regiment's "Old Guard" with their horses and caisson. Accompanying this effort are the "Arlington Ladies", an organization created in 1973, designed so that no Soldier would ever be buried alone. Another less traditional and lasting memory are when Soldiers get tattoos in order to personally honor and remember their fallen brothers and sisters. And finally, organizations never let the memory of their fallen slip away as they pay tribute to them by formally acknowledging their sacrifice at military banquets and balls with the "fallen comrade table", toast and moment of silence.

One of our newer and very popular traditions is that of the "challenge coin". Originating in the mid-1980s they were awarded to individuals for their excellent service or achievement and presented by a Commander or Command Sergeant Major. They started as small round, bronze in color, metal coins and have grown to playing card size in all shapes, sizes, colors and artwork. They have quickly become something of a collector's item. Units now have deployment coins, Sergeant Morales coins, promotion coins, etc. It has expanded far beyond the Army to all military services, law enforcement agencies, businesses and yes, the President even has a coin too. Truly one of the most coveted! The important point is never to be without a coin when a "coin check" is called. No matter where that happens, a Soldier without his or her coin must buy the next round of drinks! This harkens back to days past in Germany when prior to the implementation of the Euro, a "pfennig check" was called. A pfennig was the German equivalent of a US penny but half the size of a dime. Usually they were taped to the back of a Soldier's driver's license and held no other significance than as a way to engage at social events.

History, traditions and customs play a significant role in our lives as Soldiers, Leaders, Veterans, Retirees and Family members. They ground us in our past while preparing us for the future so that we never forget the men and women who have gone before us and the hard fought lessons that they learned. Through the symbols, memories, always embellished "war stories," and opportunities to celebrate our successes and our losses we will always remain Army Strong! Hooah!

SGM(R) Toni Gagnon Ross

From One Leader to Another
Interpersonal Communication

Command Sergeant Major James VanSciver,

Today's Operating Environment (OE) requires dynamic leadership in order to meet the myriad of challenges our Soldiers and organizations must face in the often volatile, uncertain, complex and ambiguous world in which we operate. Being able to effectively communicate the mission and intent in order to achieve shared understanding and ultimately the desired end state requires not only clear and concise guidance, but also an understanding and appreciation for the fact that Soldiers must be given the flexibility and latitude which will enable them to exercise disciplined initiative within that guidance and intent in order to execute and accomplish a given mission. Understanding how Soldiers receive and perceive that instruction is paramount to interpersonal tact.

Interpersonal skills are extremely important as they directly contribute to the leadership competency of *leads* and more specifically, *communicates*. *Army Doctrinal Reference Publication* 6-22 (*Army Leadership*) discusses interpersonal tact in paragraphs 5-11 through 5-18. It outlines the key components which influence tact and the variables (diversity, self-control, emotional factors, balance, and stability) which leaders must be cognizant of as they may have a direct effect on the leader and their subordinates. In fact, maintaining effective interpersonal communications skills ensures that both parties understand their role in developing solutions to problems which are mutually beneficial. Some may argue that tact is merely the ability to act diplomatically or with a greater sense of empathy in order to convey respect to a superior, however that respect should be mutually recognized and beneficial. Regardless, tact remains an important competency, one which should be continually developed and routinely used when communicating with subordinates, peers and superiors in order to build cohesive, effective and efficient teams.

Recognizing the variable of diversity among others within a group allows a leader to better understand how a Soldier's upbringing and other societal influences helped to shape them as an individual. Paragraph 5-13, *ADRP 6-22* states "... it is unknown how the talents of individuals or groups will contribute to mission accomplishment." Every Soldier has the potential to provide a unique perspective which may be leveraged in order to successfully plan, prepare and execute an assigned mission – be it an idea, method or tactic. Consider a unit who has an infantryman originally from the Philippines who speaks Tagalog fluently. During a tactical questioning scenario in which a person of interest is speaking in that language this Soldier now becomes a key component to mission accomplishment. Being able to employ this Soldier using his talents has now helped the team.

Throughout history we have born witness to countless examples of poor leadership where the leader has lacked self-control or the ability to self-regulate. Displaying "calm confidence" ensures that the team remains focused on the mission as the leader role models behavior which their subordinates may now emulate. In a June 27, 2012 *NCO Journal* article written by Jennifer Mattson titled "Battling Toxic Leadership" the author quotes the results of a 2011 special report stating that "The presence of toxic leaders in the force may create a self-perpetuating cycle with harmful and long-lasting effects on morale, productivity and retention of quality personnel." Based on the facts referenced in this article notwithstanding, self-control and self-regulation most definitely affects the team. Improper attitudes and dictatorial leadership creates an environment of distrust and ultimately one of dissent.

The final three components: emotional factors, balance and stability work, closely together. Each of these as personified and demonstrated by the leader can either positively or negatively affect their Soldiers. How a leader feels most definitely impacts how he or she interacts with others. Consider for a moment that one of your Soldiers has just received a Red Cross message as the result of a death in their Family. What are your actions? Do you look at it as "just" another Red Cross message or even worse, as a distracter from your current mission or do you reach out to the Soldier and let him or her know you are there for them should they need you to be? One of my commanders once told me during my initial counseling that I should "not wear your emotions on your sleeve." What he didn't mean in that statement was not to show my emotions period, but he meant that my emotions can and often do have a very big impact on the organization as a whole. An emotionally charged individual may say something in the heat of the moment that they would have otherwise not said or have a message come across wrong. Your Soldiers will follow the example which you role model for them.

ADP 6-22 states that "Leaders communicate to convey clear understanding of what needs to be done and why" and goes on to suggest that communication and influencing activities, when performed correctly, help to develop and extend trust. A leader who lacks interpersonal communication skills such as tact will erode and ultimately destroy the very bedrock of trust within an organization.

If you would like to learn more about this topic it is recommended that you read *Army Doctrine Publication*, 6-22, *Army Leadership* and it companion document, *Army Doctrine Reference Publication 6-22, Army Leadership*.

CSM James VanSciver,
500th MI BDE

From One Leader to Another
Leader Development
Command Sergeant Major Joe B. Parson

From the birth our Nation and establishment of the Continental Army there have always been Non-Commissioned Officers. Leaders within our ranks, who are charged with the day-to-day activities that maintain good order and discipline, generate readiness, conduct training, ensure the health and welfare of the force and carryout a myriad of other duties and responsibilities essential to the success of an organization, our Army and ultimately our Nation. In 1779, Inspector General Friedrich von Steuben formally standardized NCO duties and responsibilities when he published "Regulations for the Order and Discipline of the Troops of the United States." This regulation, the beginning of a long "green line" of doctrinal publications, was the first of its kind to formally identify what was required of the NCO Corps and therefore, the first step in the formal leader development process we rely on today.

Without question, the success of our Army has and will always rest upon the shoulders of its Soldiers and the support of our Nation. As actor and comedian Bill Murray so eloquently stated it, "The Army needs leaders the way a foot needs a big toe". Although this analogy may seem funny it couldn't be truer and it also suggests that leaders are an essential part of our Army's physical makeup. Recognizing how important leaders are to our Army and its success, it is imperative that we have processes and systems specifically designed for developing those leaders. So here lie our opening questions: What is leader development? Where does it take place? Quite possibly the most important question, whom is responsible for it?

The Army defines leader development as "the deliberate, continuous, and progressive process-founded in Army Values-that grows Soldiers and Army Civilians into competent, committed professional leaders of character." At the macro level, this definition clearly answers the above questions. However, for a direct and/or organizational leader this definition requires elaboration. What do we mean by "deliberate, continuous and progressive", the "where" and "how" of what we are charged to develop? What do we really mean by "growing competent, committed professional leaders of character," and the "what" we are developing within that leader? And finally, is our definition really that inclusive, meaning are we in fact charged with developing all Soldiers and Civilians, the "who" we are charged with developing into our future leaders? And we still have the unanswered question from above, "who is responsible for leader development?"

The Leader Requirements Model, what we expect leaders to "be, know and do" and the attributes and competencies which we should expect from all Army leaders, is clearly outlined in Army *Doctrine Publication 6-22, Army Leadership* and further clarified in its reference publication, Army Doctrine Reference Publication 6-22. These publications and *Army Doctrine Reference Publication* 1-0, *The Army Profession* clearly define what it means to be an Army Professional, a person of character who is both competent and committed to the Army Profession, fellow Army Professionals and our Nation. By making the statement that we are charged with developing professionals we then answer the question of "who" we are charged with developing; we are charged with developing all members of the Profession of Arms (Soldiers) and all members of the Army Civilian Corps (Department of the Army Civilians). Therefore, our leader development programs and systems must be inclusive and meet the ends of developing competence, character and commitment. So the tougher questions still remain, that of "where," "how," and "who is responsible for leader development."

Our Army Leader Development Strategy states that "leader development is achieved through the life-long synthesis of training, education, and experiences acquired through opportunities in the operational, institutional, and self-development domains." It is quite clear from this statement that leader development is not the sole purview or responsibility of any one organization or entity. Each and every member of our profession has a shared responsibility to not only development him or herself but also to develop others. It is also clear from this statement that leader development does not occur periodically or sporadically throughout one's career. It does not solely take place at a particular school, in a particular assignment or through one's individual efforts. Leader development occurs throughout all of those examples and many, many more. Unfortunately our current operational environment has created a culture and climate that does not completely embrace this view.

A fundamental flaw in many organizations is the premise that leader development is merely made up of a counseling program and a handful of leader professional development sessions. For some organizations this mindset has become further clouded either because of a deliberate view or an inattentive focus on leader development where it has become something that resides solely in the realm of professional military education. Either through deliberate planning or lack of attention, those organizations have in effect abdicated responsibility to develop their subordinates and have become overly reliant on an educational system designed to provide the fundamentals of leadership. In some cases our expectations of each domain (operational, institutional and self-development) have become somewhat skewed. A great organization places the appropriate amount of focus on training, education and experience in all three of the domains by deliberately planning, preparing, executing and assessing their organization's leader development program.

So what does this mean to you and your organization? You need to turn this strategy into a mission and this mission into a plan; so start with what you know. Across our Army and within your organization we execute a myriad of programs that directly influence leader development. A way to synchronize our efforts is by categorizing our activities as formal, semi-formal and informal processes, programs, procedures and systems. You, as a direct and organizational leader, can start by taking the time to codify each of these in your leader development plan.

Using these categories as a method to articulate a leader development plan, we have formal processes which are prescribed and often mandated in Army Regulations, Doctrine, etc. that should be clearly identified in your plan. Counseling, Evaluations, Feedback and Assessments, Professional Military Education, Structure Self-Development, Recognition and Promotion Boards, Qualifications, Certifications, Command Climate Surveys and Inspection Programs are a few of the formal aspects of leader development that should be articulated in a leader development plan. We then have less prescriptive processes that are equally as important to a leader development plan and should be linked accordingly. Items such as the Unit Training Management System, Field Training Exercises, the Organizational

Multi-Source Assessment and Feedback, Standard Operating Procedures, Ceremonies, Organizational Certifications such as Team Leader and Squad Certifications, Reception and Integration Activities, Functional Training and talent management within an organization are all semi-formal processes (items that may not be specifically mandated, but are highly encouraged) which directly relate to leader development. And finally, there are countless informal activities (items that are routinely conducted in high performing organizations but are not directed). These often have the greatest impact on leader development, yet many organizations fail to formally recognize and include them in their leader development plans. Items such as mentorship, additional duties, team-building exercises, sensing sessions, professional reading programs, and succession planning are all examples of informal processes, systems and programs that should be included in a leader development plan. Again, this is merely a way to view leader development within an organization. Below is a graphical depiction of the interrelated nature of a leader development program. The key is taking the time to articulate the significance of leader development and your plan to the members of your organization.

Some will argue that many of these formal and informal activities already take place within an organization and therefore need not be spelled out in a leader development plan. The rationale behind this statement, in many organizations, may be true. However, by not codifying these type of items in a deliberate manner within your leader development plan the organization's leadership will miss out on an opportunity to highlight the significance of leader development, and to demonstrate how many that are done on a regular basis and directly link to leader development. Again, keep in mind that leader development is "achieved through the life-long synthesis of the training, education, and experiences acquired through opportunities in the operational, institutional, and self-development domains". A plan is beyond an idea, it is the "why, how, and what" we intend to do. Therefore, it is important that we take the time to plan for leader development. Otherwise, we will be forced to rely on happenstance as our method for developing our future leaders.

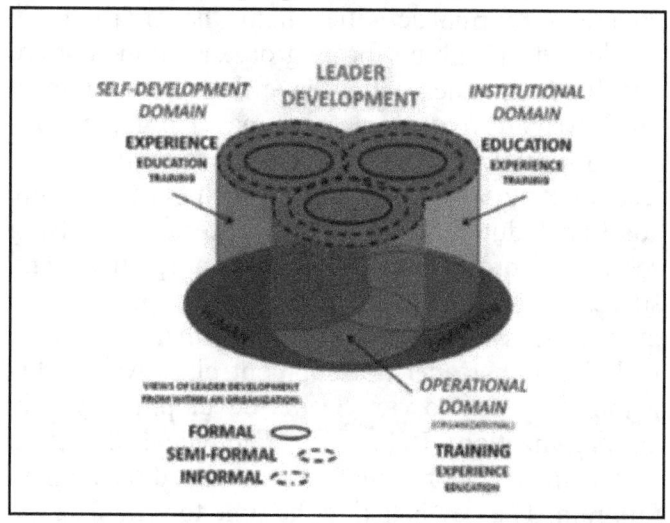

In the end, the Army is dependent upon itself, upon leaders, to develop leaders. We cannot simply advertise to hire an Army Leader in our local newspaper or in an online job listing, nor can we wait to develop a leader as the need arises. Each and every day every one of us is charged with developing the leaders of today and tomorrow. As an Army Professional, you are charged with planning, preparing, executing, and assessing leader development at your level in order to grow Soldiers and Army Civilians into competent, committed professional leaders of character. Developing leaders who are role models, who possess the attributes and competencies as described in the Leader Requirements Model, is absolutely essential to the Army's mission and future strength of our Army. This is unequivocally our collective responsibility as Leaders.

If you would like to learn more about this topic, I recommend you read the "Army Leader Development Strategy 2013," the *Army Doctrine and Doctrine Reference Publications* 6-22, *Army Leadership*, and the *Army Doctrine Reference Publication* 1-0, *The Army Profession*.

CSM Joe B. Parson
Combined Arms Center,
Leader Development & Education

From One Leader to Another
Leader Development
Master Sergeant (P) Garrick Griffin

If there has been one thing in my 22 years of military service that I could always depend on, it would be change. Developing leaders that can adapt to and overcome these changes has been the cornerstone of our military existence. During the history of our military, we have had many great leaders that have shaped and transformed the very way our Army fights and train today. It is important that, as our military begins to embark on a new era, we continue to grow great leaders. We must develop our junior Soldiers and Officers in a manner that will position them and our military for success now and in the future.

Army Regulation 600-100 defines leader development as the deliberate, continuous, sequential, and progressive process, grounded in Army Values, that grows Soldiers and civilians into competent and confident leaders capable of decisive action. As a leader of Soldiers, it will not only be a part of your daily functions to take care of your Soldiers and their well being, but you will also have to ensure that you are preparing your Soldiers for that day when they will become a leader . There are some that will say leaders are born with all the attributes needed to be successful. I would agree that some are born with the ability to lead but it is through training and experience that they become effective leaders.

It will be your job to ensure that the Soldiers you are developing into leaders are given the chance to excel at ever cost. You have to share your successes as well as your failures with them so that they can learn from your experiences. You must encourage your Soldiers to increase their knowledge by attending military institutional training as well as civilian education to help them develop. Institutional training consists of schools like the Warriors Leaders Course, the Advance and Senior Leader Courses, just to name a few. By attending college, it adds even more credibility to your future leader not only in the military but even as a civilian when they depart the service.

To be deliberate in developing your future leader, you must have a plan laid out for them to grow and prosper. You must talk with them often in both formal and informal settings to assist them in their growth. There will be times that you will need to encourage them to do things that they don't believe that they can achieve themselves. When I was a drill sergeant, I loved training new recruits and preparing them for their life in the military. That is all I wanted to do, was to train. I had a Command Sergeant Major that saw something in me that I didn't see myself. There was a Drill Sergeant of the Year competition coming up and he wanted me to represent the unit. I fought it tooth and nail but like I said before, as a leader you have to see the potential in your Soldiers, the potential that they may not see in themselves. I went to that board and won at the battalion, brigade, and installation levels. The CSM knew I would do well, but he also knew I needed that little push. You must see the potential in your Soldiers and push them in directions they can't see right now so that we help them develop into great leaders.

The process must be continuous as well. I have continued to guide Soldiers I have served with over the years. Even after you or your Soldier has moved on, you must continue to be that mentor that pushes them to reach greater heights. Many of the roads your Soldiers will head down, you have already traversed. You can provide insight and assist them in the decisions they will need to make as they make that journey down the same roads. I have always had those same leaders that I call upon when I need guidance on what actions I should take even now after 22 years. The ability for them to have that reach back is crucial, in my opinion, to leader development. Remember to assist them but don't always give them the answer. Give them some things to think about and allow them to come up with their own direction or choice. You must develop your future leaders to be thinkers that aren't afraid to make decisions.

There is a saying that I have heard that goes something like this," If you give a man a fish he will eat for a day, but if you teach him how to fish he will eat for a life time." Teach your Soldiers what right looks like. Set the example that will continue with them throughout their career. I have been blessed to have great leaders who have taught me what right looks like during my time and they have helped me be successful. Your Soldiers and future leaders are a direct reflection of you. Give them something to be proud of so that they may continue to pass the torch on well beyond after you have left the military.

It is important that you continue to grow as well in order to produce effective leaders. You must seek self-development as well as the institutional training that the Army will provide you throughout your career. I will provide you a list of books and references that have helped me throughout my career which I am certain will benefit you. Seek some of the hard jobs and assignments that will increase your knowledge and better prepare you for leading your troops. You will find it very hard to influence your Soldiers to seek self improvement when you don't have the credentials yourself. I love the Drill Sergeants Creed and I would not only ask you to read it, but if you have the chance, become one. In the creed, there is a passage that states," I will lead by example, never requiring a Soldier to attempt any task I would not do myself." There isn't much that I ask my Soldiers to do I haven't done or attempted myself. When they walk into your office can you say the same? I proudly hang my college diplomas and awards in my office to show that I am not just asking you to do something, but I have done it myself and it has gotten me to where I am now.

Developing leaders is not an easy task and there will be times when you feel like you don't think that you can do it. Don't be discouraged or give up because we have all been there. As you grow, so too will your ability to produce leaders. It is important that we continue to develop Soldiers into become leaders today so that the future of the Army will continue to be strong well after us all.

It is recommended that you take the time to read the following: "Who Moved My Cheese" by Spencer Johnson, "The One Minute Manager" by Kenneth Blanchard and Spencer Johnson, *Army Regulation 600-100, Army Leadership, Army Doctrine and Doctrine Reference Publications 6-22, Army Leadership, Department of the Army Pamphlet 350-58, Leader Development of American's Army, Department of the Army Pamphlet 600-25, Officer Professional Development Guide* and *Field Manual 7-27.7, The Army Non-Commissioned Officer Guide.*

MSG (P) Garrick Griffin
CSM Robert Austin
19th ESC

From One Leader to Another
Leader Engagement
Command Sergeant Major Allen Fritzsching

There is nothing as an important or rewarding as the privilege to lead Soldiers. Leadership is a continuous process of influence and is the lifeblood of our Army. ADP 6-22 defines an Army Leader as anyone who by virtue of assumed role or assigned responsibility inspires and influences people both inside and outside the chain of command to pursue actions, focus thinking and shape decisions for the greater good of the organization.

Throughout our history wars have been won and lost as a result of the actions taken by Leaders to ensure their Soldiers were properly trained, equipped and led during combat operations. Since the formation of the Continental Army until today Army Leaders have accepted the challenges to lead Soldiers in some of the most demanding environments under the most dangerous conditions imaginable. They have done this with great success.

To be an effective Leader you must be engaged in all aspects of the unit's mission, training plan and the training, development and lives (both professional and personal) of your Soldiers. It is extremely challenging to accomplish all of the Leader tasks necessary to be an effective NCO, but you can with great success if you are engaged. There is a distinct difference between being in charge and being an engaged leader. Leaders are professional Soldiers that know and exude Army Values. They are role models for all to emulate and are adept at motivating, teaching, coaching, counseling and mentoring. Set the example at all times. It's how you perform when no one is watching that really counts. Never do anything that will discredit you, your leaders, or your great unit. Have pride in your unit. Salute with pride!

Be the standard bearer. Set the example in appearance, personal conduct, physical fitness, competence, customs and courtesies. Do not accept mediocrity as your standard. Always try to be the absolute best at everything you do no matter how insignificant the task. Everything is a part of a bigger plan. Everything you do is important. Set goals and achieve them, don't just accept things because that is how they have always been. This is contagious and your Soldiers will emulate you which in turn will improve the formation.

Be visible and present. Engaged Leaders are visible and present at all training events, inspections, promotion and reenlistment ceremonies, unit events, etc. Be on the ground leading your Soldiers from the front both in peacetime and war. Never ask your Soldiers to do anything that you would not be willing to do yourself. Demonstrate to them that you are their Leader and you will do what you ask them to do. Your presence sends a strong message that you are an engaged Leader. Endure the hardships with your Soldiers and they will respect you.

Leaders take care of their Soldiers. Leadership is not convenient. It is your primary inherent responsibility. Communicate consistently with your Soldiers and never leave them uniformed. Know everything there is to know about your Soldiers and their Families. You can never know enough. Understand their strengths and weaknesses, goals, desires and needs. Listening is key to communicating with your Soldiers. Communicate with your Soldiers everyday and don't wait to make time for a formal counseling session. Their professional development is a continuous process. Accept that your life belongs to your Soldiers. You must make yourself available, particularly when the Soldier needs you, not just when it is convenient for yourself. If they know you are listening and genuinely care about them and their Families they will trust in you.

Conduct routine inspections routinely. Inspect something every day. Make a habit of conducting daily walk thru of the barracks and conducting in-ranks inspections. Develop a system so that you are inspecting your section and Soldiers equipment systematically and routinely. Annotate shortcomings, conduct corrective training, and provide feedback and follow-up to ensure deficiencies are corrected. Your Soldiers expect you to hold them accountable to the standard. Do routine maintenance routinely. You should inspect and maintain your equipment (vehicles, weapons, KIT, radios, etc.) weekly. Enforce high equipment readiness and maintenance standards with all your subordinates. Individual Soldier Combat Equipment (KIT) should be configured to your unit standard operating procedure. Eye protection should be worn at all times on ranges, in a tactical environment and with the helmet. Ensure that your equipment meets the TM – 10/20 maintenance standards and that you have 100% accountability. You have to go to war with what you have. If you don't maintain your equipment it will fail you in war. Soldiers must always be ready. Inspections are not designed to see how you can get ready. Inspections are designed to check your readiness.

Time is the one resource we can never get enough of, therefore it is extremely important that your time and the time of your Soldiers is managed both efficiently and effectively. Ensure that you and your Soldiers are always where they are supposed to be when they are supposed to be there in the proper uniform ready to train and execute. When you allow Soldiers to be late you have set a new standard. There is only one standard for everything we do.

Plan your training effectively while managing your time wisely so training is worthwhile. Solid, realistic, performance-oriented, tactical training is the only standard. Ensure you manage mandatory training. An untrained Soldier is a leadership shortcoming. You must have trained Combat Lifesavers and all Soldiers must be licensed to operate all assigned equipment. Every Soldier must be able to Shoot (marksmanship), Move (mounted and dismounted), Communicate (ABCS and Comms), Fight (Combative), Survive (First Aid/Combat Lifesaver), Sustain (Stewardship) and Secure (Force Protection). Soldiers expect realistic, tough, demanding training. An untrained Soldier is a Leader failure.

Be physically fit and motivated while you are conducting Physical Fitness Training. You must set the example and enforce the standard in this area. Participate in PT with your Soldiers every day. PT is a bonafide occupational qualification. We must be fit to be Soldiers and Leaders must be extremely fit to lead Soldiers. Don't accept APFT failures and overweight Soldiers. Ensure that your fitness programs are demanding. Fitness also includes wellness. Focus on comprehensive fitness, medical readiness and worldwide deployability. Unfit Soldiers are Leader Failures.

Safety and security is of the utmost importance. A violation is serious and detrimental to readiness and the mission. Do not sacrifice safety for speed. Be conscious of your surroundings and constantly reinforce operational security. Risk Assessments are mandatory for every mission. Conduct a thorough Risk Assessment and execute it. Completing a TRIPS (travel risk planning system) report is mandatory before all travel. Also ensuring that your Soldiers routinely complete the GAT (global assessment tool) will help you with identifying high risk or troubled Soldiers long before an issue might develop. Integrate the Soldier Risk Assessment Tool in to all periodic counseling sessions and prior to and after major training events and operations. Safety and security save lives.

Lead with self-discipline and impose it. Subordinates are not your buddies. Soldiers expect leaders to be highly disciplined. Review all SOPs, regulations and policies upon arrival to your unit. Enforce regulations and policies at all times. Never walk by anything that is absolutely not in accordance with a prescribed standard. If you do, you just set a new standard.

The decision-making process demands complete responsive reporting. You must keep each other informed and always ask the question, "Who else needs to know?" Finally, "bad news does not get better with time," never hold on to information for fear of the response from those being briefed. Your door should always be wide open. Use the NCO Support Channel and Chain of Command.

Exercise firm but fair leadership. Leaders award the good and take appropriate action for the wrong. Leaders don't be too lazy to write awards. Just as importantly have the intestinal fortitude to provide critical feedback to your Soldiers when they need it. Soldiers have the right to expect this type of leadership. Accepting mediocrity is detrimental to combat readiness. You must continuously teach, coach, counsel and mentor those Soldiers that fail to meet and maintain Army standards and hold them accountable if they do not improve.

Counsel regularly, every Soldier has the right to be properly counseled on time. Develop plans to support and foster your Soldier's professional growth and development. Maximize corrective training.

An untrained Soldier is a leadership shortcoming. Uniform Code of Military Justice should always be the last resort not the first option. Soldiers must understand the corrective training and not view it as harassment; it is an alternative to punitive action to correct a performance shortcoming.

Take action, use initiative, and don't always wait to be told to do something. Initiative is one of the biggest signs of great character; it really stands out. The biggest mistake that you can make is not doing anything! Ask questions. We expect you to. You are just starting out and there is a lot to learn. Read and understand the Task, Conditions and Standards. Be an expert at doctrine. Don't just take someone's word on this is how it is done. Do your research and homework before you train and conduct operations. Fully understand the Commander's intent and the operational environment. Resource your Soldiers to accomplish the mission and you run interference to reduce training distracters.

Ensure that both you and your subordinates are enrolled in professional development programs (civilian/military schooling) to enhance professional growth and promotion potential. Sacrifice now and it will pay huge dividends in the future. Ensure your Soldiers are physically, mentally, emotionally and financially ready (including their Families) to attend and successfully complete their level of NCOES. Bring to the Chain of Command's attention career issues such as retention, promotions, reassignment, retirement, reclassification, professional development, schools, etc., so that they can help you with them. You must be the biggest recruiter and career counselor in the unit.

Soldiers do exactly in war as they do in training. No seatbelts in training equals death in combat (as well as in peacetime operations). No helmets in tactical vehicles equal head injuries and death. No muzzle awareness and weapon safety checks equal negligent discharge fatalities and injuries. No eye and hearing protection equal blind and deaf Soldiers.

Continuously seek the advice of your senior NCOs and Officers. They have experience and a responsibility for your development. You must be balanced. Organize yourself so that you spend the majority of your time doing those things that are most relevant to the training, readiness and health and welfare of your Soldiers.

Lastly, you are an Ethical Standard Bearer for your Soldiers. Live the Army Values and Embody our Warrior Ethos. Remember-you are always on display no matter where you are at. Your Soldiers are watching you and they will do what you do. You are exactly who they perceive you to be and you can not fool them with your words. Your actions speak for you.

CSM Allen Fritzsching
US Army Test and Evaluation Command

From One Leader to Another
Military Bearing
Command Sergeant Major Erik Arne

There are many definitions of military bearing that can be found in countless references, one such definition and reference is that of the online "Free Dictionary" where the Soviet military defined military bearing as:

1. The element of outward appearance of a serviceman (clean and correctly arranged uniform, properly worn and adjusted equipment, manner of behavior in and out of formation) imparting a brisk military outward appearance to the individual and the entire detachment.

2. A part of individual drill instruction with the purpose of inculcating the Soldier with the habits of behavior in and out of formation and the ability to execute the drill manuals quickly and dexterously. This instruction also serves the purpose of developing in the Soldiers' unity, uniformity, and coordination during actions in motion, with arms, and in machines. The Soldier's bearing is achieved by a combination of drill, physical training, and sports.

Military bearing is far more than that, it is a discipline that should be practiced at all times, both on and off duty, by military personnel, (both US and Partner Nations), elected officials, and DoD/DA civilians. Military bearing is about demonstrating one's own pride in their profession through their outward appearance, conduct and communication. Military bearing is a courtesy, a person's manner and demonstrates their self-discipline. Today's "America's Army, Our Profession" campaign highlights the importance of military and professional bearing particularly recognizing how the Army is perceived by those within the military ranks, Governmental Agencies, Non-Governmental Agencies, the public of the United States and our Partner Nations. Our challenge is that our Army is facing a significant transition from a high operational tempo conducting unified land operations to a lower operational tempo conducting regionally aligned operations focused on worldwide geographical partnerships. Unquestionably, military bearing will play an essential role in the success of this transition across all levels of leadership, rank, and status.

A professional leader projects presence through several factors which include actions, words, respect shown to others and the manner in which they carry themselves. "Presence is not just a matter of the leader showing up; it involves the image that the leader projects. Presence is conveyed through actions, words and the manner in which leaders carry themselves. A reputation is conveyed by the respect that others exhibit, how they refer to the leader and how they respond to the leader's guidance. Presence is a critical attribute that leaders need to understand." (*FM* 6-22). Soldiers do not graduate from basic training automatically possessing military bearing even though military bearing has always been one of the general learning outcomes required of an aspiring professional. Even for the Non-Commissioned Officer, this attribute needs to be learned early on and reinforced and practiced throughout their career. There are many ways Soldiers and NCOs develop military bearing but the most effective way is through the observation of their subordinates, peers and superiors. Soldiers and even Leaders follow the example that is set for them by the people that they are in contact with. They will emulate their leaders' actions, whether good or bad. Leaders who practice good military bearing will normally have followers who do the same; leaders who do not have a "presence" normally are not respected and therefore their subordinates typically do not demonstrate the proper bearing either.

Some say that military bearing is "old school" and that our newest generation of Soldiers is beyond that. I would call foul regarding that type of remark; a professional institution should not be persuaded by generational differences, particularly in this area. I began my enlisted career in the Marine Corps and learned early on what military bearing was. In the Marine Corps military bearing is instilled in the culture of the Corps. Nothing less is acceptable and it is still that way today. Marines learn early on that respect, loyalty, duty and discipline are essential to accomplishing the mission; if they don't then they are as good as gone. One of my lasting encounters with "learning" bearing as a young Marine occurred when I was just a Corporal stationed at Camp Pendleton. As an NCO, I knew the rules regarding how to address a fellow Marine. Marines never call anyone by their first name. In fact, we would often joke that a person's rank was their first name. An example of how serious this is taken is how Marines always us the full rank title when addressing another Marine (a SSG is called "Staff Sergeant" and not just "Sergeant" as in the Army - a practice in the Army that I have never quite understood). At that time in my career my room-mate was another Corporal, CPL Steve Gutierrez, and he was the Company Training NCO. One morning I needed to visit the Company HQs to sign a few documents. When I went in to the office my Squad Leader, a Staff Sergeant, happened to be in there but I didn't immediately notice him. As I entered the office I said "Steve I'm here to sign some papers". I don't think I even got the sentence finished when a loud voice bellowed "At ease Marine! What in the world do you think you are doing? If I ever hear you call a fellow Marine by his first name,

I'll write you up on charges for disrespect!" It was, of course, my Squad Leader and that incident left a lasting impression on me and my military bearing. Of course, it was customary and acceptable when off duty and with small groups of peers to call one another by our first name.

I left the Marine Corps after my first enlistment because at the time the USMC was not a good place to have and raise a Family. In the first 18 months of my first son's life, I had spent with him approximately 45 days, not exactly the way I wanted to be a father. But after about 18 months of civilian life, I was missing the camaraderie I had found as a service member. I had started a new career and had bought a house for my Family and didn't want to go back on Active Duty, so I joined the Army National Guard. That in and of itself was a culture shock for me! Don't mistake what I am trying to say, the field artillery unit I joined was a very technically and tactically proficient unit but the unique thing about the Guard is that most units are "home town" grown. The members of a unit are often comprised of brothers, cousins, father-son combinations and now even mothers, sisters, etc. Neighbors, business owners and maybe even the Mayor are all in the same unit. At times a subordinate in the unit might be in charge of a leader in their civilian career. These types of relationships bring with them a unique set of challenges particularly in how the Soldiers communicate and conduct themselves with one another. Addressing one another by their first name, not saluting an Officer and not standing at-ease or parade-rest when addressing a superior were all considered acceptable practices. The units didn't necessarily lack discipline but they did lack bearing because of their interpersonal relationships.

I did not let this lack of military bearing and courtesy affect my own personal standards. In fact, I thrived on it and even relished in it. I decided that as a Specialist I was going to be the standard bearer for which others would follow. My first assignment was as an operations clerk in the Battalion S3 Operations Section working for the OPS SGT and Assistant S3. I would always address the AS3 and other Officers with "sir" or Captain (or whatever rank) and when given orders by the AS3 or OPS SGT I would respond with the Marine acknowledgement of "Aye Aye." I think at first I really caught them off guard and then after awhile it started to become second nature to them and they appreciated it. As time went on, I was given increased responsibility beyond that of my pay grade and respect that others of my equal grade were not given. This led to other opportunities and promotions and while I climbed the enlisted and NCO ranks, I continued to live up to my own standard and values in military bearing and courtesy. I took pride in my uniform, trying to outshine the others. I gave every job, duty and detail everything I had. I accepted constructive criticism and turned it into strength. As I was doing all of this as a sort of my own self motivation, it evolved into something called "presence." I became a heavily respected NCO in the Army National Guard by my peers, subordinates and my superiors; known as a true professional. Since becoming a first sergeant and later a Command Sergeant Major this presence was very valuable, especially after 9-11 when the Army National Guard became a much more relevant force in the war against terrorism, not just a "strategic reserve". As a Reserve Component CSM in Operation Iraqi Freedom, I often had to deal with CSMs and Commanders of the Active Army and Marine Components as well as Air Force units that we supported with security. I believe the way that I carried myself, my outward presence, enabled us to work together in order to meet our

Commander's intent and accomplish the mission. The Army National Guard has clearly evolved from those days long ago and I hope maybe in some small way I was a part of their professional evolution in standards and conduct.

We've all heard of the golden rule, "treat others as you would want to be treated," whether it was in bible study, school, at home and even in the military. Throughout my military career I've never been a shouter or a "butt kicker," I have tried to adhere to that golden rule. Because of that, I believe I was able to gain respect and was looked upon as an approachable and professional NCO.

As I stated earlier, military bearing is not just about courtesy and respect, it is also about an image. How a Soldier looks in uniform, his or her physical stature and conditioning, how they display confidence and their resilience all project military bearing. So if you look back on the definition provided in the opening paragraph you will see that it still remains true. The Soviets didn't invent military bearing, they, like most all other Armies, recognized how important it was in carrying out individual duties and accomplishing the overall mission. A person who witnesses someone in action can establish a first impression of that person pretty quickly determining what they are like and what level of professionalism he or she posses. This assessment often determines their level of loyalty and faith towards that person resulting in a deduction as to whether they will follow them or not. It comes as no surprise that if Soldiers assess not to follow then the mission will never be successful. In fact, military bearing is so recognized as a leadership trait, that it is included in the Non-Commissioned Officer Evaluation Report.

There is no doubt that as long as there is a United States there will always be a United States Army.

What the Army will look like in the years to come is difficult to ascertain. But what the Army has and will always need are professional Non-Commissioned Officers who train and care for their Soldiers, carry out and give orders and maintain good order and discipline. Future Non-Commissioned Officers who project a professional military bearing will be much more prepared to meet the missions they are assigned.

If you would like to learn more about this topic, it is recommended that you read *Army Regulation* 600-20, *Army Command Policy*, *Army Regulation* 600-100, *Army Leadership*, *Army Doctrine Publication and Doctrine Reference Publication* 6-22, *Army Leadership* and *Army Regulation* 600-20, *Army Command Policy*.

CSM Erik Arne
347th RSG, MNARNG

From One Leader to Another
Military Bearing
Command Sergeant Major Naamon Grimmett

An Army's ability to fight and win its nations wars is not solely dependent on weapons and training alone. It also rests on the attitude or climate of units, leaders and Soldiers. Find a winning Army and you will find a positive climate; the opposite is true about a losing Army. While an Army's climate is comprised of many factors, the most predominate is its Military Bearing, the way it conducts business from the top Officers and NCOs down to the most junior Soldier. If an Army possesses a positive climate at its heart, you will find a strong military bearing. Soldiers and leaders, who conduct themselves as professionals and do what is right regardless of the situation in which they find themselves, go the extra mile even when it would be easier not to in both peace and war.

Military bearing is conducting oneself in a professional manner to bring credit upon oneself and the Army at all times. It is the ability to project a commanding presence and confidence, uphold standards, and doing the hard right over the easy wrong in both good and bad situations both on and off duty. Simply acting the way Soldiers and leaders are expected to act, presenting a professional persona. Military bearing comes from pride in oneself, pride of being a Soldier, a leader and in service to the nation. The way a leader carries him or her self with the knowledge and understanding that military bearing is continuous and that his or her actions and military bearing will lead to criticism, both positive and negative. Understanding that their military bearing will define the way in which other leaders, Soldiers and the world views them. Accepting that military bearing does not end at the end of the duty day when the uniform is removed. Often the only contact the civilian population has with a Soldier is during off duty hours. This is when they will make their judgments and opinions about Soldiers and the Army in general.

Many times the first impression formed by a person or organization about a Soldier or the Army is from how Soldiers conduct themselves or by their military bearing, and first impressions do count! This is especially true when working with other branches of the Armed Forces or other nations, just as your first impression of another branch or Army is the military bearing its leaders and Soldiers demonstrate. A bad first impression may affect how much you trust and respect you show that Soldier or organization and your attitude towards working with them. The same is true when conducting operations in foreign countries. The way your unit and its Soldiers conduct themselves while executing a mission will shape the way the indigenous population will receive and accept you and your unit's actions. Always keep in mind that your success in shaping this first impression is just as important as winning any of the battles which might follow.

A leader can get a sense of a unit's military bearing almost immediately when they take a look around. It does not matter if you're a Team Leader or Command Sergeant Major, if the little discipline tarts are not being followed such as standing at "parade rest" when addressing an NCO, calling "at ease" when a senior NCO enters a room or the way NCOs and Soldiers conduct themselves when they think no one is watching. It is our job as NCOs to show a strong military bearing at all times and to instill it into our Soldiers by our example. It can be as simple as "do as I do, not as I say."

Why is having a strong military bearing important? Soldiers will always choose a leader to follow and that leader will either be good or bad. A leader's ability to maintain a strong sense of military bearing, though not always an easy task will have an immeasurable impact on Soldiers. A strong military bearing in a leader will instill pride in Soldiers. A strong military bearing among Leaders will create a sense in the Soldiers that there leader is technically and tactically proficient and a true professional leader, a leader whom they can trust, respect and place their confidence in, a leader who will take care of them. They will want to follow and be like that leader.

As NCOs we must always encompass a strong military bearing and instill it into our Soldiers. In my first few days after taking position, I was walking around the battalion area and noticed three Soldiers standing in front of the headquarters chatting. Two had their backs to me and the third was either looking past the others or did not recognize me. As I approached them with the intent to get to know some of my Soldiers and ask about their experiences in the command I noticed that one had a hand in their pocket, another had both hands tucked into his trousers. As an NCO my blood pressure began to rise, I wanted nothing more than to go over and start yelling while at the same time directing a lot of push-ups and correct the problem like my NCOs would have done 20 years ago. However, as I got closer I noticed that the Soldier facing me was a sergeant, at first this really sent by blood pressure soaring and I moved faster towards them. As I was approaching, I began to think, if a sergeant is conducting himself like this and allowing this to happen there must be a problem with his military bearing. This is when I realized that if I carried out the plan I was forming in my head I would be the one who had lost military bearing. I decided to treat this as an opportunity to educate a junior NCO and these other Soldiers. Once I was standing within a few feet of the Soldiers I was noticed and all jumped to correct themselves. Needless to say all three received a one-way, first class lecture on military bearing. I would like to say that this was the only incident of poor military bearing I witnessed over the next few days but it was not. A few days later, I conducted my first NCOPD with all of our sergeants and the topic was the significance of strong military bearing and its impact on a unit.

Much the same way that a strong military bearing can motivate and create positive effects, a loss of military bearing can have a negative effect! Take for example the two Soldiers standing with the NCO. The Soldiers were just following this NCO's example. If he did not care about his military bearing or standards then why should they? The leader that lacks a strong military bearing also risks losing the trust, confidence and most important, the respect of their Soldiers and superiors as well. The loss of military bearing has lead to Leaders being relieved of their duties. Once respect and confidence in a leader's ability is lost, it is a hard, long struggle to gain it back if ever fully regained. A Leader's poor military bearing influences, already negative in nature, will have a plague-like infection on future leaders because the current generation of Soldiers, the leadership of tomorrow's Army, will only be following the example set by their past leaders.

Military bearing is not a task that Soldiers learn in training. There are many references to assist in the study of military bearing. The NCO creed is an excellent guide to follow. The first sentence says it all, "No one is more professional than I". Other references include *ADP* and *ADRP 6-22 Army Leadership*. However, studying is not enough.

Military bearing is something learned over time by accepting and living by the Army Values and perhaps most importantly observing leaders who demonstrate and act with a strong sense of military bearing while also being part of a unit with a climate that boosts a strong overall military bearing. We must set the example now, starting with leaders. These traits will then transfer into the essentials of a good Army, its ability to train, fight and win for generations to come, as Soldiers who had leaders with strong military bearing so that they might become leaders themselves and inspire their Soldiers.

CSM Naamon Grimmett
1st HBCT, 1st ID

From One Leader to Another
Military Bearing

Command Sergeant Major Dwight Morrisey

"Our quality Soldiers should look as good as they are."

– Sergeant Major of the Army (Retired) Julius W. Gates

Pride in self, starts with pride in appearance. Army leaders are expected to look and act like professionals. They must know how to wear the appropriate uniform or civilian attire and do so with pride. Soldiers seen in public with their jackets unbuttoned and ties undone do not send a message of pride and professionalism. Instead, they let down their unit and fellow Soldiers in the eyes of the American people. Meeting prescribed height and weight standards is another integral part of the professional role. How leaders carry themselves when displaying military courtesy and appearance sends a clear signal: I am proud of my uniform, my unit, and my country. Skillful use of professional bearing of fitness, courtesy, and proper military appearance, can also aid in overcoming difficult situations. A professional presents a decent appearance because it commands respect. Professionals must be competent as well. They look good because they are good.

Military and professional bearing is projecting a commanding presence, a professional image of authority. Army leaders are expected to look and act as professionals. Soldiers and Army Civilians displaying an unprofessional appearance do not send a message of professionalism. Skillful use of professional bearing of fitness, courtesy, and proper military appearance, does. Leaders must take time to educate their Soldiers on the customs, courtesies and traditions of our Army and their unit as they greatly impact a unit's culture and climate by influencing an individual and organization's identity.

All too often, young professionals question whether it is someone else's responsibility or is it our own as an individual, an organization or as an institution to police our ranks? As I travel around to the various post, camps and stations, I have had many conversations with Officers, NCOs and Soldiers concerning this question, the question of military bearing. Most of the responses I have received were similar, in that the individual, organization and the institution have a mutually supporting responsibility; "there is a professional way you should present yourself" and "military bearing provides for an acceptable level of discipline so that a unit can function in a military manner."

In order for military bearing to be effective, the proper example must be shown and dedicated enforcement must occur at the junior NCO level. I was recently told a story about a young Officer who recently joined his new unit. When the new Platoon Leader was asked if he understood the information he was provided by his First Sergeant during his in-brief, the young Officer's answer was "Yeah, Man". A similar yet more disturbing story was that of a Soldier's response to a Staff Sergeant who directed him to complete a task in the motor pool. Clearly believing the task was beneath the Soldier to perform, the Soldier used a less than professional expletive when he responded to his supervisor and essentially refused to perform the task. That same Soldier had recently competed in the unit's Soldier of the Month competition, under the tutelage of the same NCO, where he was recognized as the runner-up. In both situations, a leader had failed this Officer and Soldier by allowing them to relax their military bearing and professionalism.

In society, neither response probably would have warranted a secondary conversation, but because of the discipline that we demand in our organizations and the Army, both of these young men ended up on the receiving side of a one-way conversation. In the Army, we must trust our leadership and we do that by training, disciplining and role modeling behavior which displays competence, character and commitment to the profession.

Many will suggest that our society has changed and a divide has been created between the norm of society and that of our military. In the military we teach young men and women to be responsible adults and productive, morale upstanding American citizens who take pride in themselves, their units and their country. For the most part, parents of these same children do everything they can to provide for them a "life better than their own". Unfortunately, as a result respect is not a value commonly taught to our children as many adults accept that maybe it is an over-rated characteristic. Discipline is no longer developed through fear of repercussion but more as a by-product of concern regarding what the individual might lose. Young athletes grow up in an environment of being proud to be on a team and part of something that is bigger than them, but seldom do we provide a similar structure for our children to be proud of who they are personally and what they represent. Moral development is a constant issue of contention between television and parents. How do you teach children to respect authority when nearly every TV channel shows someone killing a police Officer or another authority figure while glamorizing criminals, money and misbehaving youth? Some will suggest that we live in a society where we don't take responsibility for our own action. There are numerous challenges for the young men and women of our society and separating what is right and what is wrong can be a challenge for our young NCOs.

If we want to continue to be the best Army and organization in the world then implementing and enforcing an environment where a professional image is maintained is absolutely necessary. Our leaders can't be the earring, baggy pants wearing individual that our Soldiers will see as an example to follow. Soldiers need discipline and leaders need to maintain professional and military bearing in their organizations at all times. When we set the right example as leaders, then this develops that presence necessary which shows that we care about our Soldiers and helps to develop them. This presence proves to the American people that we are a professional organization, disciplined, physically and mentally tough, prepared to fight and win our nation's wars.

So the bottom line remains, we must maintain our military bearing. Society should not dictate military bearing, but "our" military bearing should provide society the confidence it needs to see us as the most professional Army in the world and the most professional organization in our country.

CSM Dwight Morrisey
Fires Center of Excellence

From One Leader to Another
An Abundance Approach to Organizational Leadership
Creating a Positive Deviance to Strengthen Combat Readiness

Command Sergeant Major John Wayne Troxell

This paper is written to provide an analysis and recommendation on strengthening our combat readiness by focusing on organizational leadership. This topic is designed to get leaders to focus less on a "problem-solving approach" to leading and more on an "abundance approach" to create or reinforce a "strive for excellence" attitude throughout the organization, thereby enhancing overall combat and organizational readiness.

For the past 12 years our Army has been tried and tested in two major combat operations in Iraq and Afghanistan conducting mostly counterinsurgency and stability operations as well as multiple deployments to other countries conducting peacekeeping, humanitarian assistance and disaster relief among other missions, as well as exercises designed to shape the environment by building partnerships and partner capacity. As we all know, units and Soldiers over that course of time have experienced multiple deployments to all of these areas. This constant "turn and burn" as sometimes referred has caused organizations to be on short timelines for reset and redeployment. Because of this it has caused some units to execute shortcuts or shoot for minimal standards as they prepare for their next deployment. What normally suffers with this attitude towards standards? Usually it is the professionalism and skills of the individual Soldier or of the organization as a whole. Leaders take on a problem solving approach to standards, accomplishment of missions or to get stuff done.

When we look at what the problem-solving approach is, it generally means that there is a deficiency or something negative or wrong that needs to be "fixed." Meaning we need to get it back to normal or to the minimum acceptable standard. Another way to say it is that less than normal is present and the task or issue at hand has taken on a "negative deviance" and needs to be brought back to normal or to the minimal acceptable standard. Examples of this include a Soldier who has failed the Army Physical Fitness Test or body fat circumference test. Generally, leaders look to get these Soldiers to just pass the PT test or tape test. An organizational example of the problem-solving approach would be to meet minimal standards of Command Supply Discipline or Mission Essential Tasks or individual and crew-served weapons qualifications. Here again leaders sometimes look to achieve the minimal standard or normal. How many times have we heard about a good leader who is known (and sometimes self-proclaimed) as a "problem-solver?" This implies that the leader knows how to take a negative deviance and make it normal. Or said differently, the leader knows how to get to the 60 percent needed to make the minimum standard. A problem-solving approach would be fine if our enemies only operated at 60 percent, or a 60 percent effort would get you promoted through the ranks. The enemies we have faced generally look for precision and efficiency when conducting attacks against us to create the most lethal effect on us, a minimal standard approach could cost lives against that kind of enemy. Also, a Soldier that shoots for the 60 percent solution with regard to their career will probably be walking the retirement stage wearing Staff Sergeant as a rank.

I propose an "abundance approach" to leading that will cause a positive deviance in everything we do and an overall strive for excellence attitude within our organizations and ranks. We have a number of units and Soldiers within our Army that have this approach and are operating at a high efficiency and performance rate. However, we still have plenty that operate in the problem-solving approach. Let's look at the Soldier who cannot pass the APFT or a tape test. Instead of just getting them to the minimal standard, let's take the abundance (or wholesome) approach and create an environment within the organization that a high fitness level is a way of life and is the cornerstone of our combat readiness. Get the overweight Soldier to focus on a lifestyle change instead of meeting the minimal standard. Let's create an attitude of "we are going to smoke this inspection" or have a focus of "we are going to be such experts with our weapons they will be an extension of our hand" to instill a "strive for excellence" attitude in everything we do. We should expect a positive deviance in everything our organizations and Soldiers do and for those that cannot meet our expectations we should have a plan that takes them from a negative deviance to a positive deviance, not just normal or the minimal standard. We should not just accept normal from our Soldiers, we should instill vitality and flow and high motivation so they can grow and develop and reach their untapped potential. Organizationally, we should not look to be just effective or efficient but shoot for excellence and extraordinary. When it comes to adaptation we should be flourishing and not just coping, and we should look to be flawless in our quality and not just reliable. This kind of approach will not only make Soldiers more excellent in how they do their duties but will create organizations that can operate in any environment, under any conditions and provide extraordinary results.

In summary, the more we instill a "strive for excellence attitude" in how we lead through an abundance approach, I submit we will see a decrease in the challenges we have affecting our current readiness and the more we will be prepared to face uncertain future conditions in our ever-changing and complex world.

I would offer up a good book to read on this abundant approach philosophy, "Making the Impossible Possible, Leading Extraordinary Performance," authored by Kim Cameron and Marc Lavine.

CSM John Wayne Troxell
I Corps and Joint Base Lewis-McChord

From One Leader to Another
Problem Solving
Sergeant Major Craig T. Lott

In today's global and highly competitive world, it is vitally important to understand the intellectual principles of problem-solving. Problem-solving deals with understanding simple to complex problems, analyzing them, and then coming up with viable solutions. Intellect deals with the capacity to use knowledge and understanding in order to meet a desired result or purpose. Using that knowledge with acquired skills is the central theme of this paper. This paper will focus on three primary skills which are essential to the capacity for problem-solving; critical thinking, oral/written communications, and collaboration. These skills by themselves are not the end all, but they are in fact critical and therefore the emphasis for this paper.

Critical thinking is the process used to analyze, interpret, synthesize, comprehend, apply and evaluate problems. Critical thinking focuses on "how" to think versus "what" to think. When used correctly, this skill will work in any facet of one's life (personally or professionally). Within institutions and schools across America including businesses (large and small), for profit, non-profit, government, non-governmental, and for the purpose of this paper, especially the military, both individuals and organizations use elements of critical thinking to solve day-to-day problems. This skill involves understanding not just your own point of view but also the multiple perspectives within and outside of your organization. Keeping and maintaining an open mind is extremely important in this process and will ultimately help you achieve your desired outcome much more rapidly.

Oral and written communications deal with the organization, structure and crafting of words. This is another skill that is vital in all aspects of life. Oral communication involves the concepts of expressing one's views clearly, concisely, and in an organized manner. Oral communication skills take patience and hours of practice. This principle centers on the ability to speak in front of audiences, large or small, and gives the speaker the confidence to deliver the message clearly and accurately.

Written communication on the other hand, is the ability to express oneself in writing. Compared to oral communications, written communications are transcribed thoughts on paper. Examples include writing a budget proposal, preparing an operations order or preparing something as routine as a counseling statement. It is the ability to clearly convey your meaning to the receiver so that they correctly understand your meaning or intent. It takes tremendous effort to master this skill but those who spend the necessary time working on this skill often reap the rewards.

The last skill related to problem-solving is that of collaboration. Collaboration is the process of working together for the greater good (teamwork). It takes recognizing that the value of the whole or the sum total far exceeds that of the individual parts. Individual parts are combined in order to formulate a total picture. This captures the essence of collaboration. The process of collaboration adds to the knowledge of problem-solving and mastering intellect. Champions of any sort understand this concept as everyone strives toward achieving for the same goal. In successful organizations, collaboration is often a hallmark characteristic that is ever-present and understood by all.

In conclusion, problem-solving, specifically analytical abilities, critical thinking and oral/written communications, is the key to success both for today and tomorrow's operating environment. The ability to understand the importance of and continually focus on the improvement of these skills both individually and collectively is paramount to the success of any organization. The point to take away from this paper is that focus on the development of these skills is both absolutely necessary and should be viewed as a lifetime pursuit.

Possessing the ability to analyze problems, establish fresh ideas and communicate effectively are keys to obtaining success and a competitive advantage. Developing these skills eases the burden of daily living and helps with reaching your desired goals. Those who take the time to master these principles gain a much needed advantage and often do not experience the same degree of challenge when attempting to reach their goals, whereas those who do not possess these skills often find themselves overburdened and less resilient.

If you would like to learn more about these skills it is recommended that you take the time to read the following: "Strategic Leadership, the Multiple Frames and Styles of Leadership" by Richard Morrill, "Critical Thinking, How to Prepare Students for a Rapidly Changing World" by Richard Paul, "Closing the Gap Between Strategy and Execution" by D.N. Sull and "The Global Achievement Gap" by Tony Wagner.

SGM Craig T. Lott
TRADOC Retention Branch

From One Leader to Another
Leadership and Your Soldiers Quality of life

Sergeant Major Dave Abbott

...My two basic responsibilities will always be uppermost in my mind – [that is the] accomplishment of my mission and <u>the welfare of my Soldiers</u>. ...I know my Soldiers and I will always place their needs above my own.

- US Army's, Creed of the
Non-Commissioned Officer

As leaders, one of our most important responsibilities is caring for our Soldiers and the Soldier's Family regardless if those in need are or are not within our direct span of control.

In caring for our Soldiers and their Families, we must ensure that we as Leaders are tightly woven into the support structure that provides those programs and services that are designed and provided to sustain, support, improve and benefit the quality of life for our Soldiers, Family members, Retirees and our civilian employees. As Leaders we also have an inherent responsibility to help provide the oversight and support to these programs and services by ensuring that the services are provided and that Soldiers are afforded the opportunity to use the programs and services. Leaders at all levels play an important role in how well the Army's quality of life programs are maintained. This requires being involved, knowing where to find these services and developing a good working relationship with the staff at their local US Army Garrison's Army Community Services (ACS) and knowing how to navigate the sources for the on-line support at:

http://myarmyonesource.com
http://militaryonesource.mil

Leaders can also help improve the quality of these programs and services by remaining an active participant in Garrison councils and by also providing feedback to the Garrison Leadership. The Army's promise to Leaders, Soldiers, Families, Retires and Civilian employees is that the Army's leadership (at all levels) will do everything within their power to deliver programs at a level commensurate with the level of their service to our nation. But this promise also comes with a caveat…that is, Leaders must than understanding what are the wants, needs, benefits and services in relation to their organization. It is imperative that leaders be able to tell their Soldiers that the Army does not take care of … (fill in the blank) for you. The point is, that many Leaders in the Army think that taking care of Soldiers is giving them everything that they want, fix every problem they bring to the leaders attention and not holding the Soldier responsible for their own actions. They routinely give them the fish rather than teaching them how to fish. The programs and services provided by the Army in order to assist the Leader in caring for their Soldier largely attempt to teach our Soldiers how to fish…that is to be Ready and Resilient.

What is quality of life, how far into one's personal life does it extend and where do the lines of leadership and personal responsibility meet? From my experience, quality of life should be looked at in three different areas: quality of life in one's working environment, quality of life in one's personal and Family environment and quality of life in one's community environment. What leadership defines as quality of life is ensuring that individuals have uninhibited and equal access to services, programs, opportunities and benefits as guaranteed as part of one's employment in the Army. One of the hardest leadership responsibilities we have is to deal with the quality of life issues and challenges of our Soldiers.

Many leaders feel that if the issue is not work related, then it is not really their problem or their responsibility. I would submit that any issue that one of our Soldiers may have should be considered as our problem as well. Proactive Leaders who know their Soldier(s) and show that they care have a greater impact on a Soldier's quality of life. Leaders who lead…not manage…are able to get out in front of those issues, which if not addressed or fixed in a timely manner, may impact the unit's mission and/or readiness.

Unlike many other occupations, being a Soldier and a Leader comes with many additional responsibilities and expectations that most employers outside of the military do or will not become involved with. As Leaders, we must understand that a fundamental part of being a Leader is ensuring that the quality of life for our Soldiers and their Families is one of our top priorities. Given the nature of our profession and the need for leaders to ensure the proper focus on Soldier quality of life issues, there is clearly a need for many of the support services we are afforded always ensuring that additional help and resources are made directly available to Soldiers, Leaders and Commanders. It is also important for leaders to understand why so much emphasis is placed on providing these program and services to help support a well-balanced quality of life for Soldiers and their Families. The established Army programs that are focused on supporting and enhancing the Soldiers quality of life issues are designed to do several things: (listed in no particular order)

- Provided programs and services are set up to afford reactive services to address currently active or emergency issues. Soldiers and Family members may be using these services on a volunteer basis or on a Command directed basis.

- Provided programs and services are set up to be used as a preventive tool. Soldiers and their Family members may be seeking these services or information on their own or as directed/recommended by their leadership in order to prevent issues.

- Provided programs and services and/or support programs that are used to train or inform our Soldiers, Families and Leaders about how programs and services can be used, what programs and services are available or where to find programs and services.

As a leader, ensuring that your Soldiers are well cared for and that those with Family members know where to find the assistance they need, will help to ease a burden and in turn, help avoid a situation that could potentially impact the Soldier's ability to perform their mission at their highest level of performance. In October 2007 after three years of combat in two theaters of war, the Army leadership found it necessary to re-focus their efforts towards the Soldier's quality of life and to reaffirm the Army's commitment of resources and leadership attention towards the quality of life of our Soldiers, Families, civilians and retirees. In response to the needs of our Soldiers and Families the Army's leadership developed the "Army Family Covenant". The Army Family Covenant, first signed by the Secretary of the Army, Chief of Staff of the Army, and the Sergeant Major of the Army pledges to provide Soldiers and their Families with a level of support commensurate with their level of service. Our role as leaders as explained earlier is to ensure that these services are readily available to all members of the Army, National Guard, Reserves and those who were assigned to missions that were not geographically close to a military installation.

Better Opportunities for Single Soldiers

As Leaders, there is one program that specifically focuses on our Single Soldiers and is designed to keep their needs and quality of life issues in view of leadership at all levels. Over the years, from my point of view, this program has lost some luster, has been or is misunderstood by some Leaders, seen as a distracter to mission accomplishment or not seen as a Commander's program. Bottom line, while there are some Leaders who do not view the BOSS program as a Commander's program, it is. Look at all of the potential contact that a leader has if involved in the BOSS program. First Sergeants, if you want to really know what is going on in your barracks...ask BOSS. If you look at all of the negative statistics, many involve Soldiers in the ages of 18 to 24 years old...that is the target audience for BOSS. Leaders at all levels need to embrace this great program, lend your support (the Soldiers will do the work; they just need your support!), encouragement, guidance and wisdom. Use BOSS as an opportunity to groom some of your up and coming Leaders. Also look at you core group of Soldiers who are actively engaged in the BOSS program, these are Leaders in the BOSS community and sadly at some Garrisons, the only ones who participate. I have to admit, that years ago I did not see the merits of the BOSS program, mainly because my senior Leadership did not see the value in the program and they did not support the BOSS efforts. Years later I get it...it is one of the best opportunities we have to make some serious progress in our Single Soldier's quality of life.

I wanted to provide a little history and a Junior Non-Commissioned Officer's perspective on the BOSS program, the following narrative is provided by SGT Adam Hughes, the current DA BOSS Representative stationed at Fort Sam Houston with the IMCOM, G-9 FMWR Staff.

In 1989, the US Army Community and Family Support Center (USACFSC) and Major Army Commands were tasked to develop a program to encourage single Soldiers to become involved in determining their recreation and leisure needs. Implementation of the BOSS program began with single Soldier focus groups. In early workshops, QOL issues emerged, along with issues relating to recreation and leisure needs. These issues were presented to the local command as part of the workshop out-brief. In 1991, the Chief of Staff of the Army formally expanded the BOSS program to include all areas of single Soldiers' lives. This change provided single Soldiers an opportunity to surface QOL issues through their chain of command. As the program evolved, single Soldiers indicated a desire to participate in activities related to community support; this interest was adopted as another component of the program. At the 1995 Army-wide BOSS conference, attendees identified the lack of BOSS guidance and program standardization as one of the top five QOL issues or concerns for single Soldiers. In 2011 USACFSC became G-9 under the Installation Management Command (IMCOM).

This program's mission is to enhance the quality of life and morale of Single Soldiers, increase retention, sustain readiness and maintain the all volunteer force supporting an expeditionary mindset and the ARFORGEN model. It is the program of choice for properly vetting and identifying Single Soldiers' perspective, ideas, feedback and input for all levels of Army planning.

What does the BOSS program do for Soldiers and Leaders? BOSS identifies Quality of Life issues and concerns, and recommends improvements through the respective chain of command. BOSS encourages and assists Single Soldiers in identifying and planning for recreational and leisure activities. Additionally, BOSS gives Single Soldiers the opportunity to participate in and contribute to their local and surrounding communities.

What are the efforts of BOSS? There are three main efforts of BOSS which are called the pillars of the BOSS Program. They are:

- Quality of life – This includes anything affecting the Single Soldier's living environment and can directly or indirectly influence their morale and personal growth/development. Quality of Life Issues are identified and raised during installation BOSS meetings or reported to the installation BOSS HQ. Issues that can't be resolved will be coordinated through the AFAP office for formatting, content and authentication. The proper execution of Quality of Life opportunities gives unit leadership the chance to enhance the morale and living environment. Soldier issues can be resolved at lowest level while unresolved issues are forwarded through AFAP. Issue examples include: Barracks improvements; Life skills; Campaigns; etc.

- Recreation and Leisure – The recreation and leisure pillar of the BOSS Program deals with influencing Single Soldiers lives by increasing their morale and welfare. By providing recreational opportunities specific to Single Soldiers, we support their inclusion as part of the "Total Army Family". Recreational and leisure events are Single Soldier planned, by the installation BOSS Council and then assisted and supported by the FMWR Advisor and the Senior Military Advisor to ensure the events are effectively executed. This is truly a way Senior Leaders and the Dept of the Army show that they provide Single Soldiers with a quality of life commensurate with the quality of their service.

- Community Service – This pillar builds a rapport with the community by supporting existing volunteer programs. It also provides visibility to the BOSS Program and the installation and gives Soldiers an opportunity to give back to the community in which they live and work.

Benefits of BOSS to the Command

- Enhance Morale and Welfare (QOL)

- Reduction of aberrant behavior (assaults/ traffic accidents, alcohol related incidents/ DUI/DWI)

- Provide Recreation and Leisure events to Soldiers

- Conduit of information between Soldier and Command

- Improve *Esprit de Corps*

- Supports Command METL

Benefits of BOSS to the Community

- Contribute to installation volunteer program

- Builds good rapport with community

- Integrates Soldiers into the community

- Builds upon the positive image of a Soldier for the community

The Bottom Line in providing Quality of Life – Leadership

As Leaders, we have a choice everyday…to be involved or to not be involved. To illustrate this point, I refer you back to 29 July 2010; then Vice Chief of Staff of the Army, General Peter Chiarelli released his report on the Health Promotion, Risk Reduction, and Suicide Prevention study that he initiated in order to determine the overall health of the force. In this report General Chiarelli noted that there were many instances where Leaders across the Army had lost the art-of-leadership in a garrison environment. To me this comment means that Leaders of all ranks and ages have either forgot how to take care of Soldiers and their Families while operating in a garrison environment, have become too pre-occupied to take care of Soldiers and Families or that they simply did not know because they had not yet been taught (by example) by another leader on how to care for Soldiers and Families. To me this comment by the Vice was a sobering call to action directed toward every Leader in our Army. While this question may have hurt a little professionally, as a Leader it caused me to think… have I lost my art-of-leadership, or have I not properly trained my subordinate Leaders to provide and ensure that those aspects of a Soldier's quality of life are met? General Chiarelli's in depth 234 page (plus annexes) report reveals to Leaders what Leaders have always known…that our responsibilities are not only to complete our mission, but to also take care of those placed in our care. This was a call to all leaders designed to get them involved, so that they know their Soldiers, and to look for those indicators that precede acts of high risk behavior or other destructive acts. The resources, programs and services that directly impact your Soldiers, Families, Retirees and Civilian Employees are available, accessible and effective!

If you would like to learn more about this topic it is recommended that you now take the time to read *AR* 215-1 for command guidance on FMWR activities, *AR* 210-50 for Housing Management or visit the following websites at:
http://myarmyonesource.com
http://militaryonesource.mil
http://www.armymwr.com
http://www.imcom..Army.mil
for more detailed information or help in obtaining the right service for your Soldiers.

SGM Dave Abbott
HQ IMCOM, Family & MWR

From One Leader to Another
The NCO Role in Mission Command
Command Sergeant Major Dennis Eger

Mission Command is a term not normally known or understood in particular amongst the Non-Commissioned Officer Corps. It will serve us well as we move into the future of Unified Land Operations to understand where it is derived and our part within Mission Command as an NCO. It is important to note up front that it is NOT an Officer term or function but a Leader term and function. Mission Command spans the spectrum from NCO to Officer and from garrison to deployed operations. Your role as an NCO is what ultimately contributes to its success or failure. The purpose of this paper is to inform the Non-Commissioned Officer Corps of how Mission Command was derived and our part in its function and success.

Throughout our military history we have heard terms such as Battle Command and Command and Control. These terms referred to how commanders would command and control their forces on the battlefield taking into account the Battlefield Operating Systems (BOS). As NCOs our takeaway during that period was often the terms "command" and "commander." We knew and understood that we were not in command and we were not commanders, thus the function must not apply to us. What we did not consider was our role as an NCO in that process. As we move forward into the future and the countless operating environments (OE) in which we might find ourselves, our role in this function has become increasingly more important.

Command and control was strictly seen as how does a commander "command and control" their forces primarily in combat. However mission command, the new term for command and control, goes much deeper. It is now one of the six war-fighting functions and many would argue the most important because it is the one war-fighting function used to link and synchronize all other functions. It also now builds on some basic principles, covers the DOTMLPF realm, and includes what it means to implement it in a Garrison environment.

Mission Command is defined in three parts: Mission Command Philosophy, Mission Command War-fighting Function (WfF), and Mission Command Systems. It is important to understand each in order to fully understand the NCO's role.

The Mission Command Philosophy is the exercise of authority and direction by the commander using mission orders to enable disciplined initiative within the commander's intent to empower agile and adaptive leaders in the conduct of unified land operations.

The Mission Command War-fighting Function is the related tasks and systems that develop and integrate those activities enabling a commander to balance the art of command and the science of control in order to integrate the remaining war-fighting functions.

The Mission Command System is the arrangement of personnel, networks, information systems, processes, facilities, procedures and equipment that enable commanders to conduct operations.

Although the prevailing word that many will see in the above is "commander", what they are failing to see is the deeper meaning in which NCOs carry out this function and help enable success on the battlefield. Decisions and/or recommendations that NCOs make in regards to mission command, directly influence the commander's decision-making process in both garrison and combat.

Within the mission command philosophy, NCOs are given the ability to exercise disciplined initiative within the commander's intent, thus empowering agile and adaptive leaders. From the young NCO being given an order and conducting troop leading procedures culminating in an action on the battlefield to the Command Sergeant Major who is giving sound advice to the commander and staff on operations or training, you are exercising and serve as a key component of the mission command philosophy. Commanders make decisions based on the circumstances and situations that surround them. You have the ability to influence those situations. Your actions and input are part of the mission command philosophy.

As a war-fighting function the commander must balance his authority with how much control they will exert. The NCO has a profound effect on those decisions. You must also understand each of the war-fighting functions and how they interact. As an NCO you exercise mission command on the battlefield with every mission in which you participate. You must take into account the intelligence you received, the maneuver plan, sustainment, protection and a myriad of other factors. If you fail to account for any of these in your planning process, the mission risks failure. Your actions on that small scale translate to the large scale for the commander as he or she also takes each into account. As you synchronize on a smaller scale the commander is taking your input and synchronizing each of the WfFs on a much larger scale. Everything that you do contributes to the commander's ability to visualize, describe, direct, lead, and assess.

NCOs directly affect the mission command system as well. The Non-Commissioned Officer is the direct voice in reporting to the commander what procedures do or do not work, issues with networks, what network would make mission success a reality, what equipment problems exist or would be better, what facilities would be best and the best use of personnel. That direct input allows the commander to make better decisions in regards to mission command in order to enable success and also helps to identify areas where NCOs might better train and prepare their subordinates.

Training is the aspect of mission command in which the NCO must not lose sight. All aspects of mission command require training, whether institutional, operational, or through self-development. This cannot be successful if the NCO does not understand the purpose of mission command and how to train it. Success in ULO can only be achieved through extensive training in which the NCO in responsible.

Six doctrinal principles exist in mission command in which all leaders should understand and practice; build cohesive teams through mutual trust, create a shared understanding, provide clear commander's intent, enable disciplined initiative, use mission orders, and accept prudent risk. As NCOs look at these principles they should immediately recognize basic leadership principles. As with the commander, you too must foster a climate of mutual trust and a shared understanding. This means ensuring for a command climate that encourages subordinates to exercise disciplined initiative and seize opportunities both on and off the battlefield. You must allow for freedom of action by your subordinates. This is what the commander does but you must do as well…this is exercising mission command.

As much of this will center on mission command in combat, we cannot lose sight of its use and importance in the Garrison environment. It is here that we hone our skills, train, and prepare ourselves for war. But above all, to become experienced at mission command, you must learn to practice it on a daily basis. You should ask yourself some basic questions; how are orders delivered in Garrison? How are they carried out? Are your subordinate units allowed to take disciplined initiative? Are you fostering a command climate in which you show that you trust what they are doing and the decisions they are making? Or, are you the leader that must micro manage everything, centralize everything, or create single points of failure? So I ask you, how are your exercising mission command in Garrison? How are you advising your commander given these circumstances?

No matter how you choose to define it, mission command is not just a commander or Officer function. The NCO is an integral part to ensuring its success through understanding, practicing, exercising, advising and training. Your exercise of the mission command philosophy has a direct impact on how the commander will make decisions within an operating environment. Whether the philosophy, function, or system; your understanding and involvement will lead to the direct success of your organization and its mission.

CSM Dennis Eger
Mission Command Center of Excellence (MCCoE)

From One Leader to Another
The Role of the NCO in Mission Command
Command Sergeant Major Norman McAfee

Mission command is the exercise of authority and direction by the commander using mission orders to enable disciplined initiative within the commander's intent to empower agile and adaptive leaders in the conduct of decisive action. It is commander-led and blends the art of command and the science of control to integrate the war-fighting functions to accomplish the mission (*Field Manual* 3-0). In *Army Doctrine Publication* 3-0; we see a slight modification of the definition: The philosophy of mission command is the exercise of authority and direction by the commander using mission orders to enable disciplined initiative within the commander's intent while guiding leaders in the execution of unified land operations. As we progressed doctrinally you can see how command and control evolved to become mission command which assists in achieving the ultimate goal of the United States Army: prevent, shape, influence, engage, deter, and win. The Non-Commissioned Officer's (NCO) role in mission command starts well before the exercise of command; it begins with the training environment.

The Army lives by the principle "Train as you fight" and doctrinally NCOs are the Army's primary trainers of enlisted Soldiers, crews and small teams. Effective mission command requires Soldiers and leaders trained to operate in ill-defined, complex and ambiguous environments. Through training, Soldiers learn how to apply disciplined initiative to act decisively while accepting prudent risks. Training assists Soldiers and leaders in developing mutual trust through a shared understanding of the unit's strengths and weaknesses. Training also reinforces the need for Soldiers and leaders to collaborate and dialog in order to achieve a greater understanding of the operational environment (*ADRP* 7-0). The NCO's role as trainer is only part of the dynamic in mission command; they are generally the principal advisor to commanders and are often confidants within the command team; as such, the NCO plays a crucial role in mission command.

When applying the Army's core competencies, Army leaders are guided by the mission command philosophy. NCOs assist the commander in execution of these orders as well as providing sound advice and perspective. The ability of Army forces to apply its core competencies in the creation a fluid mix of offensive, defensive, and stability operations depends on a philosophy of command that emphasizes broad mission-type orders, individual disciplined initiative within the commander's intent, and leaders who can anticipate and adapt quickly to changing conditions (*ADP* 3-0). Again, the NCO has an essential role in assuring these actions occur and conditions are set in order to succeed.

Mission command in the war fighting function develops and integrates those activities enabling a commander to balance the art of command and the science of control. This fundamental philosophy of command places people, rather than technology or systems, at the center. Under this philosophy, the NCO provides direction and experience in support of the commander as they drive the operations process through their activities; of understand, visualize, describe, direct, lead, and assess. They develop teams, both within their own organizations and with joint, interagency, and multinational partners. NCOs provide information and influence audiences, inside and outside their organizations. The NCO assists the commander in leading the staff's tasks under the science of control. The four primary staff tasks are conduct the operations process (plan, prepare, execute, and assess); conduct knowledge management and information management; conduct inform and influence activities; and conduct cyber electromagnetic activities (*ADP* 3-0).

The essence of decisive action is that Army forces combine offensive, defensive, and stability or civil support operations simultaneously as part of an interdependent joint force to seize, retain, and exploit the initiative, accepting prudent risk to create opportunities to achieve decisive results. Army forces employ synchronized action, both lethal and nonlethal, proportionate to the mission and informed by a thorough understanding of all dimensions of the operational environment. Mission command that conveys intent and an appreciation of all aspects of the situation guides the adaptive use of Army forces. Offensive and defensive tasks focus on the destructive effects of combat power; stability tasks emphasize constructive effects (ADP 3-07). The NCO's role in decisive action is crucial as they are typically on the ground leading these efforts with their small unit and teams. NCOs are force multipliers for commanders and provide breadth and depth to any operation.

Effective planning also anticipates the inherent delay between decision and action, especially between the levels of war and echelons of command. Sound plans draw on the fundamentals of mission command to overcome this effect, fostering initiative within the commander's intent to act appropriately and decisively when orders no longer sufficiently address the changing situation. This ensures commanders act promptly as they encounter opportunities or accept prudent risk in order to create opportunities when they lack clear direction. In such situations, prompt action requires detailed foresight and preparation (*ADP* 3-07). NCOs at all levels, particularly those serving as a Plans and Operations Sergeant, bring their experience to bear when providing their unique perspective to their Officer counterpart.

Mission command requires an environment of mutual trust and shared understanding among commanders, staffs, and subordinates. The commander's intent is a clear and concise expression of the purpose of the operation, the desired military end state, provides focus to the staff, and helps subordinate and supporting commanders and leaders act to achieve the commander's desired outcomes without further orders, even when the operation does not unfold as planned (*Joint Publication* 3-0). NCOs are key to the dissemination and shared understanding of the commander's intent.

An unexpected change in conditions may require commanders to direct an abrupt transition between phases. In such cases, the overall composition of the force remains unchanged despite sudden changes in mission, task organization, and rules of engagement. Typically, task organization evolves to meet changing conditions; however, transition planning must also account for changes in the mission. Commanders attuned to sudden changes can better adapt their forces to dynamic conditions. They continuously assess the situation and task-organize and cycle their forces to retain the initiative. They strive to achieve changes in emphasis without incurring an operational pause. Commanders in the field look to their NCOs to assist in this transitional phase in order to focus on several areas at once. NCOs can help their commanders in this effort by continually assessing and providing feedback on the mission and operational variables as well as their organizational lines of effort.

As an element of combat power, leadership unifies the other elements (information, mission command, movement and maneuver, intelligence, fires, sustainment, and protection). Leadership is a multiplier of effects; with it, organizations are focused and synchronized, resources are used efficiently, people become energized and motivated, and missions are more likely to achieve desired outcomes. Leadership serves a motivational purpose: to energize others to achieve challenging goals. An organization with effective leadership has a clear purpose, common methods, and ordered processes; sustains itself; and accomplishes its missions. Effective organizations rely on leaders to balance uncertainty, remain flexible, and provide a climate where subordinates have the latitude to explore options (*ADP* 6-22). There can be no question that NCOs are key leaders within any formation. Great organizations have great NCOs who are engaged in all facets of an operation and with their Soldiers and Families.

Influence falls along a continuum from commitment, where followers willingly act for a higher purpose, to compliance, where followers merely fulfill requests and act in response to the leader's positional power. The degree to which an individual is committed or merely compliant directly affects their individual initiative, motivation to accomplish an assigned mission, and the degree of accepted responsibility. Like commanders, NCOs expect subordinate leaders and Soldiers to commit to successful mission accomplishment. Trust, commitment, and competence enable mission command and allow the freedom of action to be operationally agile and adaptive (*ADP* 6-22). NCOs in particular rely heavily on influence which is generally experienced based in order to effect action. An NCO's span of influence is only limited by their leadership and him or herself but is virtually unlimited in regards to the impact it can have on mission success.

Clearly mission command has evolved based on operational needs in an ever-changing operational environment. In times past, we prepared for future wars focused on combating like armies largely in an offensive and/or defensive posture. With the war on terror we evolved into a counter insurgency (COIN) fight. This required us to be adaptive and find a better way to lead Soldiers in order to meet the commander's intent and achieve the mission requirements. Mission Command empowered junior leaders.

So how do you approach this topic in your unit? The Mission Command philosophy and war-fighting function must be continually studied. This can be done by conducting Non-Commissioned Officer Professional Development (NCOPD), staff rides, and mentoring. NCOPDs that discuss Army doctrine and define mission command is a good start. The effects of which can be expounded by integrating leadership scenarios and experiences. These can take the form of staff rides which are great leadership tools that allow leaders to learn from past battles, leaders, and situations. As with all of our Army doctrine, it takes leaders who require self-development in their subordinates, who tie new doctrinal principles to their organizational events, who take every opportunity to educate and develop their subordinates and who role model these principles.

If you would like to learn more about Mission Command go to *Army Doctrinal Publication* 6-0,

Army Doctrinal Reference Publication 6-0 and *Army Doctrinal Reference Publication* 3-07.

CSM Norman McAfee
261st MMB

From One Leader to Another

Standards and Discipline
An In-Depth Look at Where We Once Were and Where We Are Now

Command Sergeant Major Shelton R. Williamson

As an introduction to this short article, it is important to mention up front that compiling letters from Senior Leaders in the field who are out doing the Nation's business (leading and taking care of young Soldiers and their Families) is an extremely worthwhile endeavor. In addition to applauding this effort, it is important to note that speaking on many of these topics is extraordinarily necessary based on the strength and health of today's Army. It is fitting in many respects to discuss Standards and Discipline in our Army today. The intention here is to discuss this topic briefly from a chronological perspective specifically highlighting how Standards and Discipline have become a hallmark of our organization as an Army and how they have evolved over the years during the conduct of multiple wars and conflicts resulting in the very foundation that we stand upon both today and into tomorrow.

A little over 237 years ago, our Army was established as a result of a fierce start of the Revolutionary War between our fledging union (the United States as we know it) and the British Empire. Over the course of the Revolutionary War, led by General George Washington our Army fought in battles against a much larger and much more technically and tactically advanced Army. Our Army faced significant shortfalls and suffered many defeats at the hands of a seemingly superior force, at least in the initial stages of the war. As the revolution progressed, the Americans, as they became known, were significantly challenged by the lack of funding, equipment, personnel, formal training, and were literally considered to be "misfits" fighting against trained professionals.

Recognizing this, General Washington with the help of Benjamin Franklin, the French Ambassador at the time, made contact with Baron Fredrick von Steuben, a former Prussian Officer who was well renowned for his superior organizational skills. Von Steuben was hired by Washington to serve as the First Inspector General of the Army, with the primary responsibility of structuring, organizing and training the Army. Von Steuben quickly went to work. He would write doctrine in the evening and train small formations of Soldiers by day on drill commands that were at the time closely associated with placing weapon systems into operation and fighting formations. As he trained more of these Soldiers across the Army on manual-of-arms and drill, Washington began to recognize a significant increase in discipline across the force and it showed in ensuing battles along what we now call the east coast, including the Battle of Valley Forge and many others. Von Steuben continued this effort by training organizational leaders who would then train their small units. In 1789, Von Steuben formalized this training when he developed what was called the "Regulations for the Order and Discipline of the Troops of the United States", commonly referred to as the "Blue Book". This document became the mainstay of our Army and was not modified until the Civil War. Even though this manual, which later became the Manual for Drill and Ceremonies, was modified slightly during the Civil War, many of the tenants from the initial book remain to this day as a part of what we now refer to as "Drill and Ceremony".

As the standards and discipline of units improved, so did the success of the American Army eventually leading to victory over the British. As our Army continued to mature and take on a larger role across the globe, standards and discipline would become the very core that would separate our Army from other fighting forces around the world; often viewed by other countries as the "Gold Standard" of an Army with respect to standards and discipline. The other armies often looked at how we marched in formation, how we were consistently in the same uniform, and how strong and tactically savvy our leaders were. All of these things spoke to our standards and discipline.

Fast-forward to the late 1960s and early 1970s where the Non-Commissioned Officer became much more formally recognized with the creation of the Sergeant Major of the Army, the Non-Commissioned Officer Education System, and an "All Volunteer Army" in 1973. All of these changes and more had a significant impact on the standards and discipline of our Army. No longer did NCOs feel like they were less prepared or educated, in fact, with new schooling they felt even more empowered. This resulted in improved standards and discipline across the force creating better productivity and thus stronger and healthier organizations across the Army.

Standards and discipline are often referenced together because they work in conjunction with one another in order for an organization to be successful, especially a military organization. General of the Armies, George Washington once said "Discipline is the soul of an Army, it makes small numbers formidable; procures success of the weak and esteem to all". Great organizations are ones that exude and enforce standards and discipline much better than average organizations. The term "standard" is defined by the American Standard Dictionary as a written definition, limit, or rule, approved and monitored for compliance by an authoritative agency or professional or recognized body as minimum acceptable benchmark. Standards may be classified as (1) government or statutory agency standards and specifications enforced by law, (2) proprietary standards developed by a firm or organization and placed in public domain to encourage their widespread use, (3) voluntary standards established by consultation and consensus and available for use by any person, organization, or industry. These terminologies spark some degree of interest as they represent just one perspective, none of which are incorrect. Once established, standards (like bureaucracies) can be very difficult to change or dislodge as them become habit. As this document develops, the intent is to draw a parallel to both of these terms and explain how vital they both are to our Army's evolution and to one another. Establishment of standards represents a very good starting point for any organization.

Discipline or "military discipline" as it is often referred, is defined as the state of order and obedience among personnel in a military organization and is characterized by the men's prompt and willing responsiveness to orders and understanding compliance to regulation. Often, non-military members view all uniformed military services as organizations that have a very strict set of rules where it takes an enormous amount of discipline to thrive. Much of the perception that the Army is a very disciplined organization is true; from the time a civilian makes the choice to become a Soldier until that new Soldier walks across the parade field as they graduate from Basic training, discipline is a focal point in their training.

Over the course of our 237 year history, it has been proven time and again that discipline is the difference between winning and losing, between average and exceptional. Once standards are established in an organization, it takes discipline to follow and enforce those standards both individually and collectively. Although this might seem straight forward and relatively easy to accomplish, it can be much more difficult to achieve in practice. Using a Brigade Combat Team (BCT) as an example, it is easy to see how difficult this can be.

The Army Force Generation Cycle has a considerable impact on the life of a BCT as it comes out of the Reintegration/Reset Phase and transitions to the Train/Ready Phase. In the Train/Ready Phase, the unit begins individual training and eventually works up to collective training culminating with some type of battalion level training and most often than not, on to one of the three Combat Training Center rotations (JRTC, NTC, or JMRC). All of this training occurs over a period of time, some in a shorter time period than others. Over the course of this "train up", units that establish clear standards and have leaders that enforce those standards are normally the units that ultimately perform well at the CTC. The standards and discipline if established early in this cycle and enforced correctly result in units that are successful in their rotation and are extremely successful during combat operations. Units that fail to focus on standards and discipline often find themselves reacting to situations rather than preparing for their future mission. Wearing eye protection at all times during combat operations, carrying your rifle at the "Ready" vice slung over your back, a unit that is physically fit, a unit that has superior marksmanship skills, and a unit that conducts innovative, realistic and challenging training are all examples of disciplined units. Albeit these examples seem small and minute, they are undoubtedly the difference between an average organization and one that breeds strong disciplined leaders with high standards. In the book "About Face", by Colonel David Hackworth, he writes "The Army got rid of offending traditions, it did not replace these traditions with anything that fulfilled their basic and essential functions…to instill standards and discipline…if the Army expected its men to be effective on the battlefield, even to stay alive on the battlefield, discipline had to be the number one priority". An organization that has strong practices of standards and discipline are very successful.

Over the past 10 years, our Army has been involved in fighting and winning two wars against a very determined enemy and during the course of that time period, we as an institution have seen significant innovation across many fronts; recruitment and retention, centralized and semi-centralized promotions, functional training, professional military education, barracks/housing policies, physical readiness training, countless pieces of new equipment/technology and much more that have to a large degree, unintentionally degraded the overall standards and discipline of our Army while increasing the need for leadership that is focused on training. So what is it that we must do to re-acquaint ourselves with what made us so successful prior to our current fight? First, we cannot solely attribute the degradation in our level of standards and discipline to our fight abroad, something which we have done extremely well. The mid-level leaders we currently have in our formations are much stronger at training, preparing and performing in combat, but lack many of the garrison type skills that were present in our formations in the 1990s. One might pose the question, "well which attribute is more important to have?" The short answer is both, and the next question could be, "how can we show this generation of mid-level leaders that the 'garrison-type functions' are important?" The short answer would be to show them with hands-on application.

Make them conduct frequent inspections of their Soldier's barracks/housing. Make them lay out their OCIE along with their Soldiers. Make them conduct an in-ranks inspection of their Soldier's appearance and uniform, both utility and dress. Make them march their Soldiers from one point to another on a regular basis and not just whenever there is some type of ceremony. Make them counsel their Soldiers monthly/quarterly. Make and show them how to prepare for a Command Inspection. Make and show them how to keep common areas cleaned without the help of contractors or others. Make and show them that competing for Soldier/NCO of the Month/Quarter/Year is a "good thing". Show them that their personal and professional conduct and behavior represents more than just themselves and is representative of the US Army. Lastly, help them develop the intestinal fortitude to make on-the-spot corrections when necessary as this is essential to the standards and discipline of an organization. All of these and many more need to happen while allowing subordinate leaders the maximum latitude to operate. This is accomplished by assigning them responsibility and holding them accountable without overly managing their work.

Establishing and enforcing standards and discipline is the key to an organization's overall success and should be treated in such a way that every member of the organization understands those standards and that they are committed individually and collectively to those standards. If you can find an organization which is highly successful in combat, chances are they are one that has high standards and have strong enforcement of discipline at every level. Aristotle once wrote "We are what we repeatedly do. Excellence then is not an act but a habit…so then if we repeatedly practice high standards and discipline, and it is the creation of those habits that enable us to defeat a determined and audacious enemy."

The first quarter of calendar year 2013 is devoted to Standards and Discipline of our Army. This focus was established by the Chief of Staff and Sergeant Major of the Army in recognition that our Army still has a long way to go in order to establish a renewed sense of pride and dedication to the standards and discipline of our fighting force and our profession. Leaders at every level should take this time to train and mentor young Soldiers and leaders on a united front to continue to emphasize that standards and discipline are the hallmark of our Army. Even though this initiative is directed in order to address the rising concerns of our Senior Leaders, we should all remain confident that our Nation possesses the most lethal and professional force that this world has ever known and that we have more than enough seasoned leaders within our ranks to coach, teach and mentor our aspiring professionals on the very ideals that have made us such a successful organization for over 237 years.

CSM Shelton R. Williamson
10th Regional Support Group

From One Leader to Another
Team Building and Unit Cohesion
Command Sergeant Major Sam Young

From birth in 1775 to the present, our Army has evolved into the most dominant force on the planet, capable of fighting and winning in all environments. One of the key attributes of this success is the ability of leaders to build teams and form cohesive units. Our first Commander-in-Chief said it best, in a letter to Henry Knox, "My first wish would be that my Military Family, and the whole Army, should consider themselves as a band of brothers, willing and ready to die for each other (Washington, 1798)." During the American Revolution, untrained men would travel across the country to fight against the massive, well trained and equipped British Army. Resources were scarce and death seemed imminent. With the influence of great leadership, the colonists were able to bond together, form a cohesive unit, and fight for the Independence of our great Nation. The purpose of this paper is to emphasize the importance of team building and unit cohesion and provide a few thoughts on leadership styles and their utility.

ADRP 6-22, states that teams are developed in three separate phases. The first developmental stage is the "Formation" stage which involves the Reception and Integration of Soldiers to the unit. During this stage, the flow of communication is essential for the success of the section. The leader sets clear guidance and tells the section what he/she expects from each individual Soldier. It is also vital that the Soldier feels a level of acceptance from his/her team members. The military is a "melting pot" of different ideas and personalities. Therefore as a leader, during this stage, you need to get to know your Soldiers. Understanding the strengths and weaknesses of each team member is an essential element to success in combat.

The next stage is the "Enrichment" stage, where the Soldier begins to trust his/her leaders, peers and subordinates. Chief of Staff of the Army, General Odierno explains, "Trust is the bedrock of our honored profession -- trust between each other, trust between Soldiers and leaders, trust between Soldiers and their Families and the Army, and trust with the American people" (2012). The question arises, "How do we get Soldiers to trust their leaders, peers and subordinates?" The answer is through the implementation of an effective leadership style.

Leadership is the process of influencing people by providing purpose, direction, and motivation to accomplish the mission and improve the organization (*ADP* 6-22). Across the Army, there are several styles of leadership, which are characterized by individual traits and behaviors. Some examples of leadership styles include authoritarian, charismatic and transformational. It is hard to determine which leadership style is the best, since not all goals are the same. Depending on the situation, one style may prove more effective than another.

The authoritarian leadership style is defined as one who will rarely give subordinates the opportunity to make any suggestions, even if they benefit the organization. This type of leadership works best when a quick decision needs to be made, without the consultation of a group. However, this can be perceived as problematic when it comes to building trust within a unit. The result of this leadership style can and often will be an unsatisfactory command climate and loss of cohesion within a unit.

A charismatic style of leadership is characterized by an individuals' ability to inspire others within an organization. Subordinates are drawn to the personality and charm of this leader. Leaders who fall into this style will try to get their teams to set themselves apart from the mass of an organization. Although good for team building the downfall of this style occurs when too much emphasis is placed on the abilities of the leader. If the leader were to leave the organization, then there may be a loss of morale within the unit or team. Similar to a charismatic style is a transformational leadership style. This style is characterized by a leader's ability to motivate, while educating subordinates on their specific roles within the organization. He/she will challenge subordinates to create innovative ways to develop their own style of leadership. Both styles of leadership are proven for building trust.

Once the team is built and trust is established, Soldiers will begin to use words like "we," rather than "I." Soldiers want to be part of a team, they want to belong, and they need to be proud of who they are and what they do. Unit pride is contagious and leaders should be proud of their unit and find ways to spotlight individual, team and unit accomplishments. Develop team building events and establish a unit level competition. Ensure you support intramural sports and get the entire unit involved. Whether they are participating or cheering, it is a unit team. Design a unit t-shirt that everyone will wear with pride during unit runs, sporting events, organizational days, etc. Take every opportunity to get your Soldiers' Families involved in unit activities. These are just some examples of how to build trust, teamwork, and pride in a unit.

The final stage of team building is the "Sustainment" stage. In this stage, the team has come together, and a sense of pride is spread throughout. The leader has effectively brought together a group of individuals who are now prepared to face the challenges of war. After each section has reached the final stage of the team building process it is time to bring the unit together as a whole. While bringing individual sections together, the flow of information is essential. Leaders should share the knowledge they have gained from previous operational assignments, which will ensure that "we", as a combat force continue to evolve. When this same process is done over and over, on a slightly larger scale, the result is unit cohesion. Members of a cohesive unit have a strong bond to each other, as well as the mission.

Throughout my years in the Army, I have come across several units that could be defined as "cohesive," but only once have I actually witnessed the transformation process. Before going to this unit I had heard rumors about the lack of morale and discipline in the unit from both military and civilian personnel from across the installation. The unit was said to be the worst company sized element in the formation. We had just reorganized and were preparing to deploy. During the next several months we had to build a team and train hard, but also afford these Soldiers time to enjoy being with their Families. After meeting with the unit leaders, we arrived at a plan that each of us were confident would work. By using the examples I explained in this paper we focused on building a cohesive team. Suddenly, there was a different dynamic throughout the organization. Soldiers who once argued with each other and had no unit pride were now forming tight knit teams. The leaders knew the Family members of all the Soldiers in the formation. Spouses were baking cookies, not for her husband's "co-workers", but for his brothers in arms. Going to Iraq we were a Family, we trained hard, bonded together and were ready to do what we do best, fight and win our Nation's wars. Throughout many hardships during a fifteen month deployment we remained a cohesive unit and were successful.

If you would like to learn more about this topic, please read the references provided throughout this paper; *Army Doctrine & Army Doctrine Reference Publications* 6-22, *Army Leadership*, "Letter to Henry Knox" written by President George Washington, and "Expectations for the Future" written by Chief of Staff of the Army, General Raymond Odierno.

CSM Sam Young
United States Army Field Artillery School

From One Leader to Another
Getting Back to the Basics
Sergeant Major Dave Stewart

"We can't just step back in time."

-Sergeant Major Bryan B. Battaglia

Over the last few years in the military and more specifically the Army, we have heard our senior leaders call for a return to the "basics". However, the leaders making this call have not tried to define what the basics truly mean. How would you define the basics? Realistically, we all probably define the basics in a different way. As stated in the quote above, we simply cannot afford to go back in time. We have learned a great deal in the last decade and some of that expertise should go forward with us into the future force. What the Senior Enlisted Advisor to the Chairman of the Joint Chiefs of Staff is saying is that we must remain true to the fundamentals that make our military successful. This is a normal reaction when any organization is trying to better itself, take a football team or golfer for instance. Any football coach will tell his players that they must get back to the basics of blocking and tackling when they are struggling during a game. In order for a golfer to return to proper form, their coach will remind them of the basics of correct setup and proper grip. What these analogies point out is that getting back to the basics is the surest way to solve a crisis or help a struggling individual and/or organization. Therefore, what is the "blocking and tackling" of the Army Profession? It starts by our Army remaining grounded in its fundamentals, in the doctrine we write and practice.

You can find doctrine on the Army Profession in two publications. First, is the Army's capstone doctrinal publication, *ADP* 1, *The Army* and secondly, its companion reference publication *ADRP* 1, *The Army Profession*. Both publications highlight the five essential characteristics of the Army Profession and the certification criteria for being an Army Professional. These two things provide the framework for our identity at both the organizational and individual level and establish the fundamentals of our profession.

The five essential characteristics of the Army Profession of Trust, Military Expertise, Honorable Service, Esprit de Corps, and Stewardship are unique to our Army and our Profession. We can only remain a profession as long as these characteristics are present in our culture and maintained by its committed professionals. The trust that the American people have for our profession comes from the capability of our Army to exhibit each of the remaining characteristics (Military Expertise, Honorable Service, Esprit de Corp, and Stewardship). Our trust serves not only as an external factor linking us to the American people but it is also as an internal factor linking its members serving the Army as a vital organizing principle. These factors alone are the very reason why both the Chief of Staff of the Army, General Odierno and the Chairman of the Joint Chief of Staff, General Dempsey suggest that trust is the bedrock of our profession. Together all five essential characteristics shape our Army's identity. Identity is how we see ourselves and how others should view us through our consistent behavior and action. This makes our military profession unique from other professions. The following diagram demonstrates this linkage.

Exhibiting these essential characteristics alone is not enough. It falls on the shoulders of our certified professionals to maintain the practice of these essential characteristics. Certification is the verification and validation of an Army Professional's competence, character and commitment to fulfill responsibilities and perform assigned duties with discipline and to standard (*ADRP* 1, Initial Draft, 25 September 2012). Certification of our professionals using these three criteria is the responsibility of every member of our profession and ensures the effective and ethical application of land power. Certification in the competence or proficiency of our expert work, possessing the moral character requisite to being an Army Professional and having the resolute commitment to performing the Army's duty is vital to the continued success of our profession. This certification allows us to operate with unparalleled autonomy in the execution of our mission. Just as the five essential characteristic does for our profession, the competence, character and commitment of our professionals provides each member with an identity.

Even though the future is unknown, the Army can expect to face a continually challenging and ever-changing operating environment. Therefore, as we enter this era of transition we will continue to hear leaders across the Army suggest that we get back to the basics of our Army Profession. As Sergeant Major Battaglia suggested in the opening quote, we cannot simply step back in time. The concepts outlined in both *ADP* 1 and *ADRP* 1 give us the necessary identity to take the Army through any challenge it might face. The five essential characteristics of the Army Profession (Trust, Military Expertise, Honorable Service, Esprit de Corps, Stewardship) define this identity and must always be present. The certification criterion of competence, character and commitment are an integral part of how we vet the members of our profession and ensure that they meet the demands expected of an Army Professional. The concepts of what it means to be a profession and what it means to be a professional, provide us with the identity necessary to see our Army and our nation through even the most troubling of times. So the next time you here a leader talk about "getting back to the basics," without any further explanation, you will know what they mean and what is expected of you as a Professional.

Again, if you would like to learn more about the Army Profession, please read *Army Doctrine Publication* 1, *The Army* and *Army Doctrine Reference Publication* 1, *The Army Profession*.

SGM Dave Stewart
The Center for Army Profession and Ethic

The five essential characteristics of the Army Profession

From One Leader to Another
The Creed of the Non-Commissioned Officer

Command Sergeant Major Michael Williamson

The Creed of the Non-Commissioned Officer has existed for many years. It has been published in numerous military manuals. There are several versions of how the NCO Creed came to be. The most generally accepted version is that the Creed of the Non-Commissioned Officer began through a committee at Fort Benning, Georgia but it wasn't until 1985 that the Creed of the Non-Commissioned Officer was formalized in an official Army publication.

The creed is a celebrated document that a new or seasoned, Non-Commissioned Officer can use as an azimuth check. The NCO Creed speaks to the competencies expected from our NCO Corps. Newly promoted Soldiers often receive a copy of the NCO Creed during an NCO induction ceremony or at the time of promotion from the senior NCO within the unit, whether the First Sergeant or Command Sergeant Major.

What do these words really mean to that newly promoted Non-Commissioned Officer? The NCO Creed is more than a mere collection of words. They are words to live by professionally. The NCO Creed is a commitment that an NCO takes through his or her induction into the ranks of the NCO Corps. This is a standard by which we measure ourselves. It is especially important as the Army moves through yet another transitional period.

"No one is more professional than I." What do those words mean? They refer to obtaining and maintaining the highest military standards, to leave a legacy of selfless service and commitment to excellence for others to follow. As a professional you must uphold the highest standard of competence, character and commitment.

Over the past ten plus years there have been changes in how we train and educate our NCOs. Those shifts were necessary for the accomplishment of the mission. "I am a Non-Commissioned Officer, a leader of Soldiers." Those words are especially important, as our NCOs lead the best-trained, best-equipped, and best-educated Soldiers and subordinate leaders the country has ever known especially now as we emerge from the fight. There is no higher honor than to be a leader, a task that is to be taken seriously both on and off the battlefield. Establish and enforce standards. Soldiers are a reflection and a product of you; lead by example.

"As a Non-Commissioned Officer, I realize that I am a member of a time honored corps known as the 'backbone of the Army'." Non-Commissioned Officers make the mission happen. The NCO has been present from the beginning ensuring that the task at hand was accomplished. The realization of the time honored corps speaks to the legacy of those that have gone before and never forgetting that you came from and that you were once a Soldier not too dissimilar to those you now lead.

"I am proud of the corps of Non-Commissioned Officers and will at all times conduct myself so as to bring credit upon the corps, the military service, and my country regardless of the situation in which I find myself." The NCO Corps is self-policing and stewards of the profession. No one individual is more important than the Corps and our Army. There is not a cut off on how NCOs are expected to conduct themselves, in or out of uniform. The situations that NCOs find themselves in are constant, good or bad, and their actions matter. Doing the easy wrong over the hard right never works out well for NCOs who choose that path.

"Competence is my watch-word. My two basic responsibilities will always be uppermost in my mind---accomplishment of my mission and the welfare of my Soldiers. I am aware of my role as a Non-Commissioned Officer. I will fulfill my responsibilities inherent in that role." Training and leading Soldiers is our primary responsibility, along with the responsibility and authority for maintaining good order and discipline. To accomplish these tasks, NCOs must remain grounded in doctrine and take every opportunity to educate themselves as well as their Soldiers ensuring they are foundational strong in their profession and military expertise.

"I will strive to remain technically and tactically proficient." This is a key part of the Creed for us to remember. We have a responsibility as an NCO to become better leaders and to utilize our skills as an NCO through the use of communication, supervision, teaching, coaching, counseling, technical/tactical proficiency on current systems, decision-making, planning and use of available systems. Self-development is a fundamental aspect of this statement and one that NCOs must take ownership of in order to live by the Creed.

"I will earn their respect and confidence as well as that of my Soldiers." Respect is earned. Soldiers will always respect your position but you can only retain that respect as well as the respect and confidence of the seniors and subordinates through your daily demonstration of the principles of LDRSHP- the acronym for the Army Values ingrained into our organizational psyche. Failure in any one area will result in an immediate erosion of confidence in your Soldiers, peers and superiors.

"I will not compromise my integrity, nor my moral courage." Soldiers want and deserve a leader that they can look to as a role model. They demand that you enforce the standard and remain fair. Soldiers want you to be good at your job and they also want you to motivate them and teach them to do the right thing. One day, they too will become an NCO.

In closing, the most important thing that NCOs provide is their leadership. Competent NCOs have a positive, substantial and daily impact on Soldiers as they lead in accomplishing the task at hand. They are leaders responsible for executing the organization's mission and for its training. NCOs provide advice and guidance to the Officer Corps. This guidance and mentorship is particularly important for our junior Officers, new in their careers. Senior NCOs, with a wealth of experience, are an essential organizational link and serve as an outstanding mentor to both the enlisted personnel and the Officers within an organization. The NCO Creed is a standard by which we can measure ourselves. These are not new ideals; however, if this standard is applied correctly, it helps our Non-Commissioned Officer Corp remain focused and on track.

CSM Michael Williamson
3d Squadron, 16th Cavalry

From One Leader to Another
The Professional NCO

Command Sergeant Major Christopher J. Menton
Sergeant Major Stanley J. Balcer

Webster's dictionary defines being a professional as "characterized by or conforming to the technical or ethical standards of a profession." As Non-Commissioned Officers (NCOs) we are the "Back Bone" of the Army profession. It is our inherent duty to uphold our responsibilities, be both technically and tactically competent, quality leaders and trainers and maintain the welfare of our Soldiers and their Families. NCOs are the foundation of our Army, the rock upon which the greatest fighting force the world has ever known is built upon. Though the battlefields, uniforms, tactics and society itself may change, the NCO remains true to our history. From our earliest days crossing the Delaware with Washington to the mountains of Afghanistan today, the NCO remains the consummate professional and standard bearer for all our Army holds to be good and true.

From the outset, during the establishment of the Continental Army in 1775, the NCO Corps proved to be quite unique. It became a Corps like no other previously seen in any Army around the world. The new NCO Corps changed the way many Armies around the world would structure their forces in the years to come. Gone was the all too startling gap between the conscript Soldier and an elitist Officer Corps; the NCO stood as the experienced professional that Soldier and Officer alike came to rely so heavily upon. Standardization with duties and responsibilities were laid out in an effort to legitimize the professional role of the NCO. These duties and responsibilities were first defined by Baron von Steuben in 1776 during the early phases of the

Revolutionary War. Just as our country was being born from conflict and molded into a new nation, our Army was transformed from a rag tag, unorganized militia into a disciplined, professional fighting force. At the heart of this transformation was the Non-Commissioned Officer, with defined roles for Corporals, Sergeants, First Sergeants and Sergeants Major designed to lead this new force. NCOs became an integral part in leading their Soldiers during battle as well as administrative and other tasks. Although not as glorious, these other tasks were vital in ensuring the smooth operation of a professional fighting force. Another key factor Baron von Steuben identified was selecting quality individuals to serve within the NCO ranks, something that we still hold true today. As the Army changed and re-organized over the next two hundred and thirty seven years, so too did the duties and responsibilities of the Non-Commissioned Officer.

The Non-Commissioned Officer of today is far more educated than the fearless NCOs that stood at Valley Forge, as they receive professional military education and other functional training and education which enhances their technical and tactical knowledge. The NCO of today must also seek out personal development through the attendance of civilian education programs while simultaneously juggling the rigors of leading Soldiers, maintaining their own professional standards and dedicating time for their own Families at home. There is no place in the NCO Corps for those content with the minimum, whether that minimum be in the NCO education system, civilian education, leading Soldiers or even pushing their own boundaries during physical training. The professional NCO demands much more of themselves, as do those around them, always striving further, farther, harder and faster. They complete the minimum and then some, often well ahead of others be it when completing an online advanced or senior, ALC or SLC, leadership course or on a company run. A professional NCO is not one who rationalizes his failure to prioritize his time and effort and ends up not completing the task at hand. The true professional is one who is always physically and mentally prepared so that when he is required to attend a military school there are no reasons why he wouldn't be prepared or successful in its execution.

The NCO today is also asked to be the expert on multiple systems and procedures in order to be a well-rounded leader. The professional NCO understands this and works to ensure they are the best qualified in order to train and lead their Soldiers. As combat over the past twelve years has shown, NCOs who are able to function as a multi-faceted, subject matter expert on the multitude of systems and procedures within their purview and be able to effectively train their Soldiers in return, are quite successful. For example, a communications NCO may find himself in charge of leading a combat logistical patrol and although he might be technically competent in the communications field, if he isn't tactically competent then he endangers his Soldiers and detracts from mission accomplishment. The professional NCO also looks for well-rounded or broadening assignments throughout their career and field. Broadening your assignment selection enables you to be more versatile and able to adapt to any operating environment, be it in a home station or deployed. Being the expert and having well-rounded assignments helps to ensure that the NCO is able to set the example in all that he does.

The professional Non-Commissioned Officer is the enforcer of standards and discipline. He accomplishes this through his personal example and holding his Soldiers accountable. The Army is not a nine to five job; the professional NCO adheres to all regulations, lives the Army Values and Warrior Ethos twenty four hours a day. Being a professional, Non-Commissioned Officer is a privilege for which few are chosen. Once part of the NCO Corps, all Soldiers expect their NCOs to provide quality leadership and guidance. Whether conducting an effective counseling session with his Soldiers or teaching them how to shoot their weapon, Soldiers look to the professional Non-Commissioned Officer as their guide to learn the Army Profession. Joint operations, digital systems and working in varied cultures are just a few of the challenges that today's NCOs have adapted to.

As our Army and our Nation move forward and adapt to an ever-changing enemy presence in a non-contiguous battlefield, the professional NCO must continue to adapt as well. Those that both learn from the past and embrace the future will be best suited to lead and train the professional NCOs of tomorrow, always placing the success and welfare of their Soldiers above one's self. As the Army draws down the size of the force, there will be a two-fold affect on the NCO corps; it will become even more imperative that the seasoned, professional NCOs of today continue to groom the future of the Corps while we as an Army will only be able to select the very best for continued service. Education of systems, equipment, force structure and continued self-development will all be important to the success of the NCO. Individual and unit readiness for combat or other missions, with a strong sense of purpose, will all be dependent on the professional NCO.

History has shown that we will always need to maintain a strong, combat ready and professional NCO Corps. We must continue to build upon the foundation established by the first NCOs from 1776 by enforcing and setting the standards through our example and by training and leading our Soldiers. The success, or failure, of our Army as it transitions in an unpredictable future will hinge largely on the professionalism of the Non-Commissioned Officer; we cannot afford to fail our Army or our Nation. In a time of peace or war it is paramount that the NCO be a professional whom Soldiers look towards to lead them from the front in all that he does. From the Corporal in the garrison motor pool to the Staff Sergeant on patrol in Afghanistan, we must continue to reinforce the foundation of our Army as professionals, leaders, Non-Commissioned Officers.

If you would like to learn more about this topic it is recommended that you read *Field Manual 7-22.7*, *The NCO Guide*, *Army Doctrine Publication 6-22*, *Army Leadership*, *Army Doctrine Reference Publication 6-22*, *Army Leadership*, and *Army Doctrine Reference Publication 1*, *The Army Profession*.

CSM Christopher J. Menton
SGM Stanley J. Balcer
4BCT, 1CAV Division

From One Leader to Another
The Stripes You Wear
Command Sergeant Major John L. Murray

The NCO Corps has and will always be an important part of the United States Army and is integral to the success of its missions and daily operation. Non-Commissioned Officers are supposed to be the example for others to follow. Sometimes once we are selected for promotion or an increased position we forget about the simple things that made us and our formations successful. The following list is not all inclusive but it does clearly identify a few key points that all NCOs should remember regardless of their grade or position.

Your stripes are symbols of authority. This authority is an important privilege that must be exercised with good common sense and maturity. These are qualities that your superiors and the Army believe you possess and it is your responsibility to at all times demonstrate professional behavior. This will help to ensure their confidence in you, that their trust has not been misplaced. Never do anything that will discredit your rank and position.

Set the example. You must prove by your own actions that you deserve the privilege to lead your subordinates and that you are worthy of the respect and confidence of your superiors and peers. Your actions do speak louder than your words. Everything you do or don't do is the example that you display to others. Displaying a good example for others to emulate is part of your responsibility as a NCO.

Don't be afraid to get your hands dirty. Come to work and do your job, don't sit back and wait for other people. You must always remain technically and tactfully proficient. The only way to remain proficient is to stay current with policies and procedures, continue to work and always seek out knowledge. Don't wait for it to come to you. Don't be that type of leader which thinks that "now that I am a NCO, my job is sit back and watch others". If you stop working you will lose both your proficiency and relevancy.

Remember where you came from. Don't ever forget what it was like down in the trenches performing the daily tasks of an organization. You were once the Soldier performing the mundane, seemingly meaningless tasks, task which must be conducted in order to maintain an organization. If you think you are "too good" or "too valuable" to visit and talk to your subordinates, you will become detached and lose the "pulse" of your organization. Don't forget to give someone a simple thank-you for all of those little things that just seem to happen.

Be and look like a NCO. Your posture, the appearance of your uniform, your physical condition and your reaction to the incidents of military life all convey an impression to others. You must demonstrate to others by what you say and do that you are a master of your job and your emotions. Subordinates must feel they can rely on you in an emergency, that you are a competent NCO and an individual who habitually uses sound judgment when faced with a problem. You must be a leader, not simply a supervisor. Subordinates will follow a leader because they want to while they will follow a supervisor because they have to. You must draw upon your inner resources of personal character-courage, initiative, ingenuity and common sense. You must be able to instill in people a desire to follow you. Your vehicle in doing this is leadership.

Take responsibility for your actions. Demonstrating proper leadership indicates that you accept full responsibility and expect to be held accountable. This acceptance involves many things. Some of these include placing the health and well-being of your subordinates above your own, respect for their rights and empathy, the honest attempt to understand their problems. You must accept the fact that you are always on duty, 24 hours a day; that everything your unit does or fails to do is your concern. If you make an honest mistake, accept responsibility, learn from your mistakes and never allow them to be repeated.

Loyalty is first among the qualities that make a Soldier. Loyalty to our nation we take for granted, but we must also be loyal to our superiors, peers and our subordinates. True loyalty is more than obedience. It demands complete cooperation with the spirit as well as the letter of every order. So regardless of your private opinions, give your superiors your full support. Do not criticize nor tear apart their orders in your idle conversation. As you react toward your superiors, so will your subordinates. Constant griping is a form of moral sabotage. It weakens your authority and in time can eat away at the discipline of your organization.

Do routine things routinely. Continue to do those small things that everyone expects from a leader such as showing up on time, looking like a Soldier, displaying confidence and enthusiasm and accomplishing tasks that are given to you. These are all routine things that you should do routinely. Your superiors expect you do those things routinely. Once you start slipping you will lose the confidence your superiors have in you.

Make yourself important. Find something that needs to be done in your organization and do it. This is the essence of disciplined initiative which is vital to every organization. Show everyone that you can make a difference. Once you become an important member of the team, you will find that you will be the one that others come to for answers. Don't sit back and think that just because you wear stripes that you now know and have done everything.

Passion plus professionalism equals performance. Be passionate about your job, your Soldiers and their Families. Love your job and do everything you can to be the very best each and every day. Be professional in everything that you say and do. If you are going to do something, than do it right or don't do it at all. If you are passionate and professional about your job, you will get great performance from both yourself and from others.

If you would like to learn more about this topic it is recommended that your read *Field Manual* 7-27.7, *The Army Non-Commissioned Officer Guide* and *Army Doctrine Publication* 6-22, *Army Leadership*.

CSM John L. Murray
Army Contracting Command

From One Leader to Another
The Warrior Ethos

Command Sergeant Major Brunk W. Conley

The Warrior Ethos is a subset of our Soldier's Creed. It is the heart and soul of the Creed and is four simple, yet powerful sentences. Without the Ethos, the Creed does not stand. The Soldier's Creed was fully implemented by the Army on 13 November, 2003. Soldiers are expected to memorize it in Basic and Advanced Individual Training. However, memorization is easy, understanding is hard. The young Soldiers placed in your charge, will do better if you explain and help them understand the Ethos. Here is a way of teaching it for understanding. Steal it if you want, but it is better if you customize your lesson to fit your style.

"I WILL ALWAYS PLACE THE MISSION FIRST"

When our Soldiers join the Army, they want to be a part of an organization that is bigger than them. They want to serve their country and defend the values of our nation. This particular line is one about values. I place the mission first with little or no regard to my own personal well-being. It is bigger than any one Soldier and their individual needs. Without my pure faith and trust in the belief that my mission supports a greater good, the entire Army falls apart. Each person is responsible for their part of completing the overall mission.

"I WILL NEVER ACCEPT DEFEAT"

I love this sentence. Notice that it does not say "I will never be defeated". It says that I will never accept it. Everyone will face adversity; every Soldier will be defeated at some point in their career. Some of those defeats will be big and some small. But you never have to accept it. If you get knocked down, get back up, dust yourself off and get back at it, whatever it may be. Learn from your mistakes always seeking perfection, knowing that perfection is not likely, but it is a worthy pursuit. It is in the pursuit of perfection that individuals and units reach excellence. Excellence should be the goal.

"I WILL NEVER QUIT"

This is one of the simplest principles yet needs to be taught to our newest Soldiers and reinforced throughout their service. I was personally lucky enough to be taught this at a young age by my parents. However, not all young men and women are as fortunate. It can be taught and it can be reinforced. The best place to be taught is at the team level by a young NCO who believes it to their core.

"I WILL NEVER LEAVE A FALLEN COMRADE"

This is a very deep and powerful sentence. It has many hidden meanings other than the vision it might first evoke in ones mind's eye. I believe it is the key to our resiliency efforts. It is easy to visualize such things as flesh wounds, broken bones, bleeding and restoring breathing. But how do you apply it to a relationship, financial hardship, educational concerns, all very real issues that many of our young Soldiers face today.

Let me tackle this by asking a question. Would you ever leave a fallen Soldier if they had a broken leg? Of course, the answer is NO! Let me ask another question. Would you leave a Soldier who might do harm to themselves if you knew it? Again the answer is NO! But that is the hard part, how do you know a Soldier is hurting inside with non-visible wounds? The answer is easy to say, but hard to implement. You have to talk to them. You have to build a safe and trusting relationship in which they feel comfortable talking to you. It is by far the most difficult of the four lines comprising the Warrior Ethos. It also is the one that will truly define you as a good leader, because it is so hard to accomplish. In this new day of social media and technological advances, good old face-to-face counseling and discussion is the best way to identify unseen issues.

So in conclusion, I was lucky enough to have the Ranger Creed drilled into me as a young private in the 2/75 Ranger Battalion. I have tried to live by that creed each and every day. Now I do the same by using the Warrior Ethos each and every day. It is on my coin and it is a talk that I can give to Soldiers at a moment's notice. I believe in the Ethos and think it is one of our keys to maintaining and improving the great Army we have. I hope you find your own way to express what the Ethos means to you and share it with those under your charge.

CSM Brunk W. Conley
10th CSM of the Army National Guard

From One Leader to Another
Why the Army Professional?

Command Sergeant Major Christopher K. Greca

I was sitting in Afghanistan in the fall of 2011 when I received a call from CSM John W. Troxell, the ISAF Joint Command CSM. He had called to congratulate me on my selection to become the next Command Sergeant Major of the Combined Arms Center (CAC) and Ft Leavenworth -- you know, that post most people believe exists merely to train Majors and lock people up in jail! During this conversation, CSM Troxell told me I was the right guy to be heading up the "PoA" (Profession of Arms) for our Army. I thought to myself, "why is the CAC CSM doing anything with Powers of Attorney?" John laughed and said, you know, the Profession of Arms!?! Truly, I had no idea and I probably thought this was a "gimmick."

As I transitioned into the Combined Arms Center in November of 2011, I had the opportunity to receive in-briefs from all of the subordinate organizations to CAC. One of those organizations was the Center for the Army Profession and Ethic (CAPE), physically located at West Point, New York. During their brief, SGM Dave Stewart handed me an Army Profession pamphlet which was about 40 pages in length and I thought, "I'll read this when I get the chance, maybe?" On my flight back to Kansas I got curious so I opened up the pamphlet and read it from front to rear, highlighting the critical points and I finally had that "light bulb" moment and thought THE ARMY PROFESSION IS THE ANSWER!

Now I know that is a very bold statement but I honestly believe this to be true. I have been in the Army now for 26 years and I have never been exposed to anything more important to our Army then the Army Profession campaign of education and training. The Army Profession is or should be our identity and linkage with the American People. We are a Profession, composed of the sons and daughters of the American people. We are competent, people of character, who are committed to one another, the Army team and our Nation! Those three "C's" define our expectations of all who are part of the Army team – Civilians and Soldiers – that we all must be men and women of Competence, Character, and Commitment.

Much discussion has revolved around "who is a Professional?" The answer is plain and simple; all that wear the uniform and the civilian cohort who work in our Army are part of this team. From the moment that each take the oath of service all become "Aspiring Professionals" until they are certified by graduating from their commissioning source, Basic Combat Training and Advanced Individual Training, and/or tailored certifications for the Army Civilian Corps. At that time, all become part of the Army Profession and are expected to conduct themselves as Professionals.

As with any other profession there are certain essential characteristics that set our Army apart from any other organization. America's Army, our Profession has five essential characteristics: Trust, Military Expertise, *Espirit de Corps*, Honorable Service and Stewardship of the Profession. These "essential characteristics" are required for not only all of the members of our Profession, but as an institution it is what the American people expect and demand from THEIR Army!

Trust is the foundation in which our Army revolves and it starts with the trust the Armerican people have given to us. They have entrusted us with their sons and daughters – to train, care for, safeguard and develop them into Professionals! They expect and demand that we treat them as we would our own sons and daughters and therefore, issues like hazing, sexual assault/harassment, suicides and other preventable accidents are unacceptable! All of the issues above cannot exist in a Professional Army, not if it is comprised of men and women of CHARACTER, who are COMMITTED to one another, who know their jobs and are COMPETENT; it is impossible! If every member of the team truly espoused to the tenets of our Profession, lived up to our defined expectations and standards as a team and mitigated risk as needed, then many, if not all, of the health of the force issues we currently face should disappear. The American People trust us to get this done and it starts with each of us as Leaders and the example we set for others! Every professional must understand the impact we as "role-models" have on not just our Army, but on the American People as well. We are truly ambassadors who must be committed, role models of character, who are competent and prepared to meet the challenges this country might face in the future.

Internal to our Army the importance of "trust" is paramount and its significance to daily operations is reinforced in several Army Doctrinal Publications such as *ADP 6-22*, *Army Leadership* and *ADP 6-0*, *Mission Command*. Our leaders trust that we are taking care of and developing our Soldiers. They trust that we are training our Soldiers as charged in *Army Doctrinal Publication 7-0*, *Training and Developing Leaders*, where it states, "Non-Commissioned Officers train individuals, crews, and small teams." Our leaders expect and trust us to train them to standard and to proficiency on their critical individual tasks and drills so that as Professionals, they are competent! Trust must be earned and then sustained by not only your actions, but also the actions of your subordinates for whom you are charged to care. If they are developed to be men and women of character, who are committed to this Army and their team, competent in their tasks that support the team then this trust will be sustained!

I could continue this discussion and could honestly write a book on the importance of the Army Profession, what it means to be a Professional, and how all Cohorts: Commissioned Officers, Non-Commissioned Officers, Warrant Officers, Enlisted and Civilians must understand the importance of our Profession in the hope that all professionals might have a similar "light bulb" moment like my own. This is not a "gimmick" but rather a way of life, an identity that all who wear and/or support those wearing the uniform of a Soldier must have. One of the essential characteristics of the Army Profession is "Stewardship of the Profession", making this Army better for not only ourselves but for generations to come. We must, as Non-Commissioned Officers, continue to sustain this Army in a period of transition and make it better tomorrow than it is today. We must identify ourselves as Professionals, understand what it means to be in the Army Profession, and as Stewards of the Profession pass this information along to the youngest of Soldiers in our ranks. It is that important.

We are a Nation and Army with both challenges and opportunities. Our challenges: fiscal limitations, reduction in end strength, restructuring of the force, operations abroad, regional alignment of forces and a change in operational tempo are all opportunities - opportunities to shape this Army under the umbrella of the Army Profession. Regardless of our end strength, I am convinced that we can be stronger and more lethal than we are today if we do this right. Soldiers of character who are committed and who are competent must be the standard for all and not just for a certain MOS or certain unit but across our entire Army. An Army which revolves around trust, which is proud and filled with *esprit de corps*, filled with military expertise, committed to honorable service and finally, whose ranks are filled with those who understand that as stewards of the profession that the past 237 years have been great -- but this means nothing if we are not prepared for the future. I said previously and I'll say it again, THE ARMY PROFESSION IS OUR ANSWER; understand this and I promise we will be prepared for the challenges of the future.

CSM Christopher K. Greca
Combined Arms Center and Fort Leavenworth

Section 2

Tasks

From One Leader to Another
Quarters/Barracks

Command Sergeant Major Carlos Medina Castellano

For some time, we as an Army have been drilling down on NCOs in regards to inspecting barracks, quarters and getting to know their Soldiers on a more personal level. Many have forgotten that our NCO Creed states: "my two basic responsibilities will always be uppermost in my mind; accomplishment of my mission and the welfare of my Soldiers." Checking our Soldier's barracks and living quarters is about taking care of and looking out for their welfare.

Throughout my career, I have had the opportunity to serve in TRADOC units as a Drill Sergeant, in Divisional units as a Section Sergeant and Platoon Sergeant, and Operational and Strategic units as both a First Sergeant and Command Sergeant Major. What is constant in all instances, is the fact that NCOs are expected to check on barracks to ensure the health and welfare of their subordinates.

There are many ways to ensure Soldiers are living healthy and adhering to standards. I discovered the most effective way when I was serving in a divisional unit. We would walk through the barracks just prior to physical training to ensure our Soldiers were awake and were getting ready for first formation. While there, we quickly glanced at their rooms to ensure there was no trash piled up, no excessive beer cans, alcohol bottles, etc. Before work call, we would then check the common areas (stairwells, laundry rooms, hallways and latrines). This type of inspection was informal but enforced established standards and gave us an indication of what type of Soldiers we were dealing with (disciplined, undisciplined, heavy drinkers, smokers, non-smokers, etc.). In addition, we would conduct a battalion level quarterly ASU/Class A and barracks inspection. This gave us another opportunity to verify our Soldier's quality of life.

What we have discovered in the past few years is that young NCOs do not know what to look for when inspecting barracks and or quarters. A quick glance at the room is not sufficient. When inspecting, we need to take the time to open desk drawers, cabinets, refrigerators, stoves, windows blinds, etc. We should check for dust built up behind furniture, washers and dryers, under fridge, stove and beds. We should check bathrooms for mildew, soap scum and stains that may lead to health issues. Inspecting a room is a sequential art and a science just like inspecting paratroopers before they jump. If you don't have a process you may miss something. That is why most units maintain a barrack's standard operating procedure (SOP), which provides guidelines and checklists defining how one's room should be maintained.

Where we need more attention is the off-post and on-post quarters. All too often we realize that supervisors don't know where their Soldiers live and therefore they don't know how they are living. As a supervisor, especially of young Soldiers arriving to their first duty station looking for housing (not barracks), we should be part of the reception process. We should help our Soldiers find a decent place to live and accompany them throughout the housing inspection process, regardless of whether their quarters are on-post or off-post. By doing that, you get to see the place before the Soldier moves in, thus giving you a clearer picture of the living conditions prior to occupancy. This also shows both the Soldier and their Family that you care about their welfare. Additionally, if you know where your Soldier lives, you are now able to periodically drive by their residence just to check on things, not necessarily to inspect but to get a feel for how they maintain their residence on the outside at least.

Getting to know your Soldiers takes time, but by inspecting and observing their place of residence periodically, we often learn about those things they may not otherwise share with you during an initial or periodic counseling session. The bottom line is that we as NCOs are expected to check and enforce standards on barracks and quarters both as stewards of our government resources and as leaders of Soldiers. If we don't know what to do, we should ask someone. Many times another NCO won't share with you these standards or tips because they themselves don't know them. The "KNOW HOW" of daily operations need to be transferred from our Senior NCOs (MSG/ SGM/CSM) to our younger NCOs (SFC and below). Together we can ensure that Army traditions remain intact, that the art of inspecting is passed down to our next generation of leaders and most importantly that we are fully able to accomplish our two basic responsibilities; accomplishment of our mission and the welfare of our Soldiers.

CSM Carlos Medina Castellano
551 SIG BN

From One Leader to Another
Command Supply Discipline Program
Command Sergeant Major Clifton Johnson

The Command Supply Discipline Program (CSDP) is the apex of military leadership and is essential to maintaining the combat readiness of our Army. For the past twenty-nine years, I have served in the Army in both combat and garrison operating environments as a Multifunctional Logistician in various units which include Infantry, Air Defense Artillery, Armored Cavalry, Armor, Main Support Battalions, Corps Support Commands, Expeditionary Support Commands and Sustainment Brigades. My experience from these assignments has demonstrated the significance of individuals taking responsibility and being held accountable for both military property and equipment. Command, supervisory, direct, custodial and personal responsibilities are the five types of responsibilities recognized within the United States Army. One of the countless overarching responsibilities of a Commander is the care for government property and equipment. A commander may delegate the accountability and safeguard of property and equipment but they may never delegate their overall responsibility.

Supervisory responsibility is the relationship between superiors and the property in the possession of personnel under their supervision. The supervisor inherits this power. Accountable Officers and hand receipt holders incur direct responsibility. Direct responsibility ensures that government property and equipment is properly hand-receipted and obligates the person to care for that property and equipment.

Custodial responsibility relates to equipment waiting turn-in or pick-up by logistics personnel from the Supply Service Activity (SSA). The supply personnel at the command level turn-in and pick-up equipment from the SSA. The SSA controls the distribution and turn-in of military equipment and supplies. The supply system technician is the Accountable Officer for equipment turned in by the supply level personnel or received from other military agencies.

The supply technician has the custodial responsibility for the safeguarding of equipment a unit may issue to supply personnel or turn-in to the Defense Reutilization and Marketing Office (DRMO). Exercising prudent care to use government equipment and property is the responsibility of the individual hand receipted for the equipment. Each military member requires logistical knowledge and understanding to ensure the execution of proper supply use and accountability.

The CSDP is only as good as the system and processes further developed within a unit. It is not designed to be another layer of inspections but a sanity check for commanders and a tool to place the unit on the correct logistics azimuth. The key to success with CSDP and property accountability rests with the Non-Commissioned Officer (NCO) Corps. The NCO Corps must uniformly, consistently and aggressively instill supply discipline and supply economy throughout Army formations without exception.

The level of logistical experience of leaders and commanders requires teaching new Officers and NCOs about property accountability and CSDP. Every military member has to be actively involved in the training, execution and enforcement of the CSDP. CSDP is a way for commands to mentor and train their Soldiers through inspections to correct deficiencies and shortcomings. This allows the Soldiers to experience the correct way to conduct logistical business. An environment of performing correct property accountability, allows the Army to measure good stewardship and it shows Soldiers at all levels what right looks like. Soldiers who holistically grasp and execute CSDP greatly increase their chances of participating in the CSA Supply Excellent Award (SEA).

CSDP is every Leader's responsibility. Following and enforcing CSDP policies and procedures demonstrates personal involvement. To that end, resolution of identified accounting discrepancies requires command emphasis in order to fully support the Command Supply Discipline Program. Lack of property accountability can result in excesses and imbalances reducing the ability to generate combat power. Leadership involvement in making sure the unit is ready for combat is a huge undertaking. In order to achieve mission success, leaders must ensure that their Soldiers and their equipment are ready for the task.

The implementation and evaluation of CSDP begins with each commander providing the personal interest and direction necessary to establish an effective CSDP program. CSDP should be fully incorporated into existing resources and systems within the command in order to avoid redundancy of effort. Each level of command is required to evaluate their immediate subordinate level command's program.

The evaluation records are kept with the parent organization at the higher command level. Evaluation findings of noncompliance may be due to circumstances beyond the control for the evaluated organization. The level conducting the evaluation is then responsible for elevating the results and helping the evaluated unit meet compliance standards and policies.

The evaluation process includes a review of the property book and verification that the school trained supply personnel are assigned. The evaluator will record their findings regarding each applicable requirement in the requirement listing of the CSDP checklist. The organization's supervisor will be briefed on the findings at the completion of the evaluation. Major problems with procedures or policy will be reported to the chain of command.

The Command Supply Discipline Program is a program that works when emphasized, executed and enforced by the command. When there is minimal command involvement, it can be the downfall of any great organization. When leaders at all levels place a strong emphasis on the program, it helps to develop leaders of the future. History has proven that leaders who master accountability, truly master leadership.

CSM Clifton Johnson
US Army Logistics University
NCOA Commandant

From One Leader to Another
The Art of Counseling

Command Sergeant Major
Carlos Medina Castellano

Counseling, if done correctly, is probably the most difficult and time consuming task an NCO will perform on a daily, weekly, monthly and/or quarterly basis. If you examine Appendix C of the old *FM* 6-22, *Army Leadership*, it provides you with clear guidance on how to approach counseling, how to conduct counseling, what types of counseling there are and it even provides you with examples of counseling. Over the coming year, the new FM 6-22, which will support and further develop both *Army Doctrinal* and *Army Doctrinal Reference Publications* 6-22, *Army Leadership*, will be released and will include specific updated information and guidance on counseling and organizational counseling programs.

Across the force there are a couple of recurring questions regarding counseling, "So why are we not getting counseled like we are supposed to (Soldiers at least monthly and NCOs at least quarterly)?" And, "Where is the breakdown, the deficiency?" In large part, the answers to these questions often boil down to one fundamental conclusion; leaders do not counsel Soldiers because they are not competent or confident in their writing skills.

As an NCO, we should posses at least a basic foundation in writing competencies. The Non-Commissioned Officer Educational System (NCOES) has specified curriculum which covers effective Army writing, but that in and of itself just is not enough. The basic skills covered are rudimentary at best; therefore it is recommended that each individual leader take some level of college or advanced writing course in order to improve their writing proficiency.

Additionally, Senior NCOs who have the experience should be encouraged to conduct professional development sessions that specifically target writing techniques in order to help cultivate a learning environment in our young leaders; which leads to the next conclusion or answer to the above questions, mentoring is a form of counseling.

Mentorship can be categorized in two areas: direct and indirect mentorship. These two directly compliment the types of counseling; also direct and indirect. Most of us have experienced direct mentorship. For example, when someone in or outside of our normal chain of concern/command helped in our preparation for promotion or the NCO and Soldier of the Quarter Boards; when someone sat us down and explained to us what to do in order to get promoted; when someone shared with us their experiences and knowledge on how the NCOER system and counseling works, how to write effectively; and sometimes how to handle Soldiers issues, these are all examples of direct mentorship or counseling. Direct mentorship happens when you are being engaged by a leader or when you seek out advice from someone. There is some type of exchange (communication) of ideas between two individuals.

Indirect mentorship or counseling on the other hand, does not require a two-way exchange of ideas and/or means of communication. It can be as simple as an individual observing behavior. It could be observed or executed by anyone regardless of rank. At the most basic level it is how we learn from one another without actually going through a formal process. Some examples are when we see a leader conducting physical training, running, calling cadences, road marching, engaged in the training process with his/her Soldiers. All are examples where the actions of an individual speak more loudly than actual words; when someone role models behavior and leads by example. When we see these types of leaders in action, we are more likely to emulate their good behavior. Some might argue that indirect mentorship or counseling is the primary learning tool for all Soldiers.

Reflecting on my early years as a young Sergeant First Class and First Sergeant, I had the opportunity to serve with some great leaders who in one way or another had a positive impact on my development as an individual and as a Non-Commissioned Officer. Sometimes they sat me down to talk about how to improve the way I resolved military issues or concerns, but I must say, most of the information shared or learned did not come from a "sit down" session. Instead, it came from observations I made while they were performing their duties. I truly believe that when you are surrounded by positive people, good things will happen to you. As you develop as a leader, remember what you are charged to do: mentor your Soldiers, provide them with good examples and be a good role model for what an NCO should be, know and do.

It is a known fact, the more rank you get as a Senior NCO, the less mentoring or counseling you will receive. One of the reasons is that at the senior level, you are the professional. You are the fountain of knowledge for those young NCOs trying to be like you. You are the expert. Soldiers will seek your advice and your mentorship. They want to be counseled and mentored by you. Remember what the NCO creed states "all Soldiers are entitled to outstanding leadership," you are now charged to provide that leadership.

CSM Carlos Medina Castellano
551 SIG BN

From One Leader to Another
Counseling
CSM Jeremiah Inman

Counseling is a critical tool used to develop the Nations current force and future leaders. The true beginning of documented counseling cannot be pin pointed but has been a topic of note since Baron von Steuben's Revolutionary War Drill Manual (1794) and continues to be a topic of significance in our *Army Doctrinal Publication* and *Army Doctrinal Reference Publication* 6-22, *Army Leadership* (2012).

Taking care of Soldiers requires leaders at all levels to provide an environment where everyone is afforded the opportunity to develop to their fullest potential. This cannot happen without an active counseling program which provides constructive feedback. Counseling is an immediate way of providing feedback to acknowledge/improve a subordinate's duty performance. A complete and thorough counseling packet is also an indispensable tool for writing awards, NCOERs, supporting promotion/reduction requests, and if necessary, justifying disciplinary actions.

Education and constant/monthly quality assurance by the CSM/CDR are the only surefire method for a strong effective program. Every promotion board, Uniform Code of Military Justice action, schools request, staff/charge of quarter's duty, or barracks inspection can be an opportunity to review a few packets at a time and so as not to become overwhelmed. It is important that you provide written or verbal feedback for each packet regarding the counselors' performance, not the counselee, and wrap up a blanket or most common issues note for your entire formation of leaders. Listed below are tested and proven practices that help develop subordinates during these sessions. Counselors need not cover each of these topics in each and every session but they must discuss strengths, weaknesses and a specific plan for sustainment and improvement.

1. Soldiers in the rank of PVT through SFC will be counseled monthly and they will be counseled after major operations or significant events. This may be disruptive to the monthly schedule but the intent is that no Soldier should ever go without formal written counseling for more than a 6 week period.

2. All NCOs will be counseled using a DA Form 4856-R counseling form which will augment the DA Form 2166-8-1. Soldiers in the rank of MSG and above will be counseled, in writing, by their immediate supervisor quarterly. Accompanying both documents will be the working copy of the DA Form 2166-8, NCOER, which will be updated at each counseling session. Working copy meaning that the counselor updates bullets in PART IV, b thru f. Placing an "X" in the earned "excellence/success/needs improvement". At the end of the session all NCOs will know where their performance rating stands if the evaluation was due that month.

3. Integration and Reception Counseling will be completed within 24 hours of a Soldier's arrival. The intent of this counseling is to welcome the Soldier to the unit ensuring that they are; assigned a sponsor, in-processed through their company training room, outline unit standards, Garrison specific policies and regulations; cover unit policy letters, host nation conduct, tour of post areas, address Soldier and Family needs, and when

applicable ensure they were properly in-processed with outside agencies.

4. Initial Counseling will be conducted upon the completion of in-processing and assignment to a platoon/section/squad. The intent of initial counseling is to inform the Soldier of his duties (job description), outline specific duties and responsibilities of their newly assigned duty position, discuss what is required of him or her in order to be successful, discuss self-development opportunities such as how to register for Army correspondence and college courses; and to establish personal/professional goals. If known and prepared in a timely manner the integration and reception counseling sessions may be combined.

5. Each performance counseling session should address the following subject areas:

    a. <u>Performance</u>: Discuss all training and key events that took place during the counseling period. What to sustain and improve upon; specifically highlighting a plan of action for improvements. Explain the training path that will help improve their short falls. Discuss what will happen if improvement is not made to standard such as remedial training and the loss of off-duty/mission personal time.

    b. <u>Promotion</u>: Tell the Soldier when he or she will become eligible and when they might be recommended for promotion or the promotion board. Discuss what must be done to earn their promotion. Complimenting this, using some foresight, give the advice on areas they might begin now in order to better prepare them for future assignments, schools, civilian education, correspondence courses, etc. Some of these points need not be repeated month after month, just ensure that the Soldier fully understands the promotion system. Soldiers and NCOs who are in the primary zone for promotion but not recommended for promotion must be counseled specifically in this area at the end of each month. It is the leadership not the Soldier who decides when it is time for promotion.

c. Schools: Discuss with the Soldier the outlook for military education, what is needed to plan, prepare and execute this training and where they stand in regards to the unit's order of merit list. Assist and track your Soldier's progress of Structured Self-Development and the conduct of online NCOES requirements while ensuring they are afforded the time to complete these requirements. Make sure school packets are complete and turned in with all of the required paperwork necessary to attend the course. Army Correspondence Courses are a great individual developmental tool. Require your PVT-SGT to take them. They not only help with promotion points but also professionally develop the Soldier. Civilian education is readily available to all Soldiers at no or minimal cost. Encourage and show them how to sign up for online courses and check/assist them in their progress toward their goal/degree.

d. <u>Structured Self Development</u>: There are 4 Phases of SSD that leaders need to track: SSD I PVT-SPC, SSD III SGT-SSG, SSD IV SSG (P)-MSG, SSD V will apply to MSG (P) upon completion of United States Sergeants Major Academy. Each phase requires no more than 80 hours of online training and is mandatory for school attendance and subsequent promotion (see ALARACT 288/2010 for specific details). However, Leaders must ensure their Soldiers are taking time to complete this requirement and should address this monthly until complete.

e. <u>Re-enlistment</u>: Discuss the Soldier's options; make sure he or she knows when/if they are eligible and if necessary, how they can get their bar or flag lifted. Discuss the benefits, bonuses, unit incentives, possible assignment choices that may fit their specific situation and also discuss the possibility of their entry into the Reserve Component if their plan is it to leave active duty. Re-enlistment is now highly competitive, it is not a right, nor should everyone be eligible to reenlist. Discuss whether you are going to recommend to the commander for their retention, and if not, what they must do to become eligible.

f. <u>Goals</u>: Leaders should always counsel Soldiers on their personal and professional short term (within current enlistment period) and long term goals (in the next enlistment period and beyond). By requiring individuals to sit down with leaders and formally establish goals, it will better prepare our Soldiers for their career, provide a sense of achievement and build confidence once goals are met.

g. Safety: Discuss both on and off duty safety by covering items such as physical training, high risk operations, weapons, military and civilian vehicles, motorcycles, boating, hunting, water sports/activities, extreme/risky sports, anti-American groups and even sexual education. Impacting all of these and more are the use of drugs and alcohol. When on leave and at home station, it is okay to drink alcohol as long as it is done legally and responsibility. Drugs though are illegal, and it is important that you highlight the importance of your Soldiers staying away from them and those that wish to use them.

h. Courtesy/respect toward others and host nation: It is always important to discuss how your Soldiers should treat everyone with dignity and respect. Remind Soldiers that we are ambassadors for our country. They are looked up to as role models and expected to take charge of any threatening situation in order to keep everything safe. Your Soldiers need to understand that they are always being watched and observed. Loud and irresponsible speech in common areas like comments that suggest killing terrorists, watching folks get blown up or what person he linked up with last weekend are all discussions left better unsaid; profane and sexually-oriented conversations, arguing with post agencies, reckless driving and behavior and disrespect to our host nation are areas that damage a Soldiers' image and place every American at greater risk. Respect others, yourself, your unit, your fallen and all Families.

 i. <u>Checkbooks/credit cards/finance</u>: At least once a quarter, discuss financial responsibility to ensure that your Soldier understands how to properly use these items and that he or she is not getting in over their head. Encourage them to set up a type of savings/investment plan or attend a class given through the Army Community Services. Discourage living paycheck to paycheck. Advise them on get rich schemes and extreme interest rates. You should know when your Soldiers are planning a big purchase like buying a car; educate them on the interest rates, loans and the use of a minimal payment plan. This is taking care of Soldiers, protecting Families, preventing debt and possible distractions in both your home station and a deployed environment. Soldiers who write bad checks, miss payments or have financial issues will be required to schedule and attend financial training through ACS.

 j. <u>Force Protection/OPSEC</u>: You should discuss the impact of using computers and phones to contact home and fellow Soldiers in-country and while on leave, or even posting what you think may be harmless, such as photos on facebook. Soldiers must remember they are always serving in a potentially hostile environment and must assume that the enemy is everywhere. Safeguarding and protecting military identification, military manning, equipment specifications, training, operations and deployment/patrol dates/time lines is a must as they are not topics for open discussion. Operational security is critical to the safety of all Families, Soldiers and overall mission readiness.

6. Honesty and candor are essential to an effective counseling program. NCOs and Officers have the inherent leader responsibility to tell it like it is and should do so with tact and respect for the Soldier being counseled. In this manner, both the Army and the individual will benefit.

7. Counseling will be listed on training schedules as close to the end of the month as possible, or developed as part of the recovery/reset plan. An exception to this is during deployments/missions, the counseling may be completed upon return but a Soldier will not go more than 6 weeks without formal written counseling.

8. If a Soldier is not available for counseling because of leave, extended mission, attached elsewhere or TDY, a short statement will be placed in his or her counseling packet stating such; this is intended to show that no periods of counseling were missed and to complete the record. Upon return, the Soldier will be reminded of what is expected of him and counseled on any updates to policies that have changed in his absence.

9. Company Commanders and 1SGs will review select counseling packets monthly. Counselors are not expected to be

English majors, but spelling, grammar and neatness are important if the message is to be understood. Each time a Soldier is counseled his personal data sheet will be reviewed and updated, and their goals reassessed. The Company Commander and 1SG will ensure subordinate leaders maintain counseling packets. The Commander and CSM will periodically inspect the counseling packets on a no-notice basis and as part of their command inspection program.

10. The intent is that every Soldier is aware of how their performance is perceived by their first line supervisor. The goal is to enforce exceptional behavior, change substandard behavioral patterns and to produce a better Soldier and leader.

11. Any adverse personnel action must be documented before UCMJ action is taken. All Soldiers pending UCMJ action must receive a flag action.

12. At a minimum, counseling packets will consist of the following: unit coversheet-Company/Platoon or Section/Squad, an Enlisted Record Brief updated within the last 6 months, a personal data sheet, a high dollar item inventory, a copy of their clothing and organizational equipment record, weapons and vehicle qualification, an APFT score card, a height and weight statement, DA 4856 counseling forms, a copy of past UCMJ action, and a strip map for those living outside the area. For CPL and above, a copy of their last NCOER and current working NCOER must be included. There is no standard order for the items required in the packet; however,

they will be organized and all packets within each company will be in the same format.

Counseling has been an area of importance since the very beginning of our Army and has become even more important in our current operational environment/tempo. Do not fail your Soldiers during counseling. They need to hear their strengths and weaknesses from their leaders and more importantly, how they can improve. If we fail as leaders in counseling our future leaders will likely fail as well.

If you would like to learn more about this topic you should read *Army Doctrine Publication 6-22, Army Leadership*, *Army Doctrine Reference Publication 6-22, Army Leadership*, *Field Manual 6-22, Army Leadership* and *Training Circular 7-22.7, The Army Non-Commissioned Officers Guide*.

CSM Jeremiah Inman
197th Infantry Brigade

From One Leader to Another
Financial Management
Command Sergeant Major Joanne Cox

Even the most proficient, well trained Soldiers in the Army are of little use if they cannot effectively perform their duties or deploy with their unit when called upon. There are many aspects of unit readiness that organizational leaders from the first line leaders up must be involved in; financial readiness being one of those and one that likely merits much more focus than it may be receiving. It is not typically a high value target and doesn't usually get much more attention than ensuring powers of attorney are drawn up when needed and allotments are in place for bills. In units that are not pending deployment, it seldom gets leader attention until a Soldier's financial irresponsibility or neglect is brought to the commander's attention.

In the Human Resources Division of Combined Security Transition Command – Afghanistan, one of our areas of responsibility was accessions and recruitment. We needed to help grow the Afghan National Army (by a number I can't recall right now) and our Recruiting Assistance Teams (RATs) were doing a great job helping to recruit Soldiers from villages throughout the country by "selling" the benefits of serving and protecting their country. This is not a political military paper, so I will not go into the nation building and winning the hearts and minds aspects of the mission. The key point for this discussion is the financial incentives of their service to the Government of the Islamic Republic of Afghanistan instead of other employment options.

The paycheck is typically a prime motivator in choosing employment. And, as one would expect, a significant percentage of the Afghan men who enlisted did so in order to support their Families. We were making headway on the recruitment side of the mission but we weren't closing the gap in regards to meeting the required end strength.

Across the hall in the Personnel Actions Directorate they were trying to solve the widespread absent without leave (AWOL) epidemic. The finance section was trying to figure out how to prevent the ongoing and costly problem of Afghan pay Officers pocketing Soldier earnings when they weren't there for pay call. Each section was getting after their particular problem and was focused on developing and emplacing sustainable solutions. But by looking across the division and seeing the challenges each directorate was struggling with, it was easy to see that the root cause was the pay system itself.

In order to bolster a sense of nationality, assignments were strategically managed to ensure units throughout the country were comprised of cross sections of the Afghan ethnic groups. This meant that most Soldiers were stationed far from their homes.

They did not have access to banking systems to be able to deposit the pay they received in cash. There was no direct deposit option and no way to get the money home, except to take it there themselves. It could take days, or even weeks, for them to get home and back. During this time they were considered AWOL, which negatively affected their next paycheck. So some of them decided it wasn't worth the hassle or risks to keep serving in the ANA and chose different employment. That in and of itself, is a different discussion.

The problems generated by Soldiers not having adequate means to manage their finances were affecting the ability of the Ministry of Defense, Afghan Security Forces and Coalition Forces to reach required end strength and develop a national

Army that would eventually be able to take lead in the protection and guardianship of their own country. Soldiers' financial management, or the lack thereof, resulted in the loss of many trained Soldiers by inadvertently encouraging AWOL and desertion, feeding corruption that resulted in the loss of millions of dollars and hindering the forward progress of a country that has been at war for decades.

So, why would I subject you to such a boring story of human resource (yawn) trials and tribulations? Because it is a great example, taken outside the context of our military and our Soldiers that I could use to demonstrate how much of an impact Soldier financial readiness can have on units and the Army as a whole. A Soldier's financial readiness can directly affect where their motivation and dedication lies. Leader involvement in monitoring that readiness by coaching them on individual financial responsibility and sharing your knowledge of financial assistance services and training programs can literally mean the difference between a Soldier being able to take his or her place as an Army leader, or being separated from service.

Financial readiness affects many areas of a Soldier's life, both at home and in the unit. The Soldier's credit isn't the only thing damaged. We are all aware of how the stresses and strains of financial problems can destroy Families and personal relationships. Tensions caused by financial trouble can lead to a Family breaking up, resulting in the Soldier being distracted from focusing on his or her mission. And, unfortunately, it sometimes leads to domestic violence in the home.

Soldiers that can't properly manage their financial responsibilities degrade unit readiness. They can lose their security clearances, resulting in them not being able to do the job that they were trained and assigned to perform. They stay on our rolls and prevent us from being able to requisition a replacement. We have to find somewhere to gainfully employ them which does not require a clearance; which is often easier said than done in some units. Other Soldiers then have to pick up their duties and responsibilities. A Soldiers' financial irresponsibility also tarnishes the Army's image. Our country expects more of us as military professionals and negative behaviors or actions of an individual Soldier reflects badly upon the entire organization.

By regulation, Soldiers are required to pay their debts on time and manage their financial business in a satisfactory manner. The Army Regulation that governs Soldier and leader responsibility and actions regarding financial and debt management is *AR 600-15, Indebtedness of Military Personnel*.

All leaders need to read this regulation in order to know and understand the parameters of their Soldiers', and their own, responsibility. We all know that ensuring Soldiers pay their bills and honor their debt is one of our responsibilities. Although, it appears some leaders may not fully understand our rules of engagement in this area. For example, we do not have legal authority to force a Soldier to pay or set up allotments to pay private debts. Only civil authorities can enforce payment of private debt.

Soldiers can choose to set up allotments to pay debts to their creditors' financial institutions. They may also choose to set up automatic payment transfers from their bank accounts, if the bank offers this service. We can counsel them about possible ways to resolve the problem. Creditors, however, cannot request that a Soldier pay by allotment, send the Soldier examples of allotment forms or give them instructions on how to do it. Nor can they request that a Soldier set up a bank account from which to pay the debt.

Creditors often contact a Soldiers' First Sergeant and Commander requesting action because they know it's mandatory for Soldiers to honor their financial obligations, and that failure to do so is punishable under the UCMJ. But they must follow the procedures outlined in *AR* 600-15, Chapter 4 in order to submit debt complaints through a Soldier's Chain of Command. If commanders receive debt complaints that do not follow the procedures prescribed in this chapter, they are to return the complaint to the creditor without action.

If a commander receives a debt complaint that meets criteria in Chapter 4, he or she must take action as prescribed in *AR* 600-15. I am intentionally not going to cover the specifics so that leaders are encouraged to dig into the regulation.

Commanders cannot tolerate financial irresponsibility, neglect, dishonesty or evasiveness. If a Soldier is not trying to resolve unpaid debts promptly or receives repeated complaints of failure to pay debts, they must consider making it a matter of permanent record (IAW *AR* 600-37, Unfavorable Information), imposing a bar to reenlistment, initiating a chapter, and/or imposing punishment under the UCMJ.

If a Soldier shows negligence, disregard or unwillingness to pay his/her debts, the commander may decide whether to place a letter of reprimand, admonition or censure in the Soldier's official personnel file. The Army requires that all-inclusive information of Soldier qualifications be on file in order to prevent the selection of Soldiers for positions of leadership, trust and responsibility whose qualifications are questionable. If a commander believes it does not merit filing in the Soldier's official personnel file, he or she must continue to monitor the situation, ensure the Soldier receives appropriate guidance and help and they may consider action at a later time, if necessary.

I know this is stating the obvious, but writing bad checks is illegal. Commanders are required to respond to all dishonored check complaints. An exception is that they are not required to take any action if a Soldier rectifies a check that is not honored due to bank error, illegibility or failure to date the check within five days of being notified. Soldiers can be held responsible for bad checks written by Family members if they stand for debt the Soldier is legally liable for. That is a little piece of information that Soldiers almost always seem surprised to hear.

The way to stay ahead of this is through engaged leadership and education. First we, the leaders, need to ensure we understand the regulations and policies that apply to Soldier financial management. Then we need to make sure we teach our Soldiers their responsibilities and how to manage them. First Sergeants should review Command Financial Reports before their Commanders do and discuss anything that could be cause for concern. First line leaders need to establish trust with their Soldiers so they might feel comfortable asking for advice or assistance before their finances become a command issue.

We don't have to wait until there is a problem to address issues we know affect our Soldiers and units. Be proactive in taking advantage of available financial and debt management resources. Ask agency representatives or directors to come to your unit and provide informational briefings. Address financial responsibility in reception and integration counseling. Make use of forums like newcomer briefs to provide advice such as avoidance of payday or signature loan agencies, waiting until after they research all options before entering into local cell phone contracts, and any other financial hazards that may be unique to your area. Know your Soldiers and look for warning signs and indicators that they might be having or be at risk for situations regarding financial difficulties. Talk to your Soldiers... and listen.

If you would like to learn more about this topic it is recommended that you read the following publications: *AR 600-15, Indebtedness of Military Personnel*, 14 March 1986; *AR 600-37, Unfavorable Information*, 19 December 1986; and the Uniform Code of Military Justice.

CSM Joanne Cox
US Army NATO BDE

From One Leader to Another
Individual and Organization Equipment Maintenance

Command Sergeant Major
Carlos Medina Castellano

Oversight of individual and organizational equipment maintenance is probably one of the most important things that Non-Commissioned Officer (NCOs) must do on a daily basis and directly applies to training, readiness and welfare of our Soldiers. Leaders at all levels depend on NCOs to ensure their units are successful in combat, field training exercises, garrison and a myriad of other operational environments. This dependency derives from the fact that NCOs throughout history have been known to "make things happen" for their organizations. In order to make things happen, proper individual/ organizational maintenance is critical.

Individual equipment maintenance is extremely important due to its direct correlation to the operational readiness of any unit. It begins at initial military training with the issue of a Soldier's initial individual clothing bag items and continues throughout a Soldier's career with the continuous issue of TA-50 and other individual equipment from Central Issue Facilities (CIF) and/or rapid equipment fielding initiatives.

In support of our Army's effort in getting back to our basic leadership functions, we as NCOs are required to inspect and ensure our Soldiers are properly maintaining their individual equipment. We do this by conducting initial issue clothing inspections during the reception and integration process, followed by quarterly and/or yearly inspections of both the Soldier's clothing bag and TA-50 items. Soldiers are required to have in their possession all items in their clothing record. If a Soldier does not arrive to your unit with a copy of their record you can have your organizational supply request a copy from your CIF or you can ask your Soldier to provide you with a copy which is made available through their online AKO account under the "self service tab". NCOs are typically required to sign a memorandum for record stating that they have all of their issued items. However, this does not preclude them from being inspected periodically to ensure their equipment is both accounted for and serviceable as well. As part of an NCOs professional military education, most junior NCOs have their individual equipment inspected and accounted for during their attendance at the Warrior Leaders Course however, these requirements may not be the same for the Advanced and Senior Leader Courses (ALC/SLC), where equipment/clothing layout inspections are not required.

Unfortunately due to the widespread lack of focus on individual equipment, CIF TA-50 turn-in is probably one of the areas in which NCOs are in need of additional training. We need to be more involved in ensuring our Soldiers are maintaining their issued equipment properly and are taking the time to clean and replace unserviceable equipment prior to out-processing their respective installation. The last thing CIF personnel want to see is a Soldier attempting to turn-in dirty and/or unserviceable equipment. Most facilities actually keep track of their percentage of "first time GOs" during the turn-in process and unfortunately that number is not very high. We can help the process by pre-inspecting prior to turn-in appointments, thus ensuring our Soldiers are successful while also teaching them the importance of individual equipment maintenance and accountability and the significance of NCO involvement.

Organizational equipment maintenance is also crucial to the success of any organization. The bottom line is that without 'ready equipment" there is no "winning wars". There are countless factors that impact mission readiness but three of the most significant specifically in relation to an organization's activities are personnel, training and equipment. Our Soldiers often do very well in a combat environment because they know that if they don't take care of their equipment in combat there is strong possibility for it to malfunction and cost lives. The same focus and effort placed in combat must be placed during peacetime operations; field, training, garrison, etc.

Organizational maintenance is part of any unit's training plan. It is included on training schedules and is typically conducted at the beginning of the week. The best organizational equipment maintenance procedures I have encountered over my career have been in Divisional units, where Soldiers were required to maintain a "high state of readiness" due to the possibility of rapid deployment (within 18 hours of notification).

A key aspect of a successful organizational equipment maintenance program is ensuring Soldiers are familiar with the *technical manuals* (TMs) of the equipment they are assigned. A good Preventive Maintenance, Checks and Service (PMCS) program is absolutely imperative to ensuring equipment is working properly and any parts that may be required are on order. NCO supervision is essential during this process because we must ensure that our subordinates conduct their equipment PMCS by the book and do not take shortcuts. We also want to ensure that the correct deficiencies are annotated and that the correct parts are ordered.

Along with proper organization equipment maintenance is property accountability. The objective of every major hand receipt holder should be to sub-hand receipt their equipment to the lowest level or end user. By doing this, he or she ensures that their equipment is accounted for and maintained properly, assigning responsibility and accountability at the appropriate level and minimizes the likelihood of being held financially liable for any loss or damage to equipment.

Ultimately, NCOs are responsible for training their subordinates in all aspects of individual and organizational maintenance. The art of "maintenance" is something that is taught by senior NCOs to junior NCOs regardless of the operating environment; deployed or garrison. In order for any organization or individual maintenance plan to be successful, it takes leadership presence during maintenance and personal oversight and involvement in the professional development of our Soldiers.

CSM Carlos Medina Castellano
551st SIG BN

From One Leader to Another
Individual Training
Command Sergeant Major Chip E. Mezzaline

The Non-Commissioned Officer (NCO) is responsible for individual training. Officers have entrusted NCOs to accomplish this mission. During the period of the Continental Army, Inspector General Friedrich von Steuben standardized NCO duties and responsibilities in his "Regulations for the Order and Discipline of the Troops of the United States." His work, commonly called the "Blue Book," set down the duties and responsibilities for corporals, sergeants, first sergeants, quartermaster sergeants and sergeants major, which were the NCO ranks of that period. Although NCO duties and responsibilities have evolved since the Revolutionary War, the "Blue Book" paved the way recognizing that individual training is Sergeant's business. This is a point that is clearly specified in today's modern doctrine such as the *Army Doctrine Publication* 7-0, Training Units and Developing Leaders, where "NCOs are primary trainers of enlisted Soldiers, crews and small teams."

NCOs must remain up to date with new equipment and technology. Our Soldiers must be well prepared to operate within their Commander's intent and accomplish their assigned mission. Preparing our Soldiers begins with individual training. NCOs accomplish this through tough, realistic, individual and collective task training. This enables us to meet the challenges of tomorrow's ever-changing environment. The Army will continue to field new equipment and NCOs must remain on the cutting edge of understanding and mastery of that equipment. We must embrace technology and use it to our advantage; however, we must also maintain proficiency in skills and tasks that are not reliant on technology or technical systems. Ensure you stay proficient with those tasks that might be considered "old." The fundamentals acquired from that basic proficiency will enable you to become a more adaptive leader. A couple of examples quickly come to mind; first, the use of satellite based navigational devices has become the standard for getting from one point to another. We must also remain proficient with a map, protractor, and a compass. Your weapon, if properly zeroed, should still be accurate without your assigned optics. You can always use your iron sights. Embrace technology and incorporate it into your individual training but also ensure continued proficiency on basic (analog) Soldier skills that enable survival in any environment.

Individual training is accomplished by training our Soldiers on the individual and warrior task list. Ensure that you are training your Soldiers on the correct task. Check with your NCO support channel and chain of command to understand your unit's critical collective tasks list (CCTL) and mission essential tasks list (METL). Work with other NCOs to ensure that you stay proficient on your own individual and warrior tasks. Here are a few keys to success when it comes to training. Prior to the training, always set your Soldier's up for success. Let your Soldiers know what is expected, ensuring that your Soldiers know what training will be conducted by providing them with the task, conditions and standards. Keep them informed of the uniform and equipment standards. Have a designated area to post timelines and training schedules for training. Foster a training environment that is conducive to learning and building trust. You can do this by letting your Soldiers know that it is alright to make mistakes. If you embarrass your Soldiers they will become hesitant. In most cases it only takes patience and repetition to achieve success. Ensure that they meet the training objectives before training is complete. When planning individual training always ensure you have included time for retraining as necessary. Conduct an after action review after every training event. This will allow your training to become more effective.

Individual training is meant to focus on individual and warrior tasks. Individual and warrior tasks are those responsibilities that must be performed by the individual Soldier in order to perform a larger collective task. A Soldier must be accurate when firing their individual weapon. The task associated with this individual responsibility is 071-COM-0030, Engage Targets with an M16-series rifle/ M4 series carbine. A Soldier must accomplish this task semi-annually in order to remain proficient. Once individual tasks are accomplished to standard, his or her team, squad and section is better prepared to conduct training on a collective task. The task to engage targets with an M16-series rifle/M4 series carbine directly supports the collective tasks of react to an ambush. Warrior tasks are a collection of individual Soldier skills deemed critical to Soldier survival by the Army. Weapons training, tactical communications, urban operations, and first-aid are all examples of categories of warrior tasks. When we reach the desired level of proficiency with individual tasks we can then focus on battle drills. Battle drills are collective actions rapidly executed by the team, squad or section without applying a deliberate decision-making process. Some examples of battle drills are react to ambush, react to chemical attack, and evacuate injured personnel from a vehicle.

The primary manuals for individual and warrior task training are the *Soldier Training Publications* (STPs) and *Soldier's Manual of Common Task* (SMCT). *STP* 21-1 SMCT directly supports individual and warrior task training. You must use these manuals to plan, conduct, and evaluate individual and warrior tasks training. The manuals include the Army warrior training plan for Warrior Skill Level 1 and task summaries for all skill level (SL) 1 critical common tasks that support your unit's wartime mission. The SMCT manual is the only authorized source for individual and warrior task training. It is our responsibility to ensure that our Soldiers have access to the SL 1 STP SMCT within our team, squad, section, platoon and company areas.

There are few significant individual responsibilities for those involved with individual and warrior task training. Every Soldier must be able to perform the individual tasks that their organization has identified based on the unit's CCTL and METL. The individual Soldier is responsible for being prepared to conduct individual and warrior task training at any time the opportunity presents itself. Some of the NCO responsibilities are to help identify, plan, prepare, execute and assess the individual training that supports the unit's CCTL and METL.

Some of the more specific responsibilities of the NCO include: making the individual and warrior task training your primary focus and do not become distracted. Your Soldiers will know what is important to you by where you spend your time. When conducting individual training follow the steps in the SMCT. Set objectives for the training that you will conduct. Ensure that you plan and resource the training and take into consideration the number of personnel being trained, the time it will take to train them and the training aids that are required. For more senior NCOs, focus on the following: certification of your trainers, ensuring that they can accomplish the task to standard, assist with ensuring that the training being conducted is both effective and efficient and most importantly, participate in the training. All leaders should conduct risk management and take into consideration the environmental and safety concerns which could affect your training.

Many times NCOs find themselves looking for time to train their Soldiers. Today's Army is busy. Units should always set aside time on the training calendar to conduct Sergeant's time training. When Sergeant's time training is conducted correctly it allows NCOs to focus on the necessary individual training while empowering them to take ownership of their team, squad, etc. Get the attention of your commander and senior NCOs and work with them to get this time blocked on the training calendar to enable you to train your Soldiers on their individual tasks. Even though it is called Sergeant's time training, include your Officers in this training. This is a great opportunity for them to see how valuable this training is and will help in their understanding of why it is so important when they become a commander, plus it will ensure that they too are proficient as a Soldier.

A leader should always know what resources are available for use when conducting individual training. You must use current doctrine when conducting individual training. Most field manuals have been updated to reflect current doctrine. A great source to find the most recent and emerging Army Doctrine Publications, Army Doctrine Reference Publications, Field Manuals, and Training Circulars is the Army Doctrine and Training Publications website:

http://armypubs.Army.mil/doctrine/index.html

This website provides drop down boxes that allow you to access Administrative Regulations, Doctrinal References, Technical Manuals, Soldier Training Publications, the Soldier's Manual of Common Tasks and Army Doctrine Reference Publications. Another useful website is the Army Training Network, specifically the "NCO Corner" within the page at: https://atn.Army.mil/. This site also includes the Combined Arms Training Strategies (CATS) and allows you to search for a task by proponent or by the type of unit. This is a great resource for planning and conducting home station training.

CSM Chip E. Mezzaline
JRTC OPS GRP (BMC)

From One Leader to Another
Inspections
Command Sergeant Major Ronald Orosz

Inspections have been around since the beginning of our modern day United States Army and most likely long before an Army existed. Many types of inspections exist in the Army. Inspections consist of personnel and equipment inspections, organizational inspections, inspector general inspections, command inspections, and staff inspections to name a few. The reference for Inspections is *Army Regulation 1-201*, *Army Inspection Policy*. For the purposes of this paper I will focus on personnel and equipment inspections and staff inspections.

So why do we conduct personnel and equipment inspections or staff inspections? According to an online source, an inspection is defined as "a critical examination of somebody or something aimed at forming a judgment or evaluation." Inspections ultimately are about taking care of Soldiers. We conduct inspections because Army Regulations direct us to inspect subordinate units to ensure we are in compliance with Army directives, command directives, and guidance.

When I first joined the Army and assigned to my first unit in 1985 we conducted inspections before all training or daily activities. In garrison we conducted morning in-ranks inspections and before we went to the field we inspected our equipment to ensure we had all mission essential gear and it was serviceable.

Morning parade was conducted at 0900 hours daily and consisted of a personnel, equipment, and drill and ceremony inspection. The personnel inspection consisted of checking the uniform, boots, and headgear. Rangers were inspected for proper grooming standards. We were required to have a fresh high and tight haircut every Monday morning regardless of the circumstances and cleaned shaven every day. The uniform was checked to ensure it was serviceable, free of excess strings, and highly starched. The black boots were checked to ensure they were highly shined (spit shined) and headgear (black beret) was serviceable and the flash was clean. Our Sergeant ensured we knew how to march the formation with proper commands according to the drill and ceremony manual. Additional areas inspected were questions about MOS competency, assigned weapon, duty position, principles of patrolling, and the Ranger Creed.

Today our Army Combat Uniform (ACU) should be checked to ensure it is serviceable and generally wrinkle free. The ACU is not starched but how many times do you see Soldiers walking around with what appears to be a starched uniform? How many times do you walk in an alteration shop and see starched uniforms ready for pickup? Boots should be inspected and generally clean and not muddy with trousers properly bloused. Contrary to popular belief, our rough leather boots can be cleaned with warm water and a stiff bristle brush. Attention to detail in Garrison is just as important as completing the mission in the field. Additional items to inspect include the identification card and the identifications tags. Make sure both are present and serviceable. Check Soldiers to ensure they are properly groomed. *Army Regulation* 670-1 tells us about proper grooming standards and uniform requirements for serving in our profession. As of this writing, *AR* 670-

1 is undergoing a major rewrite to address unwritten policies such as walking and talking on cell phones. Army uniform standards are sometimes further defined or reinforced in unit standard books and policy letters which compliment Army regulations.

Equipment inspections include everything you carry or drive to the field. If you take equipment inspections for granted, you will not accomplish your mission. Take the time to program inspections into your out-load process. Check container packing lists, check vehicles, check boots, and check the contents of duffel bags and rucksacks. Mission essential gear should be serviceable and Soldiers should be qualified with their weapon and/or vehicle.

I remember as a new platoon Sergeant going on my first field exercise. The squad leaders were seasoned and had more than two years in position. While conducting a night movement to our objective, our foot patrol was stopped three different times to search for equipment in thick clear cut forest. Fallen logs and the underbrush were very thick! I would never guess who lost the equipment if I hadn't been on the patrol. Three different squad leaders lost equipment because they failed to properly secure it. The time in position of my squad leaders skewed my judgment and I failed to properly inspect. My life as platoon Sergeant was about to end if I didn't immediately address the problem. To fix the problem, my platoon leader and I did all the inspections for platoon field problems for the next 90 days. The inspections were detailed and took additional time. The squad leaders learned the expectations for inspections and the platoon leader and I changed the mindset of the platoon. After 90 days we changed to spot checking the platoon for key equipment and key duties and responsibilities.

Staff inspections are conducted as part of the overall Organizational Inspection Program (OIP). *AR* 1-201, dated 4 April 2008 says, "Teaching, training, and mentoring will be a goal of all inspections." Some of the areas inspected during staff inspections include physical security, safety inspections, and training inspections. The full list can be found in *AR* 1-201. "Staff inspections are compliance-oriented" to ensure units are following regulatory guidance through command directives and Army regulations. Each staff NCO or Officer is responsible for pairing with their counterpart in the subordinate unit to ensure compliance and assist as required. Staff inspections make units better and take care of Soldiers.

I was an operations NCO and responsible for managing the schools Order of Merit Lists (OML). My duties included inspecting the OML and if it was nonexistent I showed them what right looked like. A staff NCO fixes problems rather than leaving the unit with a problem. The unit OML is a bigger deal than just having a list of names and units. The OML is communicated to subordinate units to ensure the Soldier is tracking (through monthly counseling) when he/she goes to school and allows sufficient time for the Soldier to prepare for school. My additional duty was the Regimental Safety NCO. This duty was before the Army had DA civilians in brigade size formations maintaining unit safety records. I inspected the unit safety program to ensure NCOs and Officers were appointed as collateral safety Officer and NCO on orders by a commander. I used *AR* 385-10 as the basis and checklist for conducting my inspections. The end result from the inspection team was an increase in unit readiness.

Inspections are as important today as in the past. Some may argue inspections are more important because of the modernized equipment our Soldiers use. There is nothing magic about inspections. One common item for all inspections, regardless of type, is a detailed checklist. Checklists ensure we don't forget anything. Develop a checklist and incorporate it into your unit standing operating procedure. Inspections check the discipline and standards in the unit. Some units are more disciplined than others because of engaged leadership. Get engaged with your Soldiers and ensure they are ready to accomplish the mission.

CSM Ronald Orosz
1st Army Division West

From One Leader to Another
Success through Proper Medical Management
Command Sergeant Major Kevin B. Stuart

What is the first thing that comes to mind when you hear the term medical management? How has medical management been instrumental in our Army during the past few years? These are some of the questions that have been asked several times in recent years. I believe it is important to address these questions while reviewing the definition of leadership to understand how leaders can make a difference in ensuring our troops are being cared for in the best possible way.

Medical management is defined as the whole system of care and treatment of a sick individual. However, it can also be defined as encompassing the use of information technology for health, disease, care, and case management functions. Medical management is designed to modify medical provider behavior to improve the quality of care to patients. With regard to the military, medical management is also about leadership among Non-Commissioned Officers who play a key role on a team of US Army professionals.

Just as today's leaders have assumed many responsibilities during current conflicts and homeland defense activities, so did previous generations of NCO leaders accept the burden of heavy endeavors. The diligence, insight, and compassion of these leaders were very instrumental in building the Army's trusted reputation – a reputation of solid professional NCO leaders who advise their commanders on how to keep Soldiers healthy. These are the men and women who have provided outstanding leadership for each and every Soldier who has put their life on the line in defense of the Nation. These remarkable leaders have always endured through a wide range of duties and responsibilities, demonstrating their strength and compassion, from care on the battlefield to care of troops at home. These trusted professionals teach, coach, mentor and watch over their troops, ensuring that they are fit, ready and reliable for any mission.

The significance of medical care for Soldiers in the Army dates back as far as the Revolutionary War. During those trying days, leaders failed to focus on the medical health of their troops, which in turn weakened their military force. The lack of proper medical equipment and trained personnel from the Civil War to the Vietnam conflict resulted in many Soldiers being taken out of the fight, with some cases ending in death. Many past military leaders focused primarily on defeating the enemy instead of tending to the ill health of their Soldiers; these cases typically ranged from severe tooth decay, extreme cold weather injuries to diarrhea, and from pneumonia, encephalitis to viruses. The medical readiness of these troops could have been higher if leaders played a more engaged role in monitoring their Soldiers' health. The Nation learned a valuable lesson from these previous wars, and since the Persian Gulf War in the 1990s, NCO leaders have been much more vigilant in monitoring the well-being and medical readiness of their troops.

The Medical Protection System, or MEDPROS, is one of the various tools used by leaders today in managing the medical readiness of their troops. MEDPROS affords leaders increased visibility regarding the health of their troops, which leads to unit readiness. Many NCO leaders use MEDPROS to manage the medical readiness of each Soldier, with regard to the following: (1) Identifying the need or requirement for medical warning tags; (2) checking for annual vision screening and identifying if eyeglasses are needed; (3) checking to see if a hearing exam is warranted; (4) screening for dental readiness and annual check-ups; and (5) screening for medical profiles, among other things. Leaders who maintain keen vigilance on monitoring their Soldiers' individual medical readiness can resolve many problems among their troops while maintaining unit readiness.

The NCO leader's book is another tool used for managing the medical readiness and status of their troops. This book allows the leader to understand various aspects of the Soldier, such as hometown origin, marital and Family status, job and skill qualifications, vaccinations and medical exam history, strengths and weaknesses of job performance, home location, and calendar/appointment scheduling.

Today, those leaders who closely monitor the medical readiness of their troops will most likely have Soldiers who are fit, ready and prepared to perform their duties in any given environment. On the other hand, those NCO leaders who fail to manage the medical readiness of their troops, assuming that to do so is not their responsibility, will usually face challenges regarding troop readiness.

Several years ago, one of the units in my command was preparing to deploy to Iraq and was dealing with numerous challenges while preparing for their mission, as many of their Soldiers were not medically ready. The unit's leadership was not managing their troop's medical readiness properly and this caused a major disruption in getting the unit to fully mission capable for the deployment. The unit recognized several troops with medical problems (e.g., back pain, foot pain, and in one case, mental health issues), but the Soldiers were told to continue training and were not supported in treating their ailments. Subsequently, these troops were deployed and after a few weeks into their deployment several of these Soldiers were sent home due to the severity of their health concerns. Additionally, it caused dissension and trust issues within the entire command. Eventually, the unit was able to remedy the situation, but damage had already occurred, and this particular organization struggled throughout the deployment. The lack of medical attentiveness from the leaders caused degradation in the unit's mission readiness while jeopardizing the health of the Soldier. Good leadership would have probably prevented this from happening – but what is good leadership?

You may have noticed that "leader" and "leadership" have often been mentioned throughout this paper, but what do these terms mean? Many have described the meaning of military leadership in various ways. Some have said that leadership is the act of getting the job done. Others have said it is the art of making things happen, and still others have said that leadership is taking care of people along with doing the task at hand. However, *Army Doctrine Publication* 6-22 defines leadership as a process of influencing people by providing purpose, direction and motivation to accomplish the mission and improve the organization.

ADP 6-22 goes on to state that an "Army leader is anyone who by virtue of assumed role or assigned responsibility inspires and influences people to accomplish organizational goals. Leadership is characterized by a complex mix of organizational, situational and mission demands on a leader who applies personal qualities, abilities, and experiences to exert influence on the organization, its people, the situation and the unfolding mission." In short, Army leadership establishes the fundamental principles to accomplish the mission and care for the troops. During my military career, I have seen that Army

NCO leaders believe in teamwork and will find a way for their team to win. They understand that losing is unacceptable, creativity and diversity are essential, quitting is unthinkable, commitment is unquestionable, and victory is inevitable. Leaders know how to win, and winning means knowing your troops and managing their medical readiness at all times. NCO leaders must also continue to teach their Soldiers to accept responsibility for their actions and show them how to manage their own medical readiness (i.e., knowing what medical vaccinations are due, preparing for eye and hearing exams, and knowing the type of physical exams that are due to maintain readiness). Leaders must continue to lead with strength and compassion, and must create an environment in which their Soldiers feel valued. The care of the Soldier is the victory which ultimately leads to mission accomplishment.

The bottom line is that good leadership typically leads to success – success for the unit and its people. Leadership is taking care of people, and those leaders who effectively manage the medical readiness of their troops reflect everything that *ADP 6-22* states about leadership. Managing the medical readiness of Soldiers most certainly concerns leadership, which contributes to the success of the unit and the morale of the Soldier. Leaders who utilize their experiences and resources, such as MEDPROS and the NCO leader's book, know and understand their Soldiers, and realize their limitations, their strengths, and what makes them tick. They are right on point in taking care of their troops, because when it comes down to it, medical management is every leader's business.

If you would like to learn more about this topic, I recommend that you take time to review *Army Doctrine and Doctrine Reference Publication 6-22, Army Leadership*, at

http://armypubs.Army.mil/doctrine/DR_pubs/dr_a/pdf/adrp6_22_new.pdf
and investigate the potential uses of MEDPROS by visiting the official Army website at
https://medpros.mods.Army.mil/MEDPROSNew/

CSM Kevin B. Stuart
US Army Medical Research and Materiel Command

From One Leader to Another
Mentorship
The Cornerstone of Leader Development

Command Sergeant Major (R) David J. Litteral

I remember sitting in a conference and hearing the Command Sergeant Major of the United States Military Entrance Processing Command speak. He was giving a leader development speech to the Medical NCOs, Chief Petty Officers, and Department of the Army Civilians in attendance at the conference. He began by stating that he was there that day, solely because of a Sergeant First Class who took him aside and said, "Specialist, I am going to make you a Command Sergeant Major." So began that Soldier's relationship with his mentor.

Ironically, I recall questioning his remarks. I didn't have any Senior NCO mentors when I was growing up in the ranks. It seemed to me, at the time, that the Army didn't need Senior NCOs who have to be forced, hand-carried, or spoon-fed. I was a newly promoted Master Sergeant when I attended that conference. It took me a few years to figure out just how right that Command Sergeant Major was. You see, military mentoring is a special brand of mentoring. Unlike mentoring in the private sector or even the government sector, mentoring in the military ranks is woven into the fabric of our system of development and progression.

In ancient times Soldiering was a necessity. It was not a vocation. History records that when city-states began to form, it became necessary to protect the people who had banded together. As such, each farm or household had to send out representatives to fight and protect their lands, crops, and people. People largely rotated through leadership positions as well as followership positions. Often, leadership positions were elected for a period. Later, as in Roman times, governments grew and military service became a way to earn stature within a community. Officers were held in the highest of regard and if they had Non-Commissioned Officers within their ranks they were typically the meanest, toughest and ugliest Soldiers placed in the back of the formation to keep the troops moving forward. This was especially necessary in battle when frequently it was the desire of many men to run away from the clashing of man against man.

Throughout the Middle Ages armies grew in size and it was common to hire mercenary armies to fill in the ranks. Doing so had its disadvantages as mercenaries often went to whichever side paid them the most money. It was not unheard of for a mercenary unit to switch sides within a battle simply because of the promise of a greater share of the spoils of the vanquished. Later as nations began to form, standing armies became the more prevailing choice for nations that wanted to retain their domain.

The Continental Army of 1775 was an example of that. Upon being formed to stand up to one of the greatest armies of that era, the Continental Army was largely formed in similar fashion to that of its foe, the British. In fact, many of the early Continental Army Officers were trained by the British. George Washington was among the ranks of those having learned to fight in British style.

Despite the initial similarities in design, the young revolutionary force had to nominate and commission Officers who often had little or no formal military education. It is well recorded that General Washington openly received the assistance of Baron von Steuben who arrived from France with the strong endorsement of Benjamin Franklin. Washington made Von Steuben the Adjutant General of the Army and charged him with the responsibility of training the men and refining the process of selecting men for leadership positions.

It is unlikely that anyone has not heard of the *Regulations for the Order and Discipline of the Troops of the United States,* (The Blue Book) so I will only remark that General Von Steuben impressed upon General Washington the importance of selecting Non-Commissioned Officers. Even so, at that time NCOs were simply a force multiplier for the Officers. It wasn't until the Plains Indian Wars where Non-Commissioned Officers truly earned their place in United States' history. During the Plains Indian Wars many outposts were held by little more than a glorified squad likely led by a senior Sergeant. Left to their own devices, a group of isolated men might get into trouble. Disease and malnutrition would often plague a camp and whole units would perish. As such, it became part of the watchword of the sergeants to check on and care for the junior Soldiers. The sergeants had come a long way since the Middle Ages when they were selected for their ability to intimidate the younger troopers to engage in battle [at the tip of the Sergeant's sword]. Now it was their mission to care for the welfare of their Soldiers as well as the accomplishment of their mission. Does that phrase sound familiar?

During the late 19th Century career military service, especially for enlisted Soldiers, was not unheard of. It was however, very uncommon. This situation made the passing of information from one generation to the next very critical. Without a standing cadre of enlisted Soldiers, lessons were learned and forgotten, only to be relearned and forgotten once again. So Non-Commissioned Officers began to pass on their experiences to those who followed behind them. Sergeants literally took care of their Soldiers as well as helping them grow and develop so that the younger Soldier would be up to the task upon assuming the responsibilities vacated when the Non-Commissioned Officer moved on.

When I attended Basic Combat Training in 1980, the cadre was primarily veterans of the Vietnam War. Some were veterans of the Korean War as well. At day's end our Drill Sergeant, Staff Sergeant Larry D. Ladner, would invite the squad leaders into his office and he would tell us stories of taking care of men and mission under fire. He impressed upon us the importance of training and mentoring those entrusted to our care. I have never forgotten his words in 33 years. One might suppose it took me until I was a First Sergeant to see how important mentoring is from the mentee or the protégé standpoint.

Shortly after being appointed as Command Sergeant Major of Blanchfield Army Community Hospital one of my young Operating Room Specialists took his own life. I picked up the phone and called CSM (Retired) Jim Aplin. Jim grew up through the ranks as an Operating Room Specialist. His career culminated as the Senior Enlisted Advisor to the Surgeon General of the Army. I asked for his help in guiding me to care for my Soldiers and DA Civilians as they grieved for the loss of our comrade. He willingly listened and then helped me come up with a plan to get us back on track. He called me several times over the next few weeks to check on me.

During my seven years as a Command Sergeant Major, one of which was in a Combat Zone and the last two as the Commandant of the AMEDD Regimental NCO Academy, I always asked troopers who were attending promotion, Soldier of the Quarter, NCO of the Quarter, Year, NCO of the Cycle, Audie Murphy, etc., to define mentorship. Rarely did the troopers answer with any form of the word, "partnership" in describing the relationship of mentor to mentee or from mentee to mentor. What does that say about mentoring within the NCO Corps? Chapter 5 of the *NCO Guide* merely tells the reader that it is their responsibility to mentor.

There are many references which can help NCOs create a mentorship program within their unit. I challenge everyone to read the story of a young Major being mentored by a two-star General. The Major grew up to be President of the United States. It is the story of Dwight D. Eisenhower. The Major General (Fox Conner) also mentored Generals Omar Bradley and George S. Patton. It stands to reason that Fox Conner is among the greatest mentors this country has ever known (despite the fact most Americans have never heard of him.) For more information visit the following website at:
http://www.ausa.org/publications/ilw/Documents/LWP%2078W%20Fox%20Conner.pdf
Another good reference for establishing a mentorship program was produced by the Department of Transportation and can be found on the Air University, Maxwell, AFB., website. Please see:
http://www.au.af.mil/au/awc/awcgate/mentor/mentorhb.htm#

Where do we teach young Soldiers the importance of seeking and accepting mentoring? My experience in Basic Training was fortunate. However, what happens to most young Soldiers who raise their hand in formation because they have a question? The entire platoon learns what happens when someone asks for help. Instead of starting a career path of trust and a desire to learn, many will only raise their hand again in the most extreme circumstances. I believe our NCO Corps is among the best in the world. However, there is always room for improvement with regard to developing an environment which is conducive to mentoring. This is especially true in an era where the youth of today rely on text messages instead of face-to-face communication. Just because some of us didn't have the luxury or need to rely on mentoring when we were younger doesn't mean that some young troopers won't need to be actively mentored.

It will only be a few years before the experience of deployment and active combat become a distant memory. New Soldiers will need to rely on experienced Non-Commissioned Officers who have been there and done that. Mentoring during the next interwar period will determine the success of the junior Soldiers who will be our future NCO Corps.

CSM (R) David J. Litteral

From One Leader to Another
Physical Readiness Training
Command Sergeant Major Roger Daigle

Every Soldier must be able to deploy and conduct combat operations, anywhere, anytime. Physical readiness training gives US Army Soldiers a distinct advantage over our enemies. Not only does physical readiness training prepare the Soldier physically for combat operations it also helps the Soldier emotionally, allows them to manage stress and enables them to lead a healthy lifestyle. Physical readiness training is a very broad subject matter that is conducted at the individual Soldier through organizational level. Physical readiness training is a great opportunity for leaders to lead Soldiers. There is so much that can occur in the one to two hours that a Corporal, Sergeant or Staff Sergeant has his or her troop's undivided attention. The Army and its leaders must continue to focus on physical readiness training by highlighting its importance to our Soldiers in how it develops leaders and prepares us to operate in any environment.

Physical readiness training has been part of our Army since our inception. Although not always conducted in an organized manner as it is now, it was encouraged to benefit the Continental Soldiers physiological competence. The Soldiers that fought in the Revolutionary War were mostly farmers from the Colonies; this alone required a very healthy man in order to support the well being of his Family. As we became a nation and we expanded our presence in the United States and the world, Soldiering became a full time job rather than a militia hence requiring the Soldiers to adapt physically to the demands of military training. Physical readiness training has become so important that the Army has conducted studies by doctors to determine what are the right exercises, duration and frequency of physical readiness training. The Army has changed its physical fitness test over the years to adapt to the physical needs of our operating environment and we continue to refine in order to meet the physical demands of our next engagement. Every leader in today's Army has seen physical readiness training from one extreme to the other. We have all taken part in the morning routine where the Company conducted push-ups, sit-ups and then ran four miles as a unit. Although this may enhance a unit's esprit de corps it typically did little to help with the overall fitness of the Soldier. We have also seen units that break in to ability groups and watch as their unit's overall physical fitness stamina increased. The load the Continental Army Soldier carried was minimal and over terrain that was not extremely rugged. Today's Soldiers on every combat patrol carry in excess of 50 pounds of equipment and ammunition over extreme terrain therefore requiring a much more physically fit Soldier. The Army has deemed physical readiness training so important that after canceling the Master Fitness Trainer Course early on in the Global War on Terrorism they have reinstituted the course and are requiring units to train its leaders in all aspects of physical readiness training.

Every Leader and Soldier probably has a different view on the right way to conduct physical readiness training. These views can range from conducting combatives, running, foot marches, urban orienteering, cross fit, combat focused events, or playing intramural sports. This short list of events is great as all of these events can help to forge the Warrior Spirit and allow young leaders to form their teams. All too often though, senior leaders in organizations cannot trust their junior leaders in conducting physical readiness training because the junior leaders do not properly prepare for the training event. Every leader, no matter at what level, must train to the Task, Condition and Standard, therefore their plan must be nested in the unit's overall training management system. It is the Platoon Sergeant and First Sergeant's responsibility to ensure that the leader who is leading physical readiness training has the proper resources and is fully prepared to lead that day's activities. Although this may not be the best way to plan and prepare training, some First Sergeants will plan the events for their Company by identifying the task, condition and standard and then allow the platoons, squads, sections and teams to conduct the training event. However just because the First Sergeant has developed a physical readiness training schedule his/her responsibility does not end there. In fact, because they have prepared the organization's training schedule they must be fully engaged throughout. The First Sergeant along with the Platoon Sergeants must ensure that the leader selected to train that day is prepared. Just as in combat we don't conduct operations without conducting rehearsals; this applies to physical readiness training too. When conducting something that is not familiar to the leader, the Platoon Sergeant must ensure the leader is prepared and go through the training with the selected leader.

I am a true believer in the Army's new physical readiness training *Field Manual* (*FM*). The manual incorporates activities and/or muscle groups that a Soldier will be expected to use in today's operating environment, it has events that Soldiers conduct during their daily missions and it focuses on overall body composition rather than one component of physical training. *FM* 7-22 focuses on the Squad/Team Leader in conducting physical readiness training, this is imperative as this is how we fight. I cannot think of a better way to build teams then to allow the Squad and Team Leaders to have 60-120 minutes a day focused on physical fitness and leader training. Units must continue to be creative, ensure they don't work the same muscle groups two days in a row, make sure leaders are engaged and are conducting physical training and that their Soldiers are progressing as they continue the organization's physical fitness routine. Leaders must be sure they do not fall into a routine of training for the physical fitness test. It is okay to do push-ups, sit-ups and run but don't make it the daily routine; you and your unit will suffer. Integrate these exercises into your overall physical fitness plan, work on core muscles to better develop your Soldier's flexibility and posture, focus on functional movements, plan runs (5k individual, sprints, shuttles etc....), conduct foot marches that increase in distance and time, conduct obstacle and confidence courses and when time permits integrate sporting events which encourage friendly competition between elements. I have found that occasionally organizing sporting events can increase the competiveness of an organization. I have also found that conducting combat-related events against squads and platoons can be great for organizational morale.

It is critical for leaders to be involved in physical readiness training; they must participate with their unit, spot check junior leaders and offer incentives to the top performers. Perception is everything to today's Soldier. When they don't see their leaders at or participating in physical training they develop an attitude that physical training is not important. We must show them the importance of physical training by leading from the front while showing them that we are capable of performing the same tasks they are expected to perform. Physical readiness training when done correctly will improve a unit's combat capability, decrease injuries and illness and bond a unit. When a Soldier is physically fit, they heal faster from injuries, recover from illnesses quicker and are prepared to answer the nations call at anytime. Physical readiness training is one more way in which we can better prepare our Soldiers, our unit and ourselves to fight and win our nation's wars!

If you would like to learn more about this topic it is recommended that you read *Field Manual* 7-22, *Army Physical Readiness Training*, *Field Manual* 21-18, *Foot Marches*, *Training Circular* 3-25.150, *Combatives*, *Army Regulation* 350-1, *Army Training and Leader Development* and *Army Regulation* 600-9, *The Army Weight Control Program.*

CSM Roger Daigle
USAG Fort Huachuca

From One Leader to Another
Physical Readiness
Command Sergeant Major Joseph Jacobs

On 5 July 1950, US troops, who were unprepared for the physical demands of war, were sent to battle. The early days of the Korean War were nothing short of disastrous, as US Soldiers were routed by a poorly equipped, but well-trained, North Korean People's Army. As American Soldiers withdrew, they left behind wounded comrades and valuable equipment largely because their training had not adequately prepared them to carry heavy loads. The costly lessons learned by Task Force Smith in Korea are as important today as ever and should never be forgotten. If we fail to prepare our Soldiers for their physically demanding wartime tasks, we are guilty of paying lip service to the principle of "Train as you Fight." Our physical training programs must do more for our Soldiers than just get them ready for the semi-annual Army Physical Fitness Test (APFT). *FM* 7-22 is directed at leaders who are responsible for the planning and conduct of physical fitness training. It provides guidelines for developing programs, which will improve and maintain physical fitness levels for all Army personnel. For some, this ideology may not sound new as it has been around for quite some time.

Physical Readiness is the foundation for which all training should take place. It is meant to do so much more than prepare your Soldiers for the rigors of combat. Executed properly it will increase the effectiveness of your team, squad or section, build *espirit de corps*, instill pride and discipline and build resiliency. Yes, it is training and needs to be planned, resourced, conducted and assessed using the proper training methodology. Physical readiness plays a larger part in today's Army. Soldiers are expected to carry heavier loads, work longer hours and perform many more physically demanding activities than any time in our nation's past. As the Army begins to draw down, even greater demand will be placed on your Soldiers. We will be expected to do more with less and time will be in even greater demand, therefore proper planning and execution of Physical Readiness Training (PRT) will be all the more important. It will be essential to utilize time management and get the most out of every session. Being that our NCO Creed states "No one is more professional than I", NCOs are challenged to master their craft by becoming the subject matter expert of all aspects of PRT. Reconditioning PRT should play a huge part in your unit so that injured Soldiers return to the formation ready to perform with little wasted time.

So here are the key tasks and challenges you must meet in order to accomplish your daily tasks: Identify specific tasks that PRT enhances in support of your unit's METL. Build individuals, crews and small unit teams. Continually prepare, rehearse, execute and assess your PRT program. Evaluate PRT and conduct after action reviews with your subordinates and provide feedback to your unit leadership. Set lofty but realistic goals for the members of your team and continue to refine those goals. Challenge your subordinates as well as yourself. Always remember that you are training your replacement. Always lead from the front! Do not worry about those things that you cannot control but ensure that others are aware of the challenges you face. Do not train solely with the APFT as your focus, if your Soldiers are in shape they will always do well. Remember that the ultimate goal is to provide your subordinates with tough, realistic, challenging yet safe in execution physical readiness training. Your objective should be to develop your Soldiers' physical capabilities to perform their duty assignments and combat roles. Never forget that you are training your replacement and the future leaders of our Army.

FM 7-22 dated October 2012 should be your primary reference however; you can find some great additional information along with training videos and suggestions regarding the establishment of a program within AKO at the Army Physical Readiness Divisions AKO Website, as well as ARMYPRT.com for the most current news concerning PRT. Always remember that you alone are responsible for developing the next generation of leaders. You must strive to make them fit, resolute, skilled and disciplined in every way and it begins every morning with the fundamentals of PRT. Best of luck and "Be the Creed."

CSM Joseph Jacobs
1-15 FA BN

From One Leader to Another
Planning and Troop Leading Procedures
Command Sergeant Major Frederick Heard

As civilizations and their armies developed, so has their reliance on operational planning and preparation. Although this concept dates back to well before 6000 B.C. as documented by Sun Tzu's "The Art of War," it is a relatively new idea within the US Army, who only formally initiated the applied theory in the late 1800's. Though their military vs. civilian governance ideas were unfavorable with the American Constitution and like other military concepts, the US Army again took lessons from the Prussian military model. The US learned from the failures of the Prussian Generalstab's Schlieffen Plan philosophy that flawless planning will not trump poor strategy and execution.

The age of modern US Army planning began in 1910, just prior to World War I with the publication of "Regulations for Field Maneuvers;" though a start, it failed to address processes. The procedural shortfall was acknowledged with a 1914 *field service regulation* (FSR) publication that mentioned the void, yet again failed to provide substance. The post WWI update brought the establishment of doctrinal orders, annexes, maps, tables and guidance that leaders "first make an estimate of the situation, culminating in a decision upon a definite plan of action" (Paparone); yet again no process steps were defined. The 1932 publication, "The Staff Officers' Field Manual", outlined principles rather than unyielding rules that set the foundation for today's procedures. As a result of the growing World War II effort, the 1940 *Field Manual (FM) 101-5, Staff Officer Field Manual: The Staff and Combat Orders* addressed the intricacies and scope of planning and decision-making for a multinational effort. The updates to *FM* 101-5 in 1950 and 1954 focused primarily on the commander's estimate process. 1968's revisions of *FM* 101-5 presented the Standardization Agreement (STANAG) 2118, set problem solving techniques with flowcharts and wiring diagrams and the encouragement to "fill the gaps in knowledge of what conditions probably will be" (Paparone). In 1972, *FM* 101-5 included the introduction of the administrative staff study to focus on administrative preparations allowing for the military decision-making process (MDMP) to be used primarily for combat operations. The re-titled *FM* 101-5 was released in 1984 as the *Staff Organization and Operations* where MDMP was further developed doctrinally by adding rehearsals among other details. 1997 brought the introduction of the commander's intent and the marriage of synthesis and analysis during the MDMP process. 2005 introduced the sixth update to the original FM 101-5 and another re-titling to FM 5-0, "Army Planning and Orders Production." This publication established the link between the MDMP and troop leading procedures (TLP). The final 2010 update to *FM* 5-0 further strengthened the linkage between MDMP and TLPs through the Army problem solving methodology. The most recent version of this document, *Army Doctrine Publication* (ADP) 5-0, *The Operations Process* accompanied by its sister publications, helped to revolutionize and simplify our doctrinal references while reinforcing this linkage.

Infantry Soldiers and those who have used *FM* 7-8, eventually *FM* 3-21.8 and other similar publications have been exposed to and have utilized Troop Leading Procedures for years. It has however, only been recently that the TLP concept has broken outside the combat arms realm. This can be, in large part, directly attributed to the more than 10 years of war and the collaborative efforts across all cohorts and branches while often operating outside our traditional doctrinal roles. Troop Leading Procedures are now covered in not only the Infantry manuals but *The Operations Process* (*ADP* 5-0), the *Commander and Staff Officer Guide* (*ATTP* 5-0.1) and many others validating the relationship and dependencies between the Army design methodology, military decision-making process and troop leading procedures. This complementary relationship lends credence to the use and value of TLPs and their overall contribution to mission success.

As military leaders, we spend much of our time planning. We plan multiple courses of action, we plan for numerous contingencies and we plan for events that we pray never come to fruition. Ultimately we plan so that we are ready to confidently and successfully lead our Soldiers into a situation for which we have considered the likely scenarios and potential outcomes. Troop leading procedures give us a proven planning and decision-making process by which we can effectively and expeditiously plan, prepare and execute at the company level and below.

The TLP is made up of eight steps and although they are in serial, some steps may run parallel to one another, as do the TLP steps with those of MDMP (*FM* 3-12.8).

Step 1: Receive the mission - this could be by either completed OPORD or WARNO and later FRAGO; oftentimes the MDMP is still developing COAs when the WARNOs are issued.

Step 2: Issue a warning order - do not delay issuance which will allow your subordinates as much time as possible to begin their preparations; include as much information as possible but do not wait for all information; send a WARNO as soon as the initial assessment and time availability is determined; and follow up with other WARNOs as needed.

Step 3: Make a tentative plan - this is based on the operational variables (METT-TC).

Step 4: Initiate movement - any movement necessary for the mission preparation or execution.

Step 5: Conduct reconnaissance - though critical, personal recons of an area of responsibility (AOR) may not always be an option, at a minimum you should always conduct a map/imagery recon and intelligence must thoroughly be reviewed in order to identify information gaps in the plan and mission analysis.

Step 6: Complete the plan - results of the recon validate the course of action (COA); overlays, target lists, sustainment and signal requirements are refined; the tentative plan is updated; and coordination with higher headquarters and adjacent units is complete if available time permits.

Step 7: Issue the order - this is typically issued verbally following the standard format of the five-paragraph OPORD. Ideally the issuance would be at an AOR vantage point overlooking the objective, however due to security/other concerns this is typically done over a sand table, a map or other means.

Step 8: Supervise and refine - this step keys in on the strength of the unit's SOP, rehearsals and the NCO's role of check, check and check again. Organizational SOPs help to govern the process, the rehearsals help to strengthening the action/team and the NCO checks (PCCs/PCIs/inspections) verify Soldier/mission readiness.

Troop leading procedures are a dynamic process that will require adaptation as the operational variables change. As leaders we plan for an anticipated result based on unknown actions by a potentially hostile force; some plans go well and as history and experience has proven, others often do not. TLPs are the battle drill for small unit level planning and provide a guide to plan for a specific COA while considering possible outcomes and alternate COAs. Rehearsals, battle drills and SOPs are key in case things do not go according to plan, Soldiers and leaders must have the confidence, foundation and "muscle memory" to instinctively transition to an alternate COA or contingency and still find success.

The Army has procedures and manuals for nearly everything that you will come into contact with in Army life. Some procedures are hard structured with no gray area or room for deviation, such as the Uniformed Code of Military Justice or the rigging instructions for a parachute; others have room for interpretation and application such as troop leading procedures. TLPs provide a flexible framework due to the variables and factors associated with mission planning. Although some considerations carry more weight than others, each step is equally important and leads to a clearer picture of the impending operation. A recent Joint Readiness Training Center (JRTC) study found that leaders who used a simple GTA reference card were much more effective than those who did not on 34 of 39 measures, additionally resulting in ample time to conduct quality TLPs. Should one step be overlooked rather than assessed it weakens the subsequent steps, the operation and ultimately the Soldier's safety.

We have all heard the quote from former UN General Assembly President Vijaya Lakshmi Pandit "the more we sweat in peace, the less we bleed in war." Based on that thought, TLPs are to be used and honed during peacetime and training operations. When I was stationed in Hawaii during the mid 90's one of our sister companies was conducting a platoon live fire range where they were assaulting an objective. The company issued the order and the platoons immediately began their planning processes. By all indications things were running smoothly with the platoons rotating through a day dry fire, blank fire and live fire. The platoons then proceeded into the night iterations, again completing a dry, blank and live fire. It was when the third and final platoon went into their live fire scenario that things went wrong.

On the sixth run for this platoon, having done well on the previous five iterations, a Soldier was killed. After the investigation and interviews it was determined that the process had changed on that final iteration compared to the previous five. The critical decision that put this in action was the leader's decision to initiate fire on the objective himself rather than the M60 gunner who had done it five times previously. The Soldier positions were not easily visible due to very high and thick grass and as a result the Soldier was shot in the back by his leader. We will never know for sure but chances are that this accident could have been avoided had the leader taken the time to revisit and follow the TLPs.

In a cursory review, this should have been caught in any of the following steps: Step 2, was this change covered in a concept of operation WARNO? Step 3, METT-TC- Terrain and Weather was observation, avenue of approach and cover considered? Troops and Support Available was the change the result of a Soldier or manning issue? Or if initiating fires was a changing COA given in a FRAGO? Step 5, was a reconnaissance done of firing positions and Soldier locations in respect to the objective? Step 6, was a new plan completed with the change in initiation? Step 7, was the order issued over a sand table with locations or on the ground with exact locations? Step 8, was there a rehearsal with the new plan, what is the unit SOP for such an operation?

We are in a tough business and accidents are going to happen, however the Army gives us the tools to succeed and it is up to us to use them correctly; as in life the effort you put in will be the results you take out. Most of the lessons and procedures we study today are based on the hard experiences and gaps of yesterday. To prevent the hard lessons of times past we as leaders must coach these principles through the implementation and enforcement of standards and discipline. The goal is to set up our Soldiers and future leaders with the foundation and skills today so that they are prepared to lead and succeed tomorrow.

If you would like to learn more about this topic, it is recommended that you read the following publications; *Army Doctrine Publication* 5-0, *The Operations Process*, *Army Tactics, Techniques and Procedures* 5-0.1, *Commander and Staff Officer Guide*, *Field Manual* 3-21.8, *The Infantry Rifle Platoon and Squad*, "Improving Troop Leading Procedures at the Joint Readiness Training Center" by Evans & Baus, "US Army Decision-making Past, Present and Future" by Paparone and "The Schlieffen Plan" by Ping.

CSM Frederick Heard
536th BSB

From One Leader to Another
Promotions

Sergeant Major (Retired) Toni Gagnon Ross

Promotions are a part of every Soldier's career. Putting on that first stripe, the "mosquito wing," is the beginning of a series of promotions which are based not only on performance but on an individual's potential for additional responsibility. Army Regulation 600-8-19, Enlisted Promotions and Reductions, helps to explain the ins and outs of all enlisted promotions. The purpose of the promotion system is "to fill authorized enlisted spaces with the best qualified Soldiers." Upon entering the ranks of the Non-Commissioned Officer Corps your primary function becomes that of leadership which implies that you must develop your Soldiers. Challenging and rewarding, being a Leader of Soldiers is a great privilege. It requires perseverance, commitment, selflessness and a litany of Leadership traits, values, competencies and attributes that are developed over time.

The *Army Non-Commissioned Officer Guide*, FM 7-22.7 (*TC* 22-6), states: "As a leader, as a trainer and as a teacher, the NCO embodies the Army's past, present and future." It explains what NCOs should "be, know and do," and provides vignettes and lessons learned to assist NCOs at each of the levels of responsibility. The Leader Requirements Model, as outlined in *Army Doctrinal Publication* 6-22, *Army Leadership*, specifically identifies the leader competency of "develops" as "creates a positive environment/fosters esprit de corps, prepares self, develops others, and stewards the profession." Army Regulation 600-20, Army Command Policy, emphasizes "that effective performance counseling ensures Soldiers are prepared to carry out their duties efficiently and accomplish the mission." As an NCO you develop your subordinates for promotion through counseling, both formal and informal, discussing ways to improve while always acknowledging positive behavior. As difficult as it may seem, when counseling your Soldiers about promotion you must be honest with them and offer suggestions on how they might improve themselves both personally and professionally. You owe them the truth but delivered with tact and diplomacy just as you would like to hear it from your supervisor.

General Omar Bradley once said "I would caution you to always remember that an essential qualification of a good leader is the ability to recognize, select and train junior leaders."

This responsibility started with your Leaders selecting you for promotion and now as an NCO you too will look for those competencies and attributes in your Soldiers. You are charged with providing the right type of leadership and to convey the knowledge necessary to assist in their development. Likewise you will look to your Leaders to assist you in developing your leadership skills and preparing you for your next promotion and/or level or responsibility. As you increase in rank and position, considerable more experience will be required thus it will take you longer to be promoted than when you were a junior Soldier. It is important that during your counseling sessions you seek guidance on how to improve while realizing that improvement takes practice. You should also search the internet and other sources such as the Army Career Tracker for your specific MOS career map which should help you with identifying what schools and positions you should seek in order to broaden your training, education and experience. You should always strive to develop your Soldiers and yourself so that when afforded the opportunity to attend a school both they and you are prepared to do so.

As you work through the semi-centralized promotion system for promotions to Sergeant and Staff Sergeant you will have opportunities to assist yourself in obtaining additional points through education, physical training, weapons qualification and most importantly your appearance and communication skills. This is also true when encouraging your Soldiers. Appearing before a promotion board is always a test of your personal courage in learning to deal with the "butterflies in your stomach" and demonstrate your knowledge and confidence. Always put your uniform together using the regulation (*AR* 670-1), a ruler and a "second set of eyes". Make sure it fits and is well-pressed; check it out several weeks in advance so you have time to have alterations made if necessary. A poor fitting uniform, improperly placed awards, service ribbons and badges, unserviceable shoes or a poor haircut will set the stage for your entire board appearance. This applies to your Specialists appearing before the Sergeant board, you have an ethical and moral duty to ensure you have checked their uniforms, etc. so they have the best opportunity to succeed before the board.

Also prepare them for questions that require an opinion such as: What is the most important activity/event happening in the United States today and why do you think this? If you were the Battalion Command Sergeant Major for a day, what would you change and why? What is the most important Leadership quality and why? These are questions that test a Leader's ability to "think on their feet", present a solid response and have the personal courage to stand by their opinion. Occasionally a board member might challenge an answer to an opinion question;

all the while, your Soldier or you may agree that the board member's answer is commendable but "in your opinion" your position is the correct one. It is fine to acknowledge another's opinion but if you truly believe in your position, do not allow yourself to be swayed; to do so might be considered "waffling" or uncertainty in your answer which in and of itself can lead a much worse result than answering the question incorrectly. These are two behaviors which result in weak leadership.

Similarly, the question "Why should you be promoted to the next higher grade?" may illicit the response "Because I am the best Specialist (Sergeant) in the Army." Make sure you are prepared to answer why that is. Stumble here and you might find yourself stumbling throughout the remainder of your board appearance, compromising a successful score. No matter what happens, a Soldier must maintain their composure and military bearing throughout their board appearance. The saying "Never let them see you sweat!" is something for your Soldiers and you to keep tucked in the back of your mind at all times.

Most NCOs have a war story or two to share about their appearance before a promotion board, thus they can relate to a Soldier's board preparation and appearance. It is a learning experience to be shared so that others can benefit from your Soldiers' or your appearance before they attend a board. Developing your subordinates and yourself for promotion is inherent to your duties as a Leader. It takes hard work and a desire to succeed. It is within a Soldier's reach and a measure of preparedness and tenacity. You as a Leader are an integral part of that process. Encouragement and assistance will go a long way in supporting your Soldiers and yourself towards success.

SGM(R) Toni Gagnon Ross

From One Leader to Another
Safety and Risk Management
Command Sergeant Major Marc L. Maynard

The Army has committed huge resources to preserving combat power through advancing a culture of Risk Management. This does not mean we avoid risk altogether. The work our organization does is inherently dangerous and sometimes high levels of risk have to be assumed. Even though we cannot avoid all risk, we can manage most of it and at the same time empower our organizations to accomplish more things efficiently without unnecessary cost in combat power.

Safety and risk management as we know it today has evolved through the course of Army history. The US Army Combat Readiness/Safety Center (USACR/SC) was commissioned in 2005. It is the outgrowth of the US Army Safety Center and it traces its roots back to 1954 and the Army Accident Review Board based in the Aviation School in Ft. Rucker Alabama. It was predominantly an aviation focused endeavor until 1978 when it took on ground safety as well. The USACR/SC is the central hub organization for Army safety programs, training and investigations.

Organizational safety however does not come from having a great website, or a top-notch staff running a multi-million dollar training and awareness campaign. It comes from leaders at every level taking serious their mandate to be responsible for the forces under them. These leaders need to understand the advantages of running a risk managed operation.

First, risk management protects our most valuable asset, people. I use people rather than Soldiers for the very simple reason that we are no longer operating in a sterile Army-only environment. We now work alongside of other services and civilians as well.

The bottom line is they are all valuable and though we train to be replaceable, the fact of the matter is that experience is lost when Soldiers are replaced. The intangible past experience is not passed on to the next person. As an organization we cannot afford to lose valuable experience to mishaps. Additionally, there is a real wound to an organization when the unthinkable happens. This degrades readiness and has real costs in morale and physiological as well as mental health in our formations.

Second, in a resource constrained environment, risk management saves money by avoiding damage to Army property. As budgets get tighter, commanders are going to be forced to choose rather than fund everything. Some months will leave no money in the budget to repair that piece of equipment and training may have to be cancelled or consumables reduced to pay for the repair.

Third, since risk management is a pro-active, forward looking endeavor, better planning occurs in organizations that intentionally seek to reduce risk. The military decision-making process is not frustrated by risk management, it is enhanced. Courses of action become clearer when more information is incorporated into the process.

So how do we cultivate a culture of risk management in our organization? I believe we must promote individual safety initiative, maintain standards, invest in subject matter experts and communicate the message and the plan. The examples provided here are from my own experience. I do not bring them forth to highlight my accomplishments. These events do however specifically demonstrate the points I am trying to make regarding safety and risk management.

PROMOTE SAFETY INITIATIVE: As a young Specialist, I came upon a disaster that was about to happen when a forklift was being off-loaded from a trailer. I rolled into the area to deliver a truck load of ammunition to a tank gunnery range. After halting my vehicle and dismounting, I noticed a clearly stressed operator attempting to follow the instruction of the ground guide who was attempting to download the forklift from a low-boy trailer. As I approached the area I noticed that the passenger side wheels of the forklift were already hanging halfway off the side of the trailer. I immediately stopped the disaster from continuing by waving my arms and yelling at the operator to stop. I then asked the operator if he was okay. He was obviously not comfortable but said he was okay. I then proceeded to relieve the ground guide (a Major who at the time was not very excited about a young Specialist asking him to leave the scene) and gave instructions to the operator on how we were going to proceed. We then executed some technical maneuvers to get the forklift back on the trailer correctly and then off the trailer safely.

I feel I need to clarify this story a little. First, I was a licensed operator for that forklift with many hours experience and I knew exactly what it could do. Second, I was firm but respectful in approaching the Major and asking him to leave so I could take over the ground guide duties. I did not tell him to leave. Third and most importantly, I cared enough to act. I assumed responsibility for a bad situation because I had made an estimate from my observation that I knew how to get that forklift down and the Major clearly did not. It could have gone badly for me if I had acted from inexperience or acted without respect. Worse yet, it could have gone very badly for the operator if I did not act at all. I did not receive any awards or accolades, just some thanks from the operator and the personal satisfaction of knowing I did the right thing. As an organization we must encourage that kind of action. We must empower

Soldiers to do the right thing. I was not flogged for embarrassing the Major. I did what needed to be done and the chain of command supported me that day.

MAINTAIN STANDARDS/STICK TO THE PLAN: As a Squad Leader in a transportation platoon I was in charge of a detail collecting Class IV barrier material after the conclusion of training. Our standard operating procedure while at training was to wear our helmet and gloves when handling barrier material. One Specialist in my detail was not wearing her helmet and I instructed her to stop and go get her helmet. Needless to say, she complained about it but she complied and put on her helmet. Within five minutes, like a "Laurel and Hardy movie" she was hit on the head by a 4x4 board that rolled off the side of the 5-ton trailer. Later that afternoon the Soldier came to me and thanked me for insisting that she wear her helmet. Again, I did not receive an award or accolades, simply the thanks of a grateful Soldier and the personal satisfaction of knowing I did the right thing. We have to maintain the standard and follow the risk management plan in order to maximize the potential for safety.

INVEST IN A SUBJECT MATTER EXPERT: As the CSM of an ASB I have had the good fortune of observing the results of an integrated risk management approach that includes a full time safety Officer. In previous assignments I served largely in ground operations where the safety Officer is often merely viewed as an additional duty. I will freely admit that when I first heard that the battalion had a full time safety Officer I thought to myself; wow!, it must be nice to have nothing to do but walk around, give some briefs and review safety stuff. I had no idea how engaged and important the safety Officer is in our battalion. Granted, we are an Aviation Support

Battalion but I clearly had some cultural growing to do. What I found was that the safety Officer is a trusted key component of our organization's success. Ours in particular is a very pro-active forward looking safety Officer. As a result, resources for safe mission accomplishment are available and early risk decisions and mitigation is made to take full advantage of the available planning time. At every level in our organization there should be a safety person who is part of both the plan and the planning process.

COMMUNICATE: Use all of the available risk management tools to construct a plan and disseminate it to the lowest levels. During domestic operations in support of Hurricane Sandy disaster relief, my Battalion Commander clearly communicated the message of how important risk management was to our operation. He said "The first rule of disaster relief is to not make the problem worse, we must aggressively use risk management to insure our Soldiers do not become a part of the problem rather than a part of the solution." Our company commanders acted on those words and disseminated them to the leaders and Soldiers on the ground. They embraced risk management. Every one of our Soldiers received in-process safety briefs regarding the conditions on the ground and what to do or not do in the presence of high voltage wires and the other risks in our area of operation. Our activities and movements on the ground all had properly executed risk assessments reviewed by our BN safety Officer and approved by the Commander. Spot checks were conducted constantly by leaders at all levels to insure that the risk management controls were both understood and enforced. As a result, we enjoyed success. When we concluded operations the net result was no major accidents and only a few relatively minor personal injuries.

Culture development does not happen overnight. The safety culture I have been exposed to and enjoying in the aviation community was not started yesterday. I surely cannot take the credit for it. The success we are witnessing is further evidence of the final picture I would like to draw for you. I call it the chain of failure.

In most every cataclysmic failure there is a chain of smaller more devious human errors. If any one of those errors had been averted the catastrophe would not have occurred. For example, an unlicensed "go-to" Soldier is asked to drive a vehicle a "short" distance at night. The vehicle is not properly maintained and the convoy experiences unexpected rain. The defroster does not work and the vehicle ends up careening off the road resulting in the driver being injured or killed.

The chain of failure began with the leader not following established guidelines and sending an unlicensed operator on the road, it continued with the operator not questioning the decision to be put into that position and not conducting a good PMCS, the problem was further exasperated because the previous operator had never documented the faulty defroster. There are likely countless other contributing factors and negligent individuals in this scenario. Any one of these people could have broken the chain of failure but they chose not to. We must aggressively instill in our Soldiers the "chain-breaker" mentality where "I will be the one who does it right." Together we can make a difference. Fortunately my battalion is full of chain breakers.

In closing, I would like to leave you with this thought as a leader. When I was a First Sergeant in Afghanistan with Soldiers at 11 separate forward operating bases scattered across the entire country, I told my Soldiers "I am not here to be your friend.

You can live out your days hating me for making you uncomfortable when doing the right things and I will be thankful you got home on my watch." They all did. Break the chain of failure and create a culture of safety.

If you would like to learn more about Army Safety and the Risk Management Process you should visit the Army Safety Center website https://safety.Army.mil/, your one-stop shop for all your risk management needs. It includes tools like the Risk Management Information System, the Travel Risk Planning System, and the Ground risk Assessment Tool, just to name a few. You can also read Army Regulation 385-10, "The Army Safety Program" and Field Manual 5-19, "Composite Risk Management".

CSM Marc L. Maynard
642d ASB

From One Leader to Another
Safety
A Leadership Imperative

Command Sergeant Major Richard D. Stidley

It is difficult to overestimate the importance of safety in our Army. During our nearly 238 years of existence, preventable losses have taken a heavy toll on both our Soldiers and mission effectiveness. Statistics tell the tale: almost twice as many Soldiers died from accidents and disease as enemy action in every American conflict from the Mexican War through World War I. Accidents alone were responsible for one of every five Soldier deaths during World War II and one of every seven in Vietnam. The numbers were especially devastating during Operations Desert Shield and Desert Storm, when 62 percent of Army fatalities were attributed to non-hostile causes. Yet, even in the midst of the longest continuous conflict in our nation's history, Army accident rates have fallen to peacetime levels.

The answer is a complex one as to why. We have learned important lessons from the past, and advances in technology and protective equipment have mitigated the lethality of human error and other accident causes. That is only part of the picture, however. We have gotten better and better as an Army at managing risk, and policies and processes designed to protect Soldiers and maintain combat readiness are more streamlined than ever before. The greatest credit for our success, though, is due to the most basic elements of Soldiering: leadership and camaraderie. Leaders and Soldiers looking out for and encouraging one another to make smart decisions every day, on and off duty, have had a far greater impact on safety than any policy or piece of equipment possibly could.

As Non-Commissioned Officers, we are the firewall for Soldier safety. Notice I did not say "first line of defense" or "vanguard" or any of the fancy terminology that has dominated the safety conversation during the past few years. In my mind, our priority as leaders is to prepare our Soldiers to be their own first line of defense against accidents by making wise risk decisions, whether on a road in Afghanistan or a highway at their home station. Of course, we must lead the accident prevention effort and mentor and guide them as they find their way to a safety-focused lifestyle, but holding our Soldiers accountable for their own well-being is just as important. Getting there, however, will require us to move past some the common misconceptions about safety and embrace safety as what it really is: a critical combat multiplier in an age of tactical uncertainty.

Many new, ambitious NCOs go into their first leadership assignments with lofty goals in mind. A zero-risk policy should not be one of them. While it might seem counterintuitive, seeking to eradicate all hazards can actually hinder workable safety goals. It is entirely within our power to control and mitigate risk to acceptable levels, and we can do it without constraining Soldiers to the point of ineffectiveness. Planning for and wisely executing the mission is essential to combat readiness; safety will work to your advantage if we let it. Know your Soldiers, their individual and collective strengths and weaknesses, and build a flexible safety program that meets their needs and can be adapted as conditions change.

The line of communication between you and your Soldiers will be critically important, especially regarding safety. They should be invested in their safety program, not simply told what to do from the top down. The most successful safety initiatives are those where Soldiers "buy in" to what their leader is promoting, and asking them to participate in the process is the best place to start. I know that idea might run counter to what many of you have experienced in the Army, but safety demands inclusion. Soldiers are some of the most creative people on the planet, and I am continually surprised at the candid responses I get when talking to them about safety. You will not be any less of a leader or lose authority by asking them how you and the unit can better approach safety issues. It all goes back to letting your Soldiers take ownership of the process, enabling them to think through and solve problems themselves, all skills that will serve them well off duty.

Do not fall into the trap of thinking your Soldiers are "safer" at home station. As forces redeploy from abroad and we transition back to a smaller, peacetime Army, I fear that complacency is going to become a problem for leaders and Soldiers alike. The immediate threat of a tangible human enemy may be gone, but risk is one of the stealthiest and deadliest opponents we face. Even our worst years for accidents during the past decade, plus those of war do not compare to the hundreds of Soldiers lost annually during the long peace between Vietnam and Operation Desert Shield. Most of those fatalities were due to private motor vehicle accidents, which remain the number one accidental killer of Soldiers today. It is a tragedy for a Soldier to survive the brutalities of combat only to return home and die in a preventable accident, especially when something as simple as slowing down or wearing a seat belt could have saved him or her. There is no possible way for you to be everywhere at once, and that is why you must inform and empower your Soldiers to make smart safety decisions all the time.

Finally, and perhaps most importantly — be a safety leader, and lead by example. Soldiers are smart and they know when their leaders are just talking, not doing. For the past several years, more than half of all Soldiers killed on motorcycles have been NCOs. Unfortunately, indiscipline was involved more often than not in those accidents, and it is doubtful these leaders died on their first careless ride. The life we lead has a profound impact on our Soldiers, so we must hold ourselves to the very same standards we expect of them. You have young, impressionable men and women looking up to you now, and it is your duty to be a responsible mentor. Have fun, but always play it safe.

I commend you all for the hard work and dedication it has taken to reach this point in your careers. You have a challenging, yet immensely rewarding task ahead. For more information on safety and leadership, please visit the US Army Combat Readiness/Safety Center website at https://safety.Army.mil. Also be sure to print a copy of *Army Regulation* 385-10, *The Army Safety Program* and *Department of the Army Pamphlet* 385-10, *Army Safety Program* for your desktop reference set.

Keep up the great work, and remember, Army Safe is Army Strong!

CSM Richard D. Stidley
US Army Combat Readiness/Safety Center

From One Leader to Another
Sponsorship
Starting Off Right

Sergeant Major (Retired) Toni Gagnon Ross

A good sponsor is critical to the successful reception of an in-bound Soldier and their Family. As the old adage goes, "you only get one chance to make a great first impression;" this is especially true when welcoming new Soldiers into your unit. That first meeting and subsequent support or lack thereof will set the tone for their entire assignment with the organization.

Throughout the years, the Army has had multiple forms of sponsorship programs. In the 1980's the First Sergeant notified Platoon Sergeants of in-bound Soldiers, in turn the Platoon Sergeants or Squad Leaders appointed individual Soldiers to serve as sponsors. This was the pre-internet era so it started with an introductory letter from the sponsor explaining the unit, mission, location, and facilities along with an Army community Service (ACS) welcome packet. There may have been an exchange of letters based on the individuals; usually Soldiers with Families would share additional information about day care, schools, etc. When the new Soldier arrived, the Sponsor assisted him or her with their in-processing (again, this was before consolidated in-processing).

In the 1990s it became much easier to share information because of the internet but the program still required monitoring by the unit leadership. Soldiers were able to provide a detailed request for sponsorship to allow the gaining unit to better assist with their transition. Later it would become governed by *AR* 600-8-8, *The Total Army Sponsorship Program* instituting a scripted sequence of events to assist in providing a first-class transition. The regulation clearly stated the purpose as "a system to help commanders exercise their basic responsibility to assist Soldiers, and Families to successfully relocate into and out of their commands. Sponsorship is a commander's program in which commanders and individual sponsors are key to success."

A new Soldier's sponsorship and welcome experience forms their first opinion of a unit's morale, esprit de corps and attitude especially when a Soldier is arriving to their first unit or to an overseas assignment. In the training environment, new Soldiers will share their sponsorship information with one another. This creates excitement amongst the troops; however, imagine the disappointment of the Soldiers not receiving a sponsorship packet or worse yet, a substandard packet. This not only impacts on each Solder but their spouse, parents and possibly their extended Family. This program can also serve as an inherent marketing tool reinforcing or failing to reinforce that the Army takes care of its own.

The regulation outlines what must be done within designated timelines. Will this be a succession of form letters from the chain of command and the sponsor or will there be some sort of personalization involved? The sponsor should write the letter they would want to receive, not a letter that "checks the block." Soldiers of all ranks and experience want to feel as though they will be welcomed by and value added to their gaining unit. They are curious to hear of what awaits them and are often curious as to whether any of their friends from previous assignments are also there. The gaining unit should be thrilled to be getting a replacement; the red carpet should be ready to be rolled out for the proverbial "new guy."

Most every Soldier experiences a bit of "PCS anxiety" but the spouse and children often have greater amount of fear as they are leaving behind their friends, favorite teachers, schools, stores and the like.

They perceive the Soldier is immediately swept into in-processing, surrounded by newfound teammates to assist in their learning of the ropes within the new unit while the Spouse may feel alone. They are often left to deal with enrolling children into school, delivery of their household goods, acclimating to their new community: commissary, Post Exchange, transportation system, new doctors and dentists, and helping their children with the transition and myriad of other stressors.

The sponsor should invite questions from the in-bound spouse and children while enlisting their spouse in reaching out to the Soldier's spouse and Family. Ideally, the sponsor and their Family will provide significant information they wished they had received when they arrived to the installation, thereby always improving the organization's sponsorship program. The sponsor and the spouse should always respond to specific questions from the in-bound Soldier and Family; two of the most common of which are child care and cost of living items. Those two items are crucial when a Family plans their move and anticipate planning a new budget.

Again the internet is a great asset for ensuring timely and thorough communications. However, a successful sponsorship program takes effort and commitment on the part of the sponsor and the unit's chain of command to ensure the program is executed effectively. A Soldier, with or without a Family, who feels welcome and is excited about their gaining unit is instantly an asset once they are greeted by their sponsor. Alternatively, a Soldier who arrives without the benefit of an active and supportive sponsor is hesitant, anxious and has already been denied the leadership they deserve. Which Soldier would you prefer walk into your unit tomorrow?

SGM(R) Toni Gagnon Ross

From One Leader to Another
Sponsorship

Command Sergeant Major
Carlos Medina Castellano

During a speech at the US Army Command and General Staff College graduation in 2005, Dr. Francis J. Harvey, then Secretary of the Army, stated that Army leaders in this century needed to be pentathletes; multi-skilled leaders who could thrive in uncertain and complex environments, who were experts in the art and science of the profession of arms. He continued on to say that the Army needed leaders who were decisive, innovative, adaptive, culturally astute, effective communicators and dedicated to lifelong learning. Furthermore, as Senior Enlisted Advisors we are also charged to educate our subordinates and other leaders in subjects which are informative, interesting and relevant.

Sponsorship is one such topic and to better elaborate on this issue, I referred to the Army Leadership manual, not looking for inspiration but for collaboration. As expected, I found what I was looking for. The publication states that good leaders strive to leave an organization better than they found it and expect other leaders throughout the Army to do the same. With that said, one of the areas in which some Army organizations are not doing well is the Total Army Sponsorship Program. Like any other program within the Army inventory, if it is not managed well, than it will not meet its intended purpose.

Army Regulation 600-8-8 covers the Total Army Sponsorship Program. Its 20 short pages describe the program requirements which range from the Army Staff, to sponsor, unit and individual responsibilities. All too often it is at the unit level where the program fails to meet its expectations. Most units are not placing emphasis in assigning sponsors, getting sponsors trained or simply taking the necessary step to reach out to incoming Soldiers. They fail to realize that one of the best ways to help create a positive organizational climate is to ensure incoming personnel are assigned sponsors before their arrival.

The Army sponsorship program is designed to assist Soldiers, civilian employees and Families during the reassignment process. It also assists Families who are geographically separated from their Soldier or civilian employee sponsor because of duty requirements. It improves unit and organizational cohesion and readiness by decreasing distractions that hamper personal performance and mission accomplishment, specifically by providing support and assistance, teaching teamwork and encouraging development of a sense of responsibility. In a perfect world, every active duty Soldier on assignment instructions would receive an email, letter or some other form on contact from their gaining unit, assigning them a sponsor. However, that is not always the case.

By regulation, units are required to send a welcome letter from the Battalion Commander (for Officers), Command Sergeant Major (for enlisted Soldiers), or commander/activity director (for civilian employees) to the incoming Soldier or civilian employee within ten calendar days of their receipt of DA Form 5434 (Sponsorship Program Counseling and Information Sheet). The standard is to forward DA Form 5434 received by higher echelons within three working days of receipt; to appoint sponsors, unless the Soldier declines, within 10 calendar days of receipt of DA Form 5434; and to forward the sponsor welcome letter and information within 10 calendar days of appointment. Sponsors are also required to respond to correspondence within 10 working days of receipt.

In most cases, the latter part is not being executed in the way of a formal letter, but it is being enforced as an email or another form of correspondence between the sponsor and sponsored Soldier. The Army Community Service office is also available to provide welcome packets upon request. Units should develop their own Standard Operating Procedures (SOP) to outline the sponsorship process. In some units, updates on sponsorship are briefed during Brigade and Battalion level meetings to ensure inbound Soldiers are assigned sponsors and that contact information is accurate.

In cases where sponsors have not been successful in reaching their sponsored Soldier, other leaders (1SGs, CSMs) will make an attempt to contact the losing unit to ensure that the Soldier is notified. This is where leaders must become creative and exercise the initiative required to ensure mission success. When possible, the sponsor should plan to greet the incoming Soldier or civilian employee and Family upon arrival. The sponsorship of a Soldier typically terminates after the Soldier has in-processed and is settled-in but some units continue sponsorship like responsibilities for several months ensuring that the Soldier and their Family are fully supported and integrated into their new team.

Every Soldier in the rank of Private through Colonel (excluding Soldiers completing advanced individual training (AIT) and Soldiers making PCS moves to student detachments at long-term schools) and civilian employees through general schedule grade 15 undergoing a PCS move will be offered the opportunity to participate in the advanced arrival sponsorship program. Sponsorship is mandatory for first-term Soldiers. Long-term military schools will provide welcome and sponsorship information but they are not required to provide individual sponsors.

Gaining commanders will change pinpoint or ultimate assignments of Soldiers assigned sponsors only in rare or exceptional cases. When assignments are changed, sponsorship will be transferred and coordinated immediately with the gaining command or activity.

The Army G1 is currently developing additional measures to address assigning sponsors to Soldiers departing AIT. They are developing a pilot program in which gaining commands are required to assign sponsors prior to Soldiers being issued assignment instructions. The AIT Soldier is likely one who might benefit the most from the sponsorship program. Imagine a Soldier graduating from AIT with assignment instructions to Fort Wainwright, Alaska and moving to his gaining unit in the middle of the winter. The Soldier does not have a sponsor and does not contact the gaining unit for information prior to his or her departure. When he or she departs, they do not have the appropriate cold weather gear to endure the extreme temperatures at Fort Wainwright. Their travel plans alone, particularly if they are driving, may be treacherous with limited lodging, gas stations and cell phone reception. A young Soldier operating under those conditions without a sponsor would be open to countless, potentially catastrophic problems.

By taking appropriate action, all of the risks mentioned above can be mitigated or avoided entirely. The sponsorship program will work but only if we make it work. It takes involvement from everyone in the chain of concern; from the Soldier being sponsored, to the Command Sergeant Major signing that welcome letter and reaching out to the gaining and/or losing command. As innovative leaders, we must find a way to ensure the Army sponsorship program is both efficient and effective. If PCSing, your responsibility as a Soldier is to ensure you request a sponsor; our responsibility as a leader is to ensure your gaining unit contacts you before your departure. By doing so, your transition from one unit to another will result in a better experience for you and your Family.

A Sponsorship Flowchart Example

The process starts when the CAP Cycle is posted, upon receipt of DA Form 5434- Sponsorship Request, or when a Soldier and his or her Family arrive at a gaining unit (when not tracked on a gains roster). These include, but are not limited to Soldiers on short notice assignments and un-programmed arrivals to an organization.

↓

S1 populates a sponsorship roster based on the organizational gains roster and sends a CSM/CDR Welcome Letter as appropriate. The CSM sends an initial welcome letter which may include FRG information.

↓

Subordinate units assign a sponsor per AR 600–8–8, The Total Army Sponsorship Program and update the organization's sponsorship report as needed. S1 sends a Battalion welcome letter (with sponsor's name).

↓

The sponsor attempts to make contact. If contact is made, at a minimum the sponsor will continue to provide sponsorship to the incoming individual until he or she has settled in to the new organization. Additionally, the sponsor will forward the incoming individual an installation or organizational Welcome Packet as required. If no contact is made, the unit 1SG will notify the CSM and either the 1SG or CSM will make contact with the CSM of the individual's losing unit in order to effective link-up between the sponsor and the incoming Soldier/civilian and their Family.

The organization's sponsorship roster is updated weekly and briefed during the organization's Command & Staff and/or CSM weekly meetings.

Note 1: ACS provides Unit Sponsorship Training upon request. Sign in rosters are maintained to ensure Soldiers are trained. Soldiers must complete on-line sponsorship training.

Note 2: This flow chart takes into account additional measures to ensure incoming Soldiers are in fact assigned a sponsor. By regulation Soldiers PCSing (excluding Soldiers completing advanced individual training [AIT] and Soldiers making PCS moves to student detachments at long-term schools) are not required to have an assigned sponsor, however, the most effective organizations reach out to all inbound personnel ensuring that everyone has a sponsor.

Note 3: Every departing Soldier and civilian employee will be offered "out-sponsorship" or transition assistance if requested.

If you would like to learn more about the Total Army Sponsorship Program and the reception and integration of newly arrived personnel it is recommended that you read *Army Doctrine Publication 6-22*, *Army Leadership* and *Army Regulation 600-8-8*, *Total Army Sponsorship Program*.

CSM Carlos Medina Castellano
551st SIG BN

From One Leader to Another
The Importance of Drill and Ceremony
Command Sergeant Major Dennis Eger

Drill and Ceremony is an integral part of our military culture, deep in customs and tradition which date back hundreds of years. It is important as a military that we do not lose that part of our storied history. Over the years we have steadily lost focus on its importance, not because it was unimportant but because focusing on the fight abroad took priority. However, as Non-Commissioned Officers we must understand that the standards and discipline which drill and ceremony instilled in us are the reason why we are able to fight and win our nation's wars.

It is important to look at the past in order to prepare and propel us toward the future. Examples of drill can be seen in military forces dating back to Roman times as a means of instilling discipline and a uniform way of troop movements. It wasn't until 1778 when drill was first established in our military. Years of undisciplined military formations, movements and actions caused General Washington to seek the assistance of a Prussian Officer, Baron Frederick Von Steuben who took the first steps towards establishing drill in our military. Discipline through the use of drill ensured that troops would act to commands without hesitation. It gave them a sense of urgency and more importantly attention to detail. Drill gave the Soldier confidence in himself and his equipment while teaching him to work as a team thus instilling pride in themselves as well as their units while also establishing a means of rapidly massing and moving large formations across the battlefield.

These same principles established in 1778 still hold true today as very little has changed in regards to drill commands and functions. As an NCO it is our duty to uphold these traditions. Conducting drill and ceremony today serves the same purposes as years ago. As Soldiers enter the military one of the first things they learn is drill. This is not by mistake; drill begins to instill discipline through repetition. It teaches the aspiring professional what it means to be something bigger than him or herself and that they are just one part of a bigger organization. And if done correctly, it will instill pride in themselves and their unit.

Too often Soldiers recognize this; they see drill as a hassle or waste of time, something that keeps them on the parade field for long hours. They fail to see the details. It is our job to teach them. From the hand salute to our superiors and our colors to the uniform that they wear, it is all part of drill. It is part of instilling attention to detail, teaching them that if they can get the small things right, they will get the larger important things right. If the Soldier cannot master the attention to detail from drill, they will likely not master attention to detail in combat.

You need not look further for establishing the importance of drill than by looking at our current combat operations. The pre-combat checks and pre-combat inspections that leaders conduct are just another aspect of drill. What is their purpose? Their basic purpose is to instill discipline in the Soldier and to help them gain trust in their leaders and their equipment. If repeatedly addressed, you can begin to see discipline emerge, the development of a sense of pride and the ability to act without hesitation, just as it was in 1778.

The primary value of drill throughout history has been to prepare troops for battle and this is still the case today. Whether exercising at home station or participating in a rotation at a combat training center the objective remains the same, to mass on the enemy by using specific schemes of maneuver and formations. This is possible through constant "drill" and repetition so that it becomes second nature. This leads to disciplined Soldiers and units, on and off the battlefield culminating in confidence in self, leadership and equipment giving a sense of pride and esprit d' corps. The formations, the marching, the salutes and the parades are the little things. Understanding those and getting back to the core functions of drill are what lead to the large scale maneuver success on the battlefield.

As the war winds down what will we do? Will we put our traditions to the side or will we continue them? It is our responsibility as NCOs to go back to the fundamentals, the basics. Non-Commissioned Officers are the keepers of tradition and culture, we train Soldiers.

This solution is simple. It's holding formations during the day for accountability. It's doing in-ranks inspections to check basic uniform and equipment standards. It's taking a few minutes out of each day to allow a Soldier to march the formation. It's having Soldiers march from location to location. Each of which are basic drills that we must continue to exercise. This continues the traditions and culture of the military while teaching the discipline, standards, and attention to detail that our Army demands.

We must return to the days where prior to a Soldier's attendance at NCOES he or she is required to instruct their Soldiers in drill and ceremony. He or she must practice and ultimately demonstrate every movement from the Drill and Ceremony manual including how to extend a formation for physical training. These are the attention to detail tasks that further our culture but more importantly teach basic discipline.

A back to the fundamentals approach to drill and ceremony is our foundation for moving forward while using history as our guide. By ensuring that NCOs re-institute drill back into our formations with four components in mind; discipline, attention to detail, acting to commands without hesitation, and troop movement we will ensure success in both garrison and combat. We do not need to recruit a General who specializes in drill to make us successful. That General already exists; he resides in the Non-Commissioned Officer Corps! The Backbone of our Army!

CSM Dennis Eger
Mission Command Center of Excellence (MCCoE)

From One Leader to Another
Training Management
Sergeant Major (R) Dennis W. Paxton

The Army Training Management Model is built upon the same structure as the operations process: Planning, Preparing, Execution and Assessment. Unit training and leader development are the cornerstones of Army readiness. Through these training efforts, units are able to successfully complete missions and overcome obstacles they encounter along the way. Successful operations are dependent on the way leaders manage unit training and leader development. Entwined with the four phases of the Army Training Management Model is continuous leader involvement. A unit can only be successful if it is carefully scrutinized to determine if it has the ability to accomplish an assigned mission. Based on this evaluation, a program can be developed to bridge where a unit is and where a unit needs to be. This assessment derives the tasks that the unit must train on.

The word "task" is defined by Merriam-Webster as "a usually assigned piece of work to be finished within a certain time; something hard or unpleasant that has to be done; a duty or function." These definitions neatly describe what leaders must identify in order to make their units successful. Leaders must develop plans that, through training, education, and experience, will help develop their subordinate leaders. This process is generally easier if their units have been designated as a deployment expeditionary force (DEF) or a contingency expeditionary force (CEF) as these two categories help to prioritize a unit's training and resources. Units not designated as a CEF or DEF force must also sustain their readiness but do so largely as a matter of conducting day-to-day operations.

The tasks of training units and training leaders should happen simultaneously. As the unit is trained, the leader is also trained. This synchronization between unit and leader training provides the best use of resources and, based on good senior leader guidance, helps subordinate units and leaders achieve their training objectives. The use of mission command and mission type orders allow subordinate leaders to determine the best way to manage their training in order to achieve desired results. The key to successful training is preparation. Feedback and assessment following training ensures that either training objectives have been met, or that re-training is required.

There are three key factors that influence which tasks a Commander chooses to train: the mission, the operational environment, and most important of all, time/resources available. Because of battlefield friction, it is imperative that the Commander chooses those tasks which allow him the greatest flexibility to deal with change.

Mission Analysis, conducted while determining which tasks to train, always begins with the unit's mission. Regardless of the type of mission (named, contingency, or when building a specific capability), mission analysis is conducted to allow the Commander to determine the unit capabilities necessary to satisfactorily complete the mission. As in the Military Decision Making Process (MDMP), understanding the mission and the tasks required to complete it leads the Commander to the development of a list of necessary task groups and collective tasks the unit must train on. The Commander does not attempt to train all of the task groups or collective tasks that will support their unit's standardized Mission Essential Task List (METL), but rather opts to train fewer tasks to a higher standard. The Commander works with subordinate Commanders to determine which tasks to train and the operational environment conditions under which the tasks will be trained. The tasks trained are generally selected because of their ability to accomplish the task, as well as their ability to provide the versatility to quickly transition to another, unexpected, mission, if necessary.

Subordinate units without a standardized METL use the mission guidance from their higher headquarters (HHQ), as well as the unit's task groups and collective tasks in order to conduct their mission analysis when determining which tasks they will train their units to ensure nesting and priority of effort. This increases the likelihood that the HHQ will be able to accomplish its mission.

Smaller units who do not have a HHQ or a standardized METL must develop their METL based on their TOE or TDA mission statement, assigned mission, external guidance, and the type of operations METL they generally support. Commanders can generally use doctrinally-approved task groups and collective tasks to establish their METL. If, however, doctrinal tasks do not fit the mission, commanders develop tasks, conditions, and standards to allow the unit to meet the capabilities in its mission statement. HHQ commanders approve the unit-developed tasks and METL during their Commanders' Dialog.

Supporting training is a joint requirement between the HHQ and the installation. The HHQ provides training priorities and resources, such as evaluators, equipment, and Soldiers. The installation supports all units stationed on that installation or training on that installation with facilities, sustainment and logistics support and other training support services as needed.

Once the Commanders' Dialog is complete and the training plans are developed, Commanders provide training briefings to the next higher Commander. This meeting will formalize the training plan and the resources required, as well as ensure the higher Commander's intent is addressed in the chosen tasks. This briefing focuses on the unit training and leader development, and not the administrative details of the training. The training briefing should be concise.

The training briefing is an informal contract between commanders. The unit Commander agrees to conduct training as outlined in the plan, and the higher Commander agrees to support the training plan with required resources. If the unit is deploying to another command, the gaining unit Commander, or his representative, should also be at the training briefing. An installation representative should also be in attendance, because they manage the resources on the installation.

The training briefing should generally include -

- assessment of the unit's METL proficiency,

- collective tasks to be trained in support of the unit's METL proficiency,

- training events to be conducted and how they incorporate the collective tasks,

- resources required to replicate operational environments and support execution of training events, and

- challenges to executing the unit training and leader development guidance for the Long-Range Training Plan to subordinates.

Once the training briefing is concluded and approved, the unit Commander publishes the training and leader development guidance plan to their subordinates.

Preparation is the key to successful training and marks the transition from planning to execution. It consists of all of the activities performed by units in order to improve their ability to execute their Long-Range Training Plan. Effective training execution, regardless of the specific collective, leader, and individual tasks being performed, requires adequate preparation, effective presentation and rehearsals and thorough evaluation. Preparation begins during the planning phase and continues until the training event is completed.

As discussed earlier, the training meeting is used to synchronize the preparation for training. During the training meeting, the Commander ensures all necessary resources have been addressed and are prepared in order to conduct the training event. Preparation also includes the identification and mitigation of potential training distracters and risk issues. Part of the preparation includes informing both leaders and Soldiers of the tasks to be trained, the conditions under which they will be trained and the standard that will be used to determine if the task has been adequately trained. Prior to execution of the training, and as part of the preparation process, pre-execution checks, other inspections and rehearsals will be conducted. The training model used is up to the leader; all contingencies are addressed and the unit is prepared for task execution.

"Trainer" is a generic term which includes, but is not limited to, leaders, evaluators, observer-controllers or observer-trainers, opposing force (OPFOR) personnel and role players. Other potential trainers include every Soldier who may be required to brief a dignitary, a Soldier who has the opportunity to conduct "hip pocket" training during inclement weather or during breaks in scheduled training, or any Soldier who is either assigned a task to train another Soldier or takes it upon himself to train another Soldier. These personnel need to be identified by the chain of command to ensure they are trained to standard and rehearsed before training begins. "Training the trainers" allows the Commander an opportunity to develop junior leaders. Commanders ensure the trainers are competent, both technically and tactically, and confident on the tasks to be performed. He also ensures the trainers understand how the tasks they are training fit into the Long-Range Training Plan and higher training objectives.

Pre-execution checks are to training what pre-combat checks are to military operations. Pre-execution checks ensure equipment is present and serviceable, trainers are prepared, and training resources, such as training areas and mission-specific equipment and ammunition, are resourced. It is also the time to ensure composite risk management (CRM) worksheets (DA Form 7566) have been prepared and reviewed.

Rehearsals are always conducted before operations and early enough to conduct multiple iterations if necessary. They provide an invaluable means of ensuring actions during an operation or training are executed to standard and to time. They also provide the mechanism for leaders and Soldiers to visualize what is supposed to happen and to correct deficiencies during subsequent rehearsals.

There are many different types of rehearsals and, based on the time available, range from back briefs to combined arms. They range in both complexity and scope of participants from radio rehearsals to full-dress rehearsals conducted on replicated terrain of the operation.

Good rehearsals are not easy. They require significant work with good preparation and discipline and involve significant amounts of leader time. Because of the difficulty involved, the need to conduct "good" rehearsals becomes more important. Ultimately, conducting rehearsals at all echelons of command has proven to be a valuable use of time. They ensure the synchronization of resources arranged during the planning phase and clearly articulate the plan to all Soldiers and leaders.

Leaders use "mission type" orders by providing just enough guidance on preparation, execution, and assessment to encourage initiative from subordinate leaders. Once the order is published, unit training schedules and leader development plans may be produced. Leader development plans generally cover one week of training but may change based on Commander's input. Information included in leader development plans generally include, but is not limited to, the training audience, when and where the training will take place, the individual responsible for the training, the uniform and the required equipment.

Leader development can only occur if senior leaders give appropriate latitude to subordinate leaders to evoke initiative from them. Once training is completed, after action reviews (AAR) are also included to detail how well subordinate leaders were developed, what shortcomings need to be addressed in future training opportunities, and strengths that can be capitalized upon. This doesn't mean leaders step back and await possible failure. They teach, coach, and mentor throughout the planning, preparing, execution and assessment of the training operation.

The execution of training represents the culmination of both long and short-range planning. Execution of the plan provides the input for assessment, with assessment, re-planning, and retraining forming the foundation of improvement. Execution provides the basis for units being able to both perform their METL tasks and to adapt to changing conditions and new missions. Execution runs the gamut of individual training and execution all the way to unified action training. Leaders use a progressive training approach (crawl/walk/run) which tailors training through the short-term, near-term and long-term plans. This approach saves time by building on the proficiencies of highly-experienced Soldiers and leaders who have been trained, educated and have developed significant experience through multiple iterations of training and experience.

Recovery is not an additional task conducted at the end of training. It, in and of itself, is a training task which requires planning, preparation, execution and assessment. The previous training event which prompted a recovery phase should not be considered finished until all of the recovery tasks have been completed. Just like all other unit training events planning and preparation are just as important as the execution. The assessment of recovery is fulfilled by the inspections which follow it. Recovery should not be considered complete until all of the unit's personnel and equipment are prepared to fully function during the next training event. The final results of recovery should include the inspection, accountability and serviceability of all personnel, uniforms and equipment along with insight as to how to make the next recovery and exercise better.

The assessment of a unit is the Commander's overall responsibility. However, training and leader assessments are every leader's responsibility. Assessments are a leader's judgment of the organization's ability to accomplish a mission or task; that the training was conducted in accordance with a set standard and that subordinate leaders have been properly coached and mentored and can perform leader tasks to standard. Assessments are done throughout the training process and include assessments in both the planning and assessment phase.

Assessments are the amalgamation of many inputs; the Commander's individual experience, formal and informal feedback from trainers and evaluators, and personal observation. Leaders should not rely on a single set of inputs to assess the capability of a unit. Only by including and evaluating multiple input sources can a Commander develop a holistic understanding of the unit, task and/or leader proficiency. There are three types of assessments—

- unit,

- training

- leader

At this point, the differences between assessments and evaluations must be addressed. As stated above, assessments are the responsibility of the Commander and represent his determination that the unit can or cannot perform a task to a specific set of standards. The assessment takes into account the subjective nature of the final decision. An evaluation is not based upon the Commander's feelings or judgment, but rather it is based on the performance of the unit compared to the established standard. The Commander's feelings about how well a unit did have no bearing on the outcome of an evaluation. Because of this, results of an evaluation are generally expressed as "GO / NO GO," while the results of an assessment are expressed as trained (T), needs practice (P), or untrained (U).

The after action review (AAR) is a tool used to identify the successes and challenges which occurred during training or an operation. It allows participants to apply observations, insights and lessons learned to future training and operations. AARs can and should be a part of every type of training/operation, from individual to combined arms exercises. They do not necessarily have to take place at the end of an event. Sometimes, conducting an AAR at a pause during an event will help synchronize elements and correct deficiencies which have previously occurred.

The AAR provides an excellent opportunity to cultivate the critical thinking of all leaders. It is not meant to be a "blame game"; the AAR allows members of the unit to speak freely about what happened, where honest mistakes are freely discussed among leaders, participants and observers. The AAR is a forum which promotes understanding of what went right, what went wrong and what can be done better during future training and operations.

The AAR is not a critique. It has the following advantages over a critique—

- it focuses on key, METL-derived training objectives

- it emphasizes meeting Army standards rather than judging success or failure

- it uses leading questions to encourage participants to self-discover important lessons from the training event

- it allows a large number of Soldiers and leaders to participate so that more of the training can be recalled, and more lessons can be shared

The AAR consists of four parts:

- review what was supposed to happen

- establish what really happened

- determine what was right or wrong with what happened

- to determine how the task should be accomplished differently next time

There are two types of AARs—formal and informal. Leaders plan formal AARs at the same time they finalize their training plan. Formal AARs require more planning and preparation than informal AARs. During formal AARs, a leader facilitates a discussion of specific events based on training objectives. He provides an overview of what happened and what was supposed to happen and then the participants are able to identify what retraining needs to be done. Informal AARs are conducted after previously identified events or as on-the-spot coaching tools while reviewing Soldier and unit performance. The most significant differences between the formal and informal AAR are the amount of preparation and training aids required. Ideas and solutions gathered during informal AARs can be immediately put into effect during the continuation of training

Commanders determine the effectiveness of training with an eye on execution within the Commander's intent, achievement of training objectives and progress towards METL proficiency. The forum used to aggregate evaluations of tasks by the Commander and subordinate leaders is the training meeting. As stated earlier, the Commander uses the trained (T), needs practice (P) and untrained (U) ratings in the Digital Training Management System (DTMS) to assess their units. Based on these assessments, Commanders adjust their future planning opportunities and plans as needed. The Commander bases a subjective assessment on observed task proficiency and whether or not the training met the objectives and supported METL proficiency. Training assessments also address training support, force integration, logistics and sustainment and personnel availability. These assessments form the basis for determining the organization's training ratings for readiness reporting.

A Training and Evaluation Outline (T&EO) is a document summarizing a specific training task. It is generally composed of five elements—

- the task number and title—a clearly defined and measurable activity accomplished by individuals or organizations; tasks are specific activities that contribute to the accomplishment of encompassing missions or other requirements

- conditions—circumstances and environment a specific task is to be performed

- standards—the minimum acceptable proficiency required to perform the task under specific conditions

- task steps and performance measures—the specific steps required to conduct the task to the Army standard to include columns to annotate whether the task, as demonstrated, is rated a "GO" or a "NO GO" based on the standard

- supporting collective and individual tasks—any additional tasks that support the task noted

T&EO evaluations are an integral part of the evaluation process of a unit and the results help the Commander with his unit assessment. Ultimately, the Commander must look at each task step rated as a "GO" or "NO GO" and balance that with his specific insights and experience to determine the overall METL assessment of his unit. The T&EO also helps the Commander by defining how many times the task was evaluated and how many "GOs" the unit received on each iteration.

As the T&EOs are completed, the results are aggregated by the number of "GO" and "NO GO" tasks. Based on this, the evaluator will rate the overall task evaluated either a "GO" or a "NO GO." There is no room during the evaluation process for subjectivity by the evaluator. As stated earlier, an evaluation differs from an assessment in that the task is judged strictly against a set standard for each subtask. Once the T&EO has been submitted to the Commander, he has the responsibility to apply judgment and personal experience to the results to determine the overall T-P-U rating for the unit for each training event or task.

Every staff is different. Because of that, there is no generic set of rules to best cultivate a group of Soldiers into a coherent staff. Below are a few very broad tips which might help develop an organization's staff. These rules are not ranked in any particular order therefore the last tip in the list might have the greatest impact on your staff's proficiency level.

- Repetition breeds perfection - Doing a task poorly and not changing how that task is performed will generally lead to repetitively poor performed tasks. Every Soldier and staff should strive for incremental increases in proficiency each time a task is repeated. After performing the task over and over, it becomes something that can be done well with little preparation and little thinking.

- Use the staff's collective capabilities to prepare operations orders (OPORD) instead of merely memoranda. Building on the tip above, by enforcing the use of MDMP for each task/mission you will build a collective team, one in which each Soldier and section will understand their role in the formation of an order.

- Ensure the staff has a separate training opportunity as part of the collective training strategy of subordinate elements - There are too many times when the staff becomes the administration portion of the battalion or brigade collective task/mission with nothing to do but wait for specific training results. Use this time to develop Standing Operating Procedures (SOP) using the work that subordinate elements are doing as specific missions to track. Utilize proper radio techniques and use tracking charts, military maps and/or digital capabilities to track the activities of subordinate elements.

- During recovery, ensure the staff has time to do their own - Generally, the staff is relegated during recovery to quickly transition back to their daily gamut of garrison responsibilities. The S-1 Section is working on awards; the S-3 is working on publishing wash rack schedules or inspection times and dates; the S-6 and Maintenance Sections are fixing the broken components of vehicle and signal systems. Each of these sections requires adequate time to properly conduct their own recovery operations. If this is not adhered to, they will not be prepared for recovery inspections or worse, their equipment may not be ready for the next exercise/mission.

- Ensure the staff conducts integrated training with the elements generally attached to them - By including subordinate elements not assigned to the unit but attached for operations, the staff develops synergy and synchronization with them. This also augments the Tactical Operations Center SOP (TOCSOP) by reinforcing TOC procedures and helping to integrate systems. Without all subordinate elements being present, the physical TOC cannot be set up completely, possibly leading to discovery learning during later operations.

- Ensure a communications exercise is part of weekly maintenance and test all systems including ground-mounted radios and Army Battle Command Systems (ABCS) - Ensuring a complete maintenance ritual, checking all assigned systems is critical for the continued functionality of the TOC. Possibly more important than weekly weapons maintenance for the staff, the systems used to command and control units are critical to mission accomplishment, situational awareness and shared understanding.

- The Commander <u>must</u> give clear and concise guidance as to what he expects from each staff section - The Tactical SOP (TACSOP) and TOCSOP must be reviewed by the Commander and updated as a part of their change of command process. How each Commander sees the roles and responsibilities of his staff, as well as how he best understands information presented to him must be annotated and updated. As part of training, each staff NCO in-charge (NCOIC) must ensure his subordinates understand what the Commander expects of them and each section SOP must reflect how they will answer the Commander's vision.

- Delineation of continuous operations and practicing it - Far too many units fail to adequately prepare for continuous operations prior to major training requirements such as operations at the "dirt" Combat Training Centers (CTCs). The staff should not only anticipate the need for continuous operations, but have plans with names assigned to specific positions that outline each shift and how planning and current operations will be carried out simultaneously.

"A staff constantly needs challenging problems to solve if it's to build the attitude that it can overcome any obstacle. Tackling problems with restricted time and resources improves the staff members' confidence and proficiency, as long as they get an opportunity to celebrate successes and to recharge their batteries. Great confidence comes from training under conditions more strenuous than they would likely face otherwise." *FM* 22-100 (*Leadership*), 31 August 1999

- Use MDMP as the driver for all staff requirements - The most important thing the staff does is the synchronized preparation of orders in support of operations or training. This is a "must do." Utilize MDMP for preparing and organizing all training. While all the components might not be present, there is enough for each element of the staff to perform in order to ensure the operation or training opportunity has been well thought out.

- Get the Man-day (M-day) Soldiers involved with all processes not just the full-time Soldiers - Use collaboration sites such as Guardnet, Army Knowledge Online (AKO), or Guard Knowledge Online (GKO). A disservice is done to both the full-time Soldiers, as well as the M-day Soldiers, by not having them involved with the process. The full-time Soldiers suffer because they bear the greater brunt of the work; the M-day Soldiers suffer because they lose a training opportunity; the unit suffers because the "right" staff members might not be involved with the MDMP process because of their status.

- Include the Non-Commissioned Officers in all training and training opportunities - As stated earlier, the NCOs are the continuity of the staff and serve as the primary trainers. They do not get smarter by osmosis. They become what they are through experiential learning and by leaders and senior staff taking the time to train them properly. They become great trainers by taking the responsibility of their primary staff Officers and doing their jobs. They become close to irreplaceable by their ability to impart their accrued knowledge to the new subordinates, peers and superiors in their unit. If the NCOs are stifled and placed in a subservient position within the staff, the staff and the unit suffer.

- Take the time during planning, preparation, execution and assessment to refine SOPs - The TACSOP, TOCSOP, and Planning SOP (PSOP) are very fluid documents. Like the Commander reviewing the TACSOP and changing it to fit his persona, the TOCSOP and PSOP should be periodically reviewed, as well as annotated during operations, to determine if they are still germane. There should always be a "keeper" of the SOPs. That person should annotate changes whenever identified. Additionally, there should be a clipboard hung up somewhere in the TOC for all Soldiers to make recommendations for change in the SOPs.

- The Commander is the senior trainer for the staff - No one knows more than the Commander . . . that is why he was selected for command. As such, the Commander has responsibility for all training in his unit but is far more involved in the training of his staff than in how subordinate elements conduct rifle marksmanship. Commander, train your staff and form them into a cohesive element that understands your needs and is prepared to function in your absence.

- Staff training, like any other training requires preparation - Units do preliminary marksmanship instruction (PMI) before they transition to more advanced weapons training. Staff training requires the same level of preparation—PSOP review, understanding and generating planning tools, a thorough understanding of staff roles and responsibilities and knowledge of the appropriate doctrine are all prerequisites of successful staff training and execution.

- Develop the basic tools - Each staff section should develop a set of blank tools for their staff section or war-fighting functional area (WFF). These should include blank running estimate formats, formats for OPORDS, attachments, warning orders (WARNO), and fragmentary orders (FRAGO). Be prepared to modify them during staff training and operations.

- Establish primary and secondary reading responsibility for HHQ order analysis - It is better to have too many eyes reading the HHQ order than not enough. Too many times, units get caught in the "I didn't know that was my reading responsibility" trap. Clearly define which section is responsible for each annex and attachment. Within each section, determine who has primary and secondary reading responsibility for assigned portions of the HHQ order. Don't forget to include your enlisted Soldiers and NCOs in the plan.

- Start each operation with a blank slide deck for each briefing you plan to give - They may not always be right. They may not always be complete. They may not be exactly what the Commander wants. But they do serve as a basis for change. Prepare blank slide decks and pass them out to the staff for review prior to the operation. If you are unsure the staff will understand whose slide is whose . . . mark responsibility for the slide on the bottom.

Training a superior can be a very delicate process which must be handled with care. One wrong word or action may ruin a young Officer or create in him an attitude towards all NCOs which may last throughout their career. To begin with, NCOs should avoid approaching new lieutenants with an attitude of superiority. There is no need to try and impress the new Officer by telling him how much experience you have or to try to show him how little he knows compared to you. Approaching new lieutenants with sarcasm or intolerance is counter-productive and often causes them to stop asking questions, which can lead to serious mistakes, some of which can cause men to be killed or wounded. You should want new Officers to ask questions! Better that they ask questions and learn, than keep quiet and commit errors due to inexperience.

NCOs should act as a mentor to the new Officer and take responsibility for showing him the things he needs to learn in order to become an effective leader. It is important that the NCOs acknowledge that the new Officer is their leader and that he or she is in charge of the unit. This is very important, because the new Officer has to understand that while the success of the unit will largely result from the combined efforts of its members, as the commander, the ultimate responsibility for the unit's success or failure falls upon on him.

That being said, it is extremely important for the lieutenant to know that he can rely on his NCOs for their full support. New Officers are trained from the first day of OCS to seek the advice and support of their NCOs. They expect the NCOs to be competent and are usually very willing to accept guidance and recommendations from them. The bottom line is that NCOs should do everything in their power to ensure that new Officers quickly learn the things they need to know in order to win battles while minimizing casualties.

What can senior NCOs do to effectively support and train inexperienced Officers, particularly new lieutenants, joining a combat unit? They should do everything in their power to ensure that new Officers are oriented and "brought up to speed" regarding the tactical situation and other issues that will affect them.

They should orient the Officers on what has and is going on within the unit. It is important that they expose them to how things are done within the unit vice what was taught to them in the institutional Army or specified in field manuals, etc. Tell them what you think Officers need to focus on in order to succeed tactically while preserving the lives of their men. Make them aware of the personalities, priorities and pet peeves of the chain of command. If the battalion commander is a stickler in a particular area, tell the new Officer and let him know what to focus on in that area, etc.

Encourage them when they are having doubts. Support their decisions as best you can. Sure, many times an NCO will know how to accomplish a task more efficiently than a new Officer, but he must be careful not to become overbearing toward the new Officer and insist that things be done exactly as the NCO desires them to be. New Officers need to learn how to think and make decisions and you have to give them some room to do so. When you recommend a course of action, explain your rationale thought process to the new Officer. He'll develop faster if you ensure he knows the "why" of what you are recommending as well as the "how."

Treat the Officer with the utmost respect, especially in public. The outward display of professionalism and loyalty from NCOs will not be lost on a new Officer and he will be greatly encouraged that his subordinate leaders have accepted him as their new leader. Remember the old adage, "praise in public and reprimand in private." You are not allowed to reprimand an Officer if you are an NCO, but you can tactfully disagree with him and recommend alternatives to his plans, etc. This is always best done in private, away from the rest of the unit. Don't put a new Officer on the spot in front of people by challenging his authority. Take him aside and have a talk, you'll find that he will be much more open to considering your point of view.

If you would like to learn more about training and training management you should visit the Army Training Network website or read *Army Doctrine Publication 7-0, Training Units and Developing Leaders*.

SGM (R) Dennis W. Paxton

From One Leader to Another
Transitions
Sergeant Major Craig T. Lott

Transitions in the military are part of its culture and day-to-day life. Individuals will come and go from your organization and the service on nearly a daily basis. Like any change, it is important to remain flexible and adjust to that change when it occurs. In the simplest terms, transitions involve the process of passing from one point or stage to another. This paper will focus on two types of common transitions in the military, PCS (Permanent Change of Station) and ETS (Expiration Term of Service). Understanding the intricacies of each requires a great deal of research, planning, preparation and time management which will be the central focus of this paper. The message here will be how individuals prepare for each phase in order to best posture them and possibly their Family for success. Although a PCS and ETS transition are largely an individual action/ responsibility, it takes leader involvement in order to ensure the greatest likelihood of a smooth transition. Today's leaders understand the significance of our Army's "All Volunteer Force" and how transitions into, within and out of the service can positively and negatively impact perceptions regarding the military. At the end of the day each and every service member will experience a transition of one sort or another, therefore it is imperative that leaders at all levels educate and assist them in the process.

A PCS transition involves moving from one duty station or another based on assignment notification/ instructions often directed at the need and discretion of the Army, while ETS involves departing the military service all together either voluntarily or involuntarily for any number of reasons. The keys to success in either situation start with understanding how to best research, plan, prepare and manage one's time in the process. Individuals who embrace the concepts of transitioning find it easy to adjust when the times comes. Installations across the Army have established programs and agencies to assist in this process, some of which include the Army Community Service, the Army Career and Alumni Program, the Veteran's Administration and the Department of Labor. All of which can assist with conducting research in a number of areas including details on your gaining installation, employment opportunities in a particular area and services offered at your next location. One's research is only limited by their interest and motivation.

Planning and preparing for a transition include a myriad of activities. A good starting point to capture those activities are the organizational and unit clearing checklists. Although you may be several months away from your actual PCS or ETS it never hurts to ask for a copy of those checklists in advance in order to first, gain an appreciation for what will be expected of you and second, to add to those lists items not already identified. An example of those additional items for a married Soldier might be including the close out of your children's schools and pick-up of their school records, while for a single Soldier it might be when to schedule for your internet to be shut off. The point here is that there are countless small details that must be planned for in order to ensure success. Leaders must remain engaged throughout this process as they have the training, education and most importantly, the experience.

With regard to time management, the typical time for a transition depends on the circumstances and each individual; therefore the allocated time for a transition is largely on a case by case basis. For a PCS move, the normal timeframe is six-nine months from the time of notification. However, in some cases, report dates change and can be shorter based on current Army priorities, the needs of the gaining command and even the needs of the Soldier and their Family. For an ETS, Soldiers typically plan to leave the service well in advance and therefore have a greater lead time. Because there is generally a longer period of time available for their planning and preparation, Soldiers are now authorized to attend the mandatory Transition Assistance Program two years in advance of their ETS. The obvious exception is a Soldier being involuntarily separated which significantly reduces their planning time. Leaders are also required to conduct pre-separation counseling a year prior to a Soldier's ETS. The goal is to ensure that each individual Soldier is the utmost prepared before their ETS which may include a civilian/government resume, a letter of intent if attending college or an actual job offer.

In conclusion, transitions (PCS/ETS) are part of military life. It takes proper research, planning, preparation, and time management. The focus of this paper was to highlight these concepts as individuals prepare for these life-changing events. Those who have lived through one or both of these experiences can attest to the importance of taking a deliberate approach. It is imperative to understand that transitioning is a life altering experience and when embraced properly can be a rewarding experience for everyone associated.

If you would like to learn more about this topic it is recommended that you take the time to read or visit the following: *AR 601-680, The Army Retention Program, AR 600-8-8, Total Army Sponsorship*

Program, the ACAP (Army Career and Alumni Program), the TAP (Transition Assistance Program).

SGM Craig T. Lott
TRADOC Retention Branch

From One Leader to Another
Unit Training Management
Sergeant Major Don Rose

After more than 11 years of combat, have our Officers and NCOs lost their ability to plan, prepare, execute and assess quality training at the brigade, battalion, and company level? Since the start of the war, with shortened dwell times and back to back deployments, the planning and resourcing of training events were frequently driven by the higher headquarters, and in many cases, the execution of the training was supported with external mobile training teams, contractors or other external capabilities. As we draw down our forces in Afghanistan and face reduced training resources, commanders and leaders must be innovative and take full ownership for individual and collective home station training. Commanders and Senior Non-Commissioned Officers must reinvigorate the art and science of Unit Training Management (UTM) in our junior leaders—how to properly plan, prepare, execute and assess training, focusing on mastering the basics at the individual, crew and small team level with quality home station training. Learning the science of UTM is easier than learning the art, which leaders achieve with the experience of senior leaders coaching, teaching and mentoring our junior leaders to excellence.

When I reflect back on all the units I have had the privilege to serve in over the years, I ask myself, what made a few of them stand out more than the others? The best units conducted tough, realistic, performance-oriented and standards-based training that focused on the fundamentals. The leadership, both Officers and Non-Commissioned Officers, were always present and personally leading, assessing and training their units. They understood mission command before they knew it by name. They knew how to train units and individuals because they read the doctrine and practiced UTM skills during multiple assignments. Leaders in these high performing units knew the importance of "Training to Train" and would never allow untrained leaders to train their Soldiers.

Do our leaders understand the philosophy and principles of Mission Command as outlined in Army Doctrine Publication (ADP) and Army Doctrine Reference Publication (ADRP) 6-0, "Mission Command?" Do our young Commanders and NCOs know their roles in UTM? Have they read and do they understand the principles of training and leader development in ADP and ADRP 7-0? Do they know how to integrate both training and leader development objectives into their unit training plan? Do our leaders know what training support enablers and training management tools are out there to help them conduct training within their organizations such as the Army Training Network (ATN) and the Combined Arms Training Strategies (CATS)? This information paper talks to those essential skills and knowledge.

Effective Commanders use the principles of mission command to empower their subordinate leaders to conduct unit training and leader development at all levels. *ADP* 6-0 states, "Mission Command is the exercise of authority and direction by the commander using mission orders to enable disciplined initiative within the commander's intent in the conduct of unified land operations." The six principles of mission command are to build cohesive teams through mutual trust, create shared understanding, provide a clear commander's intent, exercise disciplined initiative, use mission orders, and accept prudent risk. We must train to become a force with adaptable leaders and versatile units. Units must be able to conduct decisive action through the application of offensive, defensive, and stability operations tasks.

Training, education, and experience occur in three domains. The **institutional domain** is the Army's training and education system that encompasses Initial Military Training (IMT), Professional Military Education (PME), functional training, cultural and language training, and troop schools. The **operational domain** is where individual, leader and collective training occur per the commander's unit training plan while at home station, CTCs, during joint and combined exercises, at mobilization centers and while deployed. The **self-development domain** is learning that supports planned, goal-oriented learning that reinforces and expands the depth and breadth of an individual's knowledge base, self-awareness, and situational awareness. It applies to both military and civilian cohorts within the Army Profession in three variations. 1) Structured self-development, 2) Guided self-development, and 3) Personal Self-development. Self-development is a critical aspect of leader development and individual success. It requires continuous self-assessment to determine individual gaps in skills, knowledge, and attributes to develop a personal plan to mitigate these gaps, fostering a life-long learning ethos in leaders at all levels.

Individual training is the foundation of a unit's ability to conduct its mission and focuses on proficiency of individual skills, i.e. warrior tasks and individual Military Occupational Skills (MOS) based upon skill level. In order for a unit to conduct an assigned mission its members must be proficient in their MOS and skill level to create capable squads and platoons. As a young NCO, a Sergeant Major once told me: "do not become overly focused on the culminating event. If you and your Soldiers master the basics, with little additional training, you can successfully execute nearly any mission."

Collective training is the primary focus of unit training in the operational domain. It builds upon individual skills learned in all three domains and introduces additional skills which support the unit's mission. Unit training focuses on building readiness and collective task proficiency to execute on the unit's Mission Essential Tasks (MET).

One of the most critical and often misunderstood requirements is the leader development program within our units, required by *AR* 350-1. The Army's leader development program encompasses all three of the training domains – operational, institutional, and self-development. Leader training requires synchronization between these to ensure that it is continuous and progressive throughout a Soldier's career. Leader development is critical to ensure we deliver quality, performance-oriented, standards-based training to our Soldiers. Good leaders develop good training and education, and good training and education produces good leaders. Soldiers that are trained by untrained leaders leads to less than optimal training outcomes and results in "the blind leading the blind." Always expose Soldiers to what right looks like and the only way to do this is to make sure you train your leaders before they train their Soldiers.

Leaders accomplish this through the application of the Army's principles of leader development when leaders and units develop training strategies, plans and programs. As leaders develop training objectives, they develop leader development objectives. As leaders we must demonstrate to our subordinates the attributes and competencies as outlined in *ADP* 7-0 *Training Units and Developing Leaders*.

Commanders are the units' primary training manager. However, all leaders must take ownership of training within their units, with NCOs taking ownership of training for individual Soldiers, teams and small crews. NCOs must be part of the unit training plan from beginning to end. Commanders must exercise mission command in order to allow subordinates to determine how to train their Soldiers. Commanders need an <u>understanding</u> of the higher commander's intent and <u>visualize</u> the culminating event and the key collective tasks the unit must train in order to achieve the end state. Commanders then <u>describe</u> their vision to their staff and <u>direct</u> the training. Commanders then <u>lead</u> the unit during training. How can you influence a subordinate leader's development if you never observe them in action with their Soldiers and provide them honest, helpful feedback? Finally, the Commander and NCOs must <u>assess</u> training. Without knowledge of their weaknesses and additional guidance from their leaders, subordinates tend to stay in their comfort zone, training tasks that are already proficient rather than tackle the tasks that need improvement. Leaders need to identify areas for improvement and develop plans to increase proficiency through training.

We achieve this by providing bottom-up input into the training plan and by conducting quality, performance-oriented, standards-based training to build confident, adaptive and agile leaders and versatile units. Training begins the moment Soldiers enter the Army and continues until the day they depart, but it must build upon previous skills and knowledge—i.e., it must be progressive and sequential over a Soldier's career. The challenge is determining in which domain we conduct the training and at what level. When you plan training for your unit, ensure that you apply the principles of unit training, as defined in ADP 7-0 *Training Units and Developing Leaders*.

The Army Principles of Unit Training

- Commanders and other leaders are responsible for training.

- Non-Commissioned Officers train individuals, crews, and small teams.

- Train to standard.

- Train as you will fight.

- Train while operating.

- Train fundamentals first.

- Train to develop adaptability.

- Understand the operational environment.

- Train to sustain.

- Train to maintain.

There are many well-developed references and resources available to guide leaders while planning and executing training. *ADP* 7-0 provides the concepts for how the Army trains units and develops leaders, while *ADRP* 7-0 and the Army Training Network provide the details for those concepts. The Unit Training Management feature found on the Army Training Network (ATN) is a web-based method of delivering unit training management to the Army in the form of modules, tutorials and examples. *ADP/ADRP* 7-0 provides the doctrine; ATN provides the "how-to."

A critical component of the "how to" are the Combined Arms Training Strategies (CATS) that are digitally delivered to the Army via the Digital Training Management System (DTMS) and ATN. CATS provide trainers HQDA-approved doctrinal training strategies, replacing Army Training and Evaluation Programs (ARTEP) and Mission Training Plans (MTP) (ALARACT 164/2005). They provide leaders with everything they need to know about required for training their particular unit—from mission essential tasks to exercises to gain proficiency on those tasks, and the resources needed to plan, prepare, and execute the exercises, I.E. training aids, devices, simulators and simulations (TADSS). They are a descriptive (not prescriptive) unit training tool which provides leaders a task-based, event-driven strategy to train for missions, functions and capabilities. CATS are based upon the unit's design, equipment, manning and Table of Equipment (TOE) or Table of Distribution and Allowances (TDA). They provide a recommended crawl, walk and run progressive training methodology for the unit to systematically build and sustain task proficiency by providing comprehensive information for each training event, including purpose, execution guidance and expected outcome. CATS identify the training audience, milestones, duration of the event, and required classes of supply.

DTMS and ATN provide Soldiers with easy access to the proponent-approved Training and Evaluation Outlines (T&EO) which contain the task, conditions, standards, performance steps and performance measures required to accomplish training. Within DTMS, commanders and trainers have access to digital tools which can facilitate construction of customized training plans and events. DTMS provides the ability to see the plan on a calendar.

The training management process mirrors the operations process. As with any operation, thorough, proper planning is essential to training. Quality training is determined by analyzing the units' mission and ability to complete the mission. The Army has standardized the METL for Brigade and above units, so that the Army can answer the question "Ready for what?" Given the Brigade's HQDA-standardized METL, Battalion and Company Commanders develop their unit Mission Essential Tasks (METs) that supports and 'nests' with the Brigade's METs. To complete the analysis, each Commander must understand the mission of their unit, the higher commander's guidance, and refer to his unit METL to understand what capability the unit requires for the mission. The commander will use this information along with input from his/her subordinate leaders to conduct mission analysis. Units identify what Key Collective Tasks (KCTs) they must train, and the time and unique resources necessary and available. The commander then determines specified and implied tasks, which become the unit's KCTs. During the Commanders' Dialogue, Commanders obtain approval from their higher commander of the proposed KCTs, the current and projected rating of these, and they identify the required resources to execute their training plan. Later, the commander briefs their unit training plan (Training Briefing) to their higher headquarters and they agree to a "contract" with the higher commander providing the necessary resources. The subordinate commander executes the training plan.

Preparation is the next step of training management. A key component of unit training management is the training meeting. Training meetings are an essential function in order to help manage training in units. Training meetings provide an opportunity for junior leaders to provide bottom-up input which is critical to determining training requirements. During training meetings commanders identify/refine training objectives, determine support requirements, identify evaluators, identify Observer-

Controller/Trainers (OC/Ts), identify opposing forces, complete PCCs/PCIs, determine if and when the unit will conduct rehearsals, and build training schedules. Training and certifying the trainers, conducting PCIs, etc. is all essential to successful training. Many units utilize the Eight Step Training Model as a TTP when preparing training for their units. Although not included in *ADP/ADRP* 7-0, it is a commonly accepted practice and is found on ATN. To assist units, the Leaders Guide to Company Training Meetings is posted on ATN, easily downloadable for review/use. ATN also has excellent videos on how to conduct company, battalion, and brigade training meetings.

Commanders must assess training and leader development in their units to ensure objectives and standards are met. Through this assessment the commander will determine if the unit met their training and leader development objectives and if the training plan requires changes. After Action Reviews (AARs) are a great tool to assess training. Whether formal or informal, AARs allow leaders to recognize what they need to sustain and improve—either as they complete the rest of the training or as they consider requirements for future training or retraining and recovery. Leaders must ensure they allocate time on their unit training calendar for AARs. The Leaders Guide to After Action Review is also posted on ATN.

As units plan future training it is important to take the time to identify and become familiar with the training support resources on your installation. At each installation the Director of Plans, Training, Mobilization and Security (DPTMS) manage and oversee the installation's ranges, training areas and facilities, Training Support Centers (TSC) and Mission Training Complexes (MTC). There are many different TADSS, for example: OPFOR clothing,

MILES, simulations such as JCATS, Games for Training, and virtual simulators such as CCTT and AVCATT-available at the TSC and in the MTC to enable leaders to train in a more realistic training environment. While, live, virtual, constructive, and gaming enablers can be used individually, the more that can be employed simultaneously, the more realistic the training environment.

I realize this paper does not lead you through from start to finish on how to develop a unit training plan. There are no easy solutions to building and executing a training plan. It takes a desire to learn/ relearn training management skills and knowledge, organization, innovation, attention to detail in planning and preparation, the ability to analyze the readiness of the unit and its leaders, and the ability to determine the most effective and efficient ways to develop leaders and achieve training objectives. As a leader responsible for training with a focus on home station training you might ask yourself, where do I start? You can begin by familiarizing yourself and your Soldiers with the new Army doctrine. Next, visit your installation's DPTMS and become familiar with all the training areas and training facilities on your installation. Go online to the Army Training Network and explore the training resources designed to assist you in developing a training plan. Finally, I would say "take personal responsibility for training your Soldiers".

After 11 years of war in multiple theaters, the Army is once again in transition. To ensure that we are prepared to continue to succeed in today's fight while preparing for the next, we must reinvigorate the training culture across all three training domains. This only happens if we recognize that the best trainers are the best leaders, the best leaders are the best warfighters, and the best warfighters are what we want.

SGM Don Rose
Combined Arms Center – Training

Section 3

Responsibilities

From One Leader to Another
Behavioral Health within a Comprehensive Soldier Fitness Plan

Command Sergeant Major Charles V. Sasser Jr.

From the US Army's beginning on through the Civil War, WWI, WWII and numerous other campaigns and conflicts, Soldiers have experienced a varied assortment of approaches with regards to their mental, physical, emotional and spiritual well-being. Medical care in the military has included services provided by the regimental surgeon and surgeon's mates after battle up to and including the progressive treatments seen on today's modern battlefield. After WWII there were conflicts between the various services being provided as they each had developed their own forms of treatment. Not long after that period the Civilian Health and Medical Program of the Uniformed Services (CHAMPUS) was established in order to address the lack of active duty dependent health care. CHAMPUS was also plagued with issues and underwent numerous changes. Through the early to late 90's, the department of Defense (DOD) created the TRICARE system to replace CHAMPUS. TRICARE has also undergone several reforms and to date has several options and programs for active duty and reserve component service members and their dependants. Over this past decade we have witnessed several new programs and systems. In fact, we now have more medical services than any other time in our history; unfortunately there are also many redundancies within these programs and services.

What young NCOs should take away from this is the importance of knowing the programs and systems available, and perhaps more importantly that they know their Soldiers and their Families in order to know how to best support them with their needs.

As you assume your role as a leader you need to talk with your Soldiers within the first few months as you assess their performance, capabilities and potential in order to understand their personal history. Engage them as a leader who truly wants to make them better. You will only be able to achieve so much by merely knowing what they have accomplished or failed to accomplish since your time with them. For example, knowing that one of your Soldiers was raised in a home where the parent did not take the time to prepare them for life beyond their walls can give you an insight as to why they might behave in a certain way. An example of which might be an environment in which the Soldier was never held accountable for their actions. There are countless examples that might be given but the bottom line is that our Army is made up of Soldiers with very diverse backgrounds which, at the end of the day, shape how they react, cope and perform in the Army.

Here are just a few suggestions as to how a leader might get in front of potential Soldier issues, problems and challenges. Start by establishing a relationship with any and all Behavioral Health (BH) providers that you and your Soldiers have access to. Make yourself an appointment and discuss your own issues even if they are small with the various providers. This will not only help you but also give you a sense of the experience so that you can better explain it to your Soldiers. In fact, every Soldier should have the experience of speaking with these providers as it will help them both personally and professionally while helping to eliminate the stigma often associated with seeking help. This can be accomplished rather easily over a three to four month period by prioritizing your Soldiers with more serious issues first. If you are deploying you should begin this effort at least six months before your departure. From that point forward, you should continue to provide support to those with lingering issues by leveraging those services available while deployed and by leveraging the expertise of your Chaplain. It is important to remember that patience is a key aspect in this effort. Some issues might be addressed through a few sessions while others may require extensive support. Remember, just because you deploy that doesn't mean support isn't needed, in fact, it is often quite the opposite case.

Because you should know your Soldiers better than anyone, you should create a list of questions which will help you identify them as a low, medium or high risk or you might use a red, amber and green system. You should be careful about how and who you use these terms with; first because you are not a behavioral health specialist and these are not medical or BH conclusions, secondly, you don't want your Soldiers to be unnecessarily labeled.

A sample list of items you might use to help identify the risk level of your Soldiers might include: their age, their rank, their number of previously completed combat or dangerous deployments, the length of time since their last deployment, previous history or involvement in verbal or physical altercations, any act of self-harm or suicidal ideations, past history of home/Family/personal problems, financial hardship, past UCMJ or legal issues, social challenges, alcohol or drug related issues, a decline in their performance, if they are a leader have they stopped enforcing standards, any previous behavioral health issues/treatment, Soldiers that arrived within three months of deployment or deployed late, and medical/health/fitness concerns.

Affording your Soldiers a place where they can "decompress" (a place where Soldiers can relax and therefore feel more comfortable about talking openly) while operating in a home station or deployed environment is an excellent tool.

Leader continuity is also a key aspect to the continued treatment and recovery of a Soldier. If key leaders change out all at once Soldiers may feel abandoned or even become lost in the medical system which could place them back at square one in their treatment plan. Doing our best to start and ultimately finish clinical support with the same service provider, be they the Chaplain or other medical provider is key to success.

Another item to consider is to send the occasional letter to your Soldiers' Family, which you can accomplish in a garrison or deployed environment. It should cover what you are doing in regards to the behavioral health support of your Soldier without providing personal or sensitive information. This is a good way to get and keep them involved in their Soldier's treatment and recovery process. You might address such things as expectation management, the reality of forming new patterns, their patience and what has changed. You might address the process their Soldier is going through such as the how, why and what programs/agencies/resources that are using.

This is also a good time to address the stigma often associated with seeking help and how their support encourages their Soldier to seek help. You may also provide a basic timeline, signs or symptoms which help to identify PTSD, discuss the Soldier Readiness Process and reverse SRP process and even provide a list of on/off post and online agencies.

All of these things combined with your own resourcefulness and initiative can and will continue to build a healthier, physically and mentally equipped and ready Army.

If you would like to learn more about the points offered in this paper and other behavioral health issues/services it is recommended that you visit your local medical treatment facility and clinical behavioral health services team at your post, camp or station.

CSM Charles V. Sasser Jr.
1st Infantry Division CSM

From One Leader to Another
Behavioral Health
NCOs Helping Soldiers

Command Sergeant Major Sheldon Chandler

"What do you mean First Sergeant? You're kidding me; there are military police and an ambulance in front of his house right now. I'll be right there! I can't believe it; Specialist Jones just killed himself. How did I not see the warning signs? I knew he had some issues when we redeployed, but he was one to suck it up and drive on. He was a good Soldier, I didn't want to screw him over and let the commander think he was some nutcase." Unfortunately, similar scenarios like this play out in the Army almost every day leaving NCOs riddled with guilt. The brutal effects of combat, multiple deployments, and difficulties coping have taken their toll on our Soldiers and their Families. It is the obligation of leaders across the Army, especially our NCO Corps, to dedicate our collective efforts to understand, prevent and react to behavioral health issues within our ranks.

The two greatest barriers a Soldier faces in seeking out behavioral health treatment are shame and the fear of jeopardizing their careers. It is imperative that NCOs across the Army, at all levels, inculcate the fact that it is acceptable to seek assistance. To coach, teach and mentor a Soldier to ask for help should be no more difficult than teaching the Warrior Tasks. It is essential that we embrace the fact that a Soldier's mental health is as equally important, if not more important than their physical readiness. To get Soldiers the required help and remove the stigma of seeking out assistance, we must first mitigate the bravado associated with the normal Army life. NCOs have heard them all: "Hooah Sergeant, I'm good", "You know me, I don't sweat the small stuff", or an all time favorite "See the shrink? I'm not nuts." It is crucial that we not accept these kinds of responses; we must actively listen to our Soldiers and encourage them to seek help. We must have the ability to quickly identify the warning signs and risk factors of suicide. Arguably, no leader in our Army is better positioned to accomplish this task than the "first line leader." It is the Team Leader or Squad Leader who will be the first to recognize a problem.

Leaders across our Army, especially the NCO Corps have and continue to make tremendous progress in confronting this serious issue; however, we are not completely there. As reported in the Army Gold Book Report, "in FY2011, 280,403 Soldiers received outpatient behavioral healthcare and 9, 845 Soldiers received inpatient behavioral healthcare". Although these numbers appear staggering, optimistically these results can be attributed to greater health care accessibility, increased leader involvement and a reduction in the stigma associated with seeking behavioral health treatment. There is still much work to be done; within your formations there are many Soldiers still struggling with behavioral health issues. We must foster a climate of trust and openness where Soldiers feel at ease seeking assistance from their leadership. Over the last eleven years, over a million Soldiers have answered the call for service and we dare not leave a Soldier wounded by behavioral health issues.

Our most senior leaders within the Army are extremely engaged; leading the charge through fundamental policy changes and revising regulatory guidance to combat the challenges of behavioral health issues within our ranks. Senior leaders are keen to the fact that behavioral health issues may manifest themselves in many forms such as misconduct, post traumatic stress, depression, substance dependence, disciplinary infractions and regretfully suicide. Each of these issues is deserving of a method or policy to mitigate and ultimately eliminate them from our military; however, none of these issues are more permanent than suicide. It is an action that is irreversible and is a tremendous loss to our Army team.

One particular example of senior leader involvement is the Army's Suicide Senior Review Group (SSRG). "The SSRG is a monthly review by the Army's senior leaders, commanders, and health/risk program managers which review every suicide in our Army. Its primary focus is to review the transitions and stressors associated with each suicide and identify lessons learned in order to improve leader surveillance, detection, and response to military stress. The SSRG also critiques policy and programs associated with Soldier transitions and stress, behavioral health issues, high-risk behavior, stigma, and leadership implementation to inform necessary adjustments or new policy/program formulation." (Army 2020, Generating Health & Discipline in the Force, 2012)

Although our most senior leaders are implementing change to policies and procedures, the most critical change is that of culture. It is extremely important that we change the paradigm concerning Soldiers seeking assistance. Unless we shift the paradigm and make positive strides in our Army culture, suicides will continue in our Army at an increasing pace. As an NCO Corps we play a critical role in advancing our culture. Soldiers who suffer from a behavioral health issue should be treated no differently than any other Soldier. A Soldier struggling through a behavioral health challenge should not be criticized, ridiculed or labeled as weak for seeking help. It is quite the contrary. A Soldier who is willing to step forward and ask for help possesses an incredible amount of personal courage, character and strength.

"It is a devastating loss when one of our own, whether a Soldier, Civilian, or Family member dies by suicide" (SMA Chandler, 2012). In October 2012, there were 20 potential suicides among active-duty Soldiers of which five were confirmed and 15 still remain under investigation. Within this year there have been 166 potential suicides where 105 were confirmed and 61 are still under investigation. In 2011, unfortunately 165 active duty Soldiers took their own life. Even more staggering were the 1,012 suicide attempts. Suicide in our Army has not only impacted the active force but also the Army National Guard and Army Reserve. This year alone, there have been 114 potential (not on active duty) suicides which 83 were confirmed as suicides and 31 remain under investigation. In 2011, the Reserve Component lost 118 Soldiers to suicide. In total, over the last two years, almost 1,600 Soldiers attempted or successfully took their own life. Each of these incidents negatively impacted a spouse, Family, loved ones, friends, and a member of a team, squad, unit, and our Army (DoD News Release #907-12, 2012).

The role of the NCO is critical to the prevention of suicides and combating behavioral health issues in our Army. In order to be successful though, we must first understand what would cause a Soldier to take his or her own life. Most suicides, attempts and ideations are reactions to an intense feeling of loneliness, worthlessness, hopelessness, helplessness and/or guilt. We may ask ourselves, "How can the American Soldier fit in this category? Are they not tough? Do they not have the resiliency to bounce back?" Soldiers are tough and extremely resilient, but the stressors of combat, military life and other traumatic experiences can have an adverse and often cumulative impact on even the most hardened and resilient Soldier.

Does a Soldier feel a sense of loneliness when they lose their spouse and children to divorce because of the stress of multiple deployments? Does a Soldier face a sense of worthlessness when they could not extract their battle-buddy from an emblazed MRAP? Is there a sense of hopelessness when a Soldier is criticized and mocked by his fellow Soldiers for seeking help? Is there guilt when a fellow Soldier switched places in the turret for the ride back to the FOB and that brother-in-arms lost their life to an IED? These are all very real questions and situations that could be impacting Soldiers within your ranks. "As a NCO Corps and 'the backbone of our Army', we are in the best position to be the Army's first line of defense. It is vital that we know our Soldiers, the resources available to help them when they are in crisis, and not overlook the risk factors and warning signs" (SMA Chandler, 2012). We must know our Soldiers and understand when they are struggling and get them the help that they need.

It is imperative that each NCO be familiar with the warning signs of suicide. When a Soldier experiences a combination of any of the following his NCO and chain of command should be more vigilant:

- Talk of suicide or killing someone else
- Giving away property or disregard for what happens to one's property
- Problems with girlfriend (boyfriend) or spouse
- Acting bizarre or unusual (based on your knowledge of the person)
- Soldiers in trouble for misconduct (Article 15, UCMJ, etc)
- Soldiers experiencing financial problems
- Soldiers who have lost their job at home (Reserve Component)
- Those Soldiers leaving the service (retirements, ETS, etc)

When they experience any one of the following warning signs; Soldiers should be immediately seen by a helping provider:

- Talking or hinting of suicide
- Formulating a plan to include acquiring the means to kill oneself
- Having a desire to die
- Obsession with death (music, poetry, artwork)
- Themes of death in letters and notes
- Finalizing personal affairs

- Soldiers who have lost their job at home (Reserve Component)

- Giving away personal possessions

NCOs must know the associated risk factors if they are to help combat suicide in our Army. These risk factors increase the probability of serious adverse behaviors or physical health. They raise the risk of an individual being suicidal, but it does not mean they are suicidal.

- Relationship problems

- History of previous suicide attempts

- Substance Abuse

- History of depression or other mental illness

- Family history of suicide or violence

- Work related problems

- Transitions

- A serious medical problem

- Significant loss (death of loved ones, loss due to natural disaster, etc)

- Current/pending disciplinary or legal action

- Setbacks (academic, career, or personal)

- Severe, prolonged, and/or perceived unmanageable stress

- A sense of powerless, helplessness, and/or hopelessness.

In conclusion, our primary charge as NCOs is to train and lead Soldiers. The Army needs us now more than ever to combat one of the most catastrophic challenges of our time. We must come armed not with a basic load of ammunition, but the knowledge, ability and compassion necessary to support and lead our Soldiers in their time of need. We must educate our Soldiers on the importance of behavioral health and removing its associated stigma. Soldiers within our ranks need to know it is okay to ask for help without the fear of shame or negative impact on their career.

We must use resources such as the Comprehensive Soldier and Family Fitness program, Master Resilience Trainers, Military Family Life Consultants, Chaplains and the Chain of Command to assist these great Soldiers. We should integrate behavioral health training into counseling sessions, leader development programs, and Family support activities not only to train our Soldiers, but also our Army Families. NCOs provided with the opportunity to attend any level of resilience training should seize the opportunity and pass their knowledge to seniors, peers, and subordinates. It is critically important that we learn and grow together to maximize the effectiveness within our ranks and overcome this critical issue. Remember the <u>ACE</u> method and make a difference!

A - Ask your buddy? Have the courage to ask the question while remaining calm…Are you thinking of killing yourself?

C - Care for your buddy. Calmly control the situation, do not use force, and be safe. Actively listen to show understanding and produce relief and remove any means that could be used for self injury.

E - Escort your buddy and never leave them alone. Escort to the chain of command, Chaplain, behavioral health professional, or primary care provider or call the National Suicide Prevention Hotline.

The Army has lost far too many great Soldiers and American heroes to behavioral health issues; we must put an end to this catastrophic trend. It is our obligation as leaders across the NCO Corps to dedicate our collective efforts to help those in need and remove the stigma associated with seeking out behavioral health treatment. An engaged leader can make a difference!

CSM Sheldon Chandler
502d Military Intelligence Battalion

From One Leader to Another
Corrective Training
Command Sergeant Major Kevin Bryan

Commanders lead our armies and discipline is kept in check through their application of the Uniformed Code of Military Justice (UCMJ). NCOs are further empowered with the responsibility to enforce the punishment set forth by the Commanding Officer and to administer corrective training for those cases which UCMJ actions are not warranted.

There are times when UCMJ actions are not the method that should be utilized. UCMJ should never be the rule or first measure to be taken; it should only be an alternative when the leadership feels that no other kind of action will change the outcome of the Soldier's attitude or performance. Therefore, corrective training is the best tool for adjusting attitudes for those Soldiers that may need extra attention, but not deserving of UCMJ punishment.

Corrective training when executed properly is an extraordinary tool. Corrective training is for those that have been identified to need additional training. Corrective training if completed in a timely manner and with the appropriate allocated time may eliminate the need for UCMJ actions in the future. However, do not use this tool as punishment or label it as punishment because only a commander may impose punishment. Routinely when a Soldier's time is taken away from him or her in order to help them meet the standard, it can serve as a wake-up call helping them pay attention to the important things that effect them and their fellow team members.

Part of the reason corrective training is often not used is because it is NCO resourced; meaning that the NCO is the one standing over or supervising the Soldier ensuring that the task is performed correctly, no matter how long it might take. The lazy leader will chose the easy path and process the necessary paperwork internally so that the Commander imposes UCMJ punishment, thereby requiring none of their own time to be sacrificed. These types of leaders fail to realize that their chain-of-command can often directly link lazy leaders and ill-disciplined Soldiers in their formation.

There are a few situations in which corrective training should be the leader's first means for problem resolution; the lack of military discipline which is founded upon self-discipline, the lack of respect for authority, and failure to live up to the principles of our Army Profession. Military discipline must be developed by individual and group training which will create a mental attitude resulting in proper conduct and obedience to military authority. Commanders should consider administrative corrective measures before deciding to impose non-judicial punishment. One of the most effective administrative corrective measures is extra training and/or instruction (including on-the-spot corrections). For example, if Soldiers appear in an improper uniform, they are required to correct it immediately; if they fail to make it to formation on time, then they must practice coming to formation on time. If Soldiers have training deficiencies, they will be required to complete extra training or instruction in subjects directly related to their shortcoming.

Keep in mind that the training, instruction, or correction administered to the Soldier in order to correct said deficiency must be directly related to the deficiency. It must be oriented so that the Soldier's performance in his or her problem area is improved. Corrective measures may be taken after normal duty hours. Such measures must assume the nature of training or instruction and should not be addressed or misconstrued as being punishment. Corrective training should continue only until the training deficiency is overcome. Corrective training properly executed and transparent across the formation will decrease the likelihood that future UCMJ action will need to be imposed by the Commander.

Most Soldiers today make enough money as to not care if they lose money through UCMJ action but they do value their free time and therefore if the NCO remains involved and implements corrective training for Soldiers that fail to meet the standard, then fellow Soldiers within their formation will see that time being sacrificed and therefore self-correct before action is taken against them. Short comings like making it to formation on time, not being in the proper uniform, hair not to standard, "no-shows" to medical appointments are all easily addressed through corrective training and should always be within the NCO's purview and ability to address, not something that the commander should tackle through the application of UCMJ, at least not initially.

For those wishing to learn more about this topic, additionally information can be found within *Army Regulation* 600-20, *Army Regulation* 27-10 and the *Manual for Courts-Martial*.

CSM Kevin Bryan
555 ENG BDE

From One Leader to Another
Legal Action

Command Sergeant Major James Norman
Master Sergeant Kevin Henderson

Non-Commissioned Officers play a vital role in the administration of legal actions on behalf of the Commander. The key to adjudicating legal action begins with proper leadership, mentorship and counseling.

The quality of the typical Soldier in the Army is high. A small group of Soldiers, however, continue to occupy a significant amount the Commanders time with misconduct and lack of discipline. Some Soldiers cannot or will not perform their duties effectively. The first step must be an attempt to motivate the Soldier, assist in solving their problems and ensure the chain of command is responding to their needs. Leadership is still the best cure.

Commanders play a major role in the military justice system by setting policies and enforcing discipline within their units. Leadership techniques, reinforced by a strong Non-Commissioned

Officer Corps, provide the best means by which to enforce discipline. Sometimes, however, it is necessary to use punitive measures, such as court martial, or punishment under Article 15, UCMJ.

Rehabilitative Measures

A Soldier who engages in minor acts of misconduct often does so as a result of simple neglect, ignorance, bad habits or similar reasons.

Counseling

Counseling remains the best tool to remedy those acts of minor misconduct. Counseling consists of advising the Soldier of their strengths and weaknesses, paying particular attention as to how best utilize their strengths while also helping to improve upon their weaknesses. Soldiers should be counseled often on their performance. When counseling becomes necessary because of unsatisfactory performance or conduct, an effort must be made by the counselor to learn what provoked the misconduct, why the Soldier failed to maintain the required standards or the reasons behind an unresponsive attitude. Counseling should be done at the lowest level possible within the chain of command/NCO support channel.

Corrective Training

Corrective training or instruction is one of the most effective non-punitive disciplinary measures available to a commander. It is used when the Soldier's duty performance has been deficient and the Soldier would benefit from extra training. The training may be conducted outside of normal duty hours. Corrective training may be authorized or directed by the Soldier's commander or by any NCO in the Soldier's chain of command/NCO support channel. Corrective training must be directly related to an observed deficiency and must be oriented toward improving the Soldier's performance in the problem area.

Revocation of Off Post Pass Privileges

A pass is an authorized absence from post or place of duty. Passes are for a relatively short period to provide respite from the working environment or for other specific reasons, at the end of which the Soldier is actually on-post, at his place of duty, or in the location from which the Soldier regularly commutes to work. Passes are not a right but a privilege to be awarded to deserving Soldiers by their commanders. Soldiers may be denied the privilege as a result of their conduct, to meet operational requirements, or for temporary administrative control. Denial of pass privileges merely withdraws the Soldier's privilege to be absent from their post or place of duty. Since the

Soldier has full access to facilities on the installation, denial of pass privileges is not a form of restriction or an adverse administrative action. A Soldier should be given written notification that their pass privileges have been withdrawn. Notice should include the period of revocation. During this time, the Soldier may be required to sign in and out of the unit and to provide his destination and estimated time of return.

Rehabilitative Transfer

When a Soldier is experiencing problems in a unit and does not respond to counseling, the chain of command should consider a rehabilitative transfer to another unit. A change in commanders, associates, or living and work areas may resolve a Soldier's problems. Reassignment should be between at least battalion-size units.

Reduction in Enlisted Grade

An enlisted Soldier in the grade of Private (E-2) and above may be reduced one grade for inefficiency after serving in a unit for at least 90 days. Inefficiency is a demonstration of characteristics which clearly show a lack of abilities and qualities required and expected of a Soldier of that grade, MOS and/or experience. Acts of misconduct may be considered when determining whether a Soldier should be reduced for inefficiency. This includes actions taken under the Uniformed Code of Military Justice or civil court convictions. Reduction for inefficiency may not be used in lieu of Article 15 punishment, for a single act of misconduct, or to reduce Soldiers for actions for which they were acquitted at court-martial. Solders in the rank of Private (E-1) through Specialist (E-4) *may* be considered for reduction of one or more grades. Soldiers in the rank of Sergeant (E-5) or above must be considered for reduction of one or more grades. Reduction boards are required in all cases unless reduction is mandatory, the Soldier is in the grade of E-4 or below, or the Soldier waives the board in writing.

Non-judicial Punishment

Punishment may be imposed under Article 15 of the Uniformed Code of Military Justice for minor offenses. Punishment under the provisions of Article 15, UCMJ provides the commander with a prompt and efficient means of maintaining good order and discipline, while promoting positive behavior changes in Soldiers without the stigma of a court-martial conviction.

If counseling and other administrative measures are not appropriate or adequate to deal with certain misconduct, a commander should consider imposing non-judicial punishment under the provisions of Article 15, UCMJ. The purpose of non-judicial punishment is to correct, educate and reform offenders who have shown they cannot benefit by less stringent measures.

Two criteria must exist for a commander to impose punishment under Article 15. First, the Soldier to be punished must have committed an offense in violation of the UCMJ. Second, the crime must be of a minor nature. The term "minor" ordinarily does not include misconduct which, if tried by a General Courts Martial, could be punished by dishonorable discharge or confinement for more than one year. This is not a hard and fast rule, however, and the circumstances surrounding the offense must be considered. Summarized Article 15s should be imposed for only the most minor of offenses.

Administrative Separation

A commander may take, or initiate, administrative action whether or not charges have been or will be preferred or dismissed. The governing regulation for the administrative separation of enlisted Soldiers is AR 635-200.

Reasonable efforts should be made to identify Soldiers who exhibit the likelihood for early separation, and to improve their chances for retention through counseling, retraining, and rehabilitation before initiating separation proceedings other than for fraudulent entry. Soldiers who do not demonstrate potential for further military service should, however, be separated to avoid the high costs in terms of pay, administrative efforts, degradation of morale, and substandard mission performance

Court-Martial

The goal of the military justice system is to achieve justice *and* maintain good order and discipline in the service. As in all American criminal courts, courts-martial are adversarial proceedings. That is, lawyers representing the government and the accused vigorously present the facts, law and arguments most favorable to their side following approved rules of procedure and evidence. Based upon these presentations, the military judge decides questions of law. The members of the court martial, as a jury, or the military judge in a trial by military judge alone, apply that law and decide questions of guilt or innocence. A court-martial conviction above the Summary Courts-Martial level constitutes a federal conviction.

This short paper is not intended to make you, the reader, an expert in legal actions. Therefore it is recommended that if you would like to learn more about this topic you take the time to read the following references: *Army Regulation, 600-8-19, Enlisted Promotions and Reductions, Army Regulation 27-10, Military Justice"* and the *"Manual for Courts Martial.*

CSM James Norman
MSG Kevin Henderson
1st Cavalry Division

From One Leader to Another
The Role of the Company level NCOs in preventing Sexual Assault

Command Sergeant Major David Davenport

During a recent visit to United States Army Europe, Army Chief of Staff, General Raymond Odierno said, that sexual assault and sexual harassment "are inconsistent with our values. It's not consistent with the trust we expect to have between Soldiers. As part of the Army profession, it really is about our values, our moral and ethical values. It is also about what I consider to be the basic component and fundamental foundation of the profession, which is trust." Commanders are responsible for preventing sexual assaults in their organizations and for creating a climate that encourages victims of sexual assault and sexual harassment to report incidents without fear of reprisal. But have you stopped for a moment and thought, what does that mean for us as professional Non-Commissioned Officers (NCO), which live by a creed that states that "my two basic responsibilities will always be uppermost in my mind...accomplishment of my mission and the welfare of my Soldiers" to end this crime of Sexual assault that erodes the bonds of trust of Soldiers, essential for military units to succeed and puts all members of the military team at risk?

I believe that Commanders and NCOs at all levels are important to eliminating this crime, but none as important as those who serve within Company level organizations across our Army; for it is those leaders at Company level that have the most supervision and interaction with our Soldiers who must help to establish a climate of trust that will encourage victims of sexual assault and sexual harassment to report incidents without fear of reprisal. For NCOs,

I would like to suggest we aid our Commander's accomplishment of this mission through education and discussing the topic with our Soldiers, aiding in the development and implementation of local sexual assault prevention strategies that demonstrate the commitment of the Command, and by setting the example in conduct and action of the Army Values.

Of course Commanders and Command Sergeant Majors (CSM) at higher levels are critical in setting the conditions to be successful as in any military operation by providing resources, training and manning. Although money is one of the first resources that come to mind, and is important to sustaining a quality program, I would like to suggest providing the resource of time. Not only time for the units to conduct the training, discussions and events, but your time as a leader by going down and taking part in company level activities so that Soldiers can hear and see your commitment to the mission of eliminating sexual assaults rather than in some mass formation or being bored to death with PowerPoint slides at a stand-down event. Identify in your training guidance your expectations of the program, make sexual assault reporting a part of your Commanders Critical Information Requirements (CCIR), and saturate the topic within the Command that it's a crime and goes against our core Army Values.

It goes without saying that your best Soldiers are needed to face the toughest of challenges. Sexual assault is a tough and complex crime that needs only the best Soldiers to serve as Sexual Harassment Assault Response Program (SHARP) Coordinators. A lot of thought must go into who will fill this critical role on the Commander's staff. Further, it is my opinion that you must look beyond the certifying checklist and into the character, personal communication skills, compassion and reputation within the organization.

It is more than filling out a certification packet and meeting a report to higher headquarters of just having the position filled; I would ask myself, does the Sergeant First Class SHARP coordinator have the intangible skills necessary to handle the highly sensitive and personal situation when a Soldier has been a victim of this crime of assault?

Both of these points were highlighted during a recent USAREUR Women's Forum hosted by the Commander and myself that featured subject matter experts (SME) and over 50 female Soldiers in various grades. Many of the information sessions were followed by small group discussions led by the SMEs that explored their concerns on the topic and developed strategic recommendations to better our overall program for USAREUR. Throughout the comment sheets and After Action Review (AAR), participates stated that they wanted "to see more leaders at the training so that Soldiers could hear their commitment to the program and the importance of having the right person as the SHARP coordinator that will take action while treating the victim with dignity and respect."

As we come back to Company level leadership, before you can enforce a standard, you must know what the standard is and how it is applied. The same is true about sexual assault. Soldiers need to know it's a crime that will not be tolerated in our Army and the role that the SHARP has in prevention of this crime. NCOs need to know who and how to contact the SHARP coordinator. We need to correct inappropriate behavior and jokes when witness them from our Soldiers and civilians. How easy is it to review the crisis hotline phone numbers and unit points of contact during in-processing, reception/ integration counseling, or how about conducting a terrain walk of the Garrison agencies and first responders that will be called upon in a time of crisis either as part of scheduled training or sponsorship? We must educate NCOs and Soldiers on the standard so that we can take action. The education has to come in other forms than memos posted on a unit bulletin board, a poster taped to a wall or a monthly celebration with information displays; it takes leaders sitting down and talking to their Soldiers, correcting and holding Soldiers accountable for inappropriate behavior and setting the example of conduct and behavior for all to see.

Once we are informed, we must begin an open and honest discussion on the subject of sexual assaults. One such topic is the fact that it is a crime that not only affects women, but men as well. Challenging norms, culture and stereotypes though discussion not only allows for the standard to be taught, but also allows for NCOs to be seen as the example addressing this crime facing our Army. Partnering with or supporting garrison production plays such as *"Can I Kiss You?"*, discussing with our Soldiers what does consent really mean, leveraging NCOs when they return from SHARP MTTs, Training forums, or by stander intervention training to share with Soldiers what they learned from their training all go a long way to beginning the discussion on the program and the Army standard, how this crime of sexual assault violates our Army's core values, erodes the bonds of trust of Soldiers and puts all members of the military team at risk.

Our Army is one of action! NCOs, as the backbone of the Army, must take a role in developing and implementing your local sexual assault prevention strategies that prevent this crime from occurring in the first place. We know what the statistics say; the majority of victims are under 24 years old, in the grade of PVT to SPC. The majority of perpetrators are male under the age of 25 in the grade of PVT to SPC. Typically the assault occurs on the weekend, alcohol is involved and the victim is new to the unit. So what are we NCOs doing about this analysis? Does the unit Charge of Quarters (CQ) have specific checks that they are required to make to ensure safety, security and policies are being enforced, are they more frequent during the late hours on the weekend, and does the Staff Duty NCO and other NCOs make random checks to ensure compliance? Are the squad leaders truly engaged with their Soldiers to know what they are doing this weekend? Just as NCOs are trained on our Army's Battle Drills...do they know how to handle a sexual assault? Many would say that these are simple steps to make, but I found time and time again that they are not known or understood at the Company level. As NCOs work with their Commanders, these strategies must have the goal of preventing any further assaults on Soldiers, enhance awareness and the use of Army and community resources, and reinforce that sexual assaults are not consistent with our Army Values and erodes that trust of our Soldiers.

The Secretary of the Army, Honorable John McHugh stated, "All of you are dedicated to eliminating this threat. And it's a threat to our cohesion of our units, a threat to our units and a threat to our very humanity." Hopefully I have made the case to get at this crime of sexual assaults. Commanders and NCOs at all levels are important to eliminating this crime facing our Army, but none as important as those that serve a Company level organizations in our Army; for it is those leaders at Company level that have the most supervision and interaction with our Soldiers and they have the immediate ability to establish a climate of trust that will encourage victims of sexual assault and sexual harassment to report incidents without fear of reprisal.

Our role as NCOs to aid our Commander's in the accomplishment of this mission and ending this crime must come through educating and discussing the topic with our Soldiers, assisting in the development and implementation of local sexual assault prevention strategies that demonstrates the commitment of the Command, and by setting the example in conduct and action of the Army Values. These may seem to be simple tasks, so it is now time for the backbone of our Army to stand up and take action as we have done so many times in the history of our Corps by living up to our chare: "accomplishment of my mission and the welfare of my Soldiers."

CSM David Davenport
United States Army Europe

From One Leader to Another
Suicide Prevention through Effective Communication

Command Sergeant Major Mark H. Oldroyd

You can prevent suicide! Leader actions, words and example play a huge part in building resilience in our Soldiers, Families and our Army in general. This past September our Army took a major step towards preventing suicides by ensuring all Soldiers recognize just how huge and tragic the loss of a single Soldier, Family member or Army Civilian is and how we all must do our part to prevent it. During our global fight against terror, we have lost over 7,000 Soldiers killed in combat, and another 18,000 wounded in action. Similarly, we have suffered losses to suicide at nearly one a day, and countless numbers who are psychologically wounded by both the cumulative effects of combat and the lingering questions that the suicide phenomenon has caused.

Some might argue that resilience is inherent in our upbringing, Family values and core belief, believing that some are more prone to suicide than others. To understand just how false this is, we have to recognize that everyone has a "breaking point." No one is immune to the lingering effects of the struggles and stress in our everyday lives which often conspire to leave us feeling helpless, frustrated and unable to counteract our depression.

So what gives one person the drive to see the good, remain optimistic and work to overcome their challenges, while another succumbs to their feelings of hopelessness and begins a downward spiral into despair? That is a difficult question. What we know with some level of certainty is that there is a recognizable pattern in the lives of those who attempt or actually do commit suicide before the act occurs.

We are able to recognize by analyzing the Soldier's life and the events leading up to their suicide that similar circumstances often exist; relationship issues, loss of self-esteem, isolation, trouble with authority, or substance abuse. Their effects often conspire against us by hitting all at once and spin a person's mental state out of their control.

So how can we as an NCO prevent, rather than just identify, this act? We have to build resilience daily through effective communication. We attack the negative aspects that build into suicidal ideation with engaged leadership, effective communication and prepared formal and informal counseling. How we see ourselves, either positively or negatively, stems in a large part from the feedback of our leaders. Our self identity as a contributing member of a group is essential to our "shield of resilience."

Jan E. Stets and Peter J. Burke wrote in their book "A Sociological Approach to Self and Identity" that, "Humans have the ability to reflect back upon themselves…they are able to regard and evaluate themselves." Further, "when one's self is encapsulated as a set of symbols to which one may respond to itself as an object, as it responds to any other symbol, the self has emerged. The responses of the self as an object to itself come from the point of view of others to whom one interacts." Our military culture centers on the formation of a common set of values, entrusted to us through our commitment and performance in order to meet a common set of challenges.

As an aspiring professional, we emerge from our initial indoctrination, basic training, and we integrate into the larger collective called the Army. We continually face challenges stimulated by an ever-changing set of variables and external processes such as time, place and circumstance. All the while we are continually trying to conform to both an individual and unit identity to which we, as a self aware member, are obligated to contribute in order to achieve collective success. We count on a hierarchy of experienced leaders to steer our youngest members through the crucible of training and ultimately engagement in combat. Suicide prevention would seem to be a daunting challenge when viewed from this context. However, if we approach it as a series of small tasks against a defined enemy, we can quickly see how we, as leaders, can contribute to the process through our daily communication with our Soldiers and their Families.

Performance Counseling, that monthly formal interaction with our Soldiers, must be fulfilling, ensuring that we encompass all that our collective group might face, broken down to build the individual's resilience against adversity, while arming our Soldiers with a sense of purpose and motivation that will allow them to meet the challenges they might face. *FM* 6-22, provides guidance or the "science" behind counseling subordinates, but to build resilience leaders must also be armed with the "art" and technique of an effective counselor. We know that proper preparation is the key to good performance. We practice battle drills extensively to ensure our ability to react quickly without thinking. Can we practice our preparation for counseling in such a manner? In fact we can, we can polish our skills to a level where we, as a leader, are able to place known data on a format in our mind's eye which might allow us to better focus on the skills necessary for effective counseling.

Format is a technique that many leaders will vary; the essence of building resilience stems from an optimistic and positive approach. How do we communicate to a subordinate Soldier in a way that the Soldier is motivated and believes they can achieve? We must start by motivating ourselves. We must believe in our Soldiers, in ourselves and communicate that belief. We do this by researching and knowing our subject matter. A format for counseling viewed in this manner will over time shape the leader. But to start we obviously must use a basic format to ensure we cover all that is pertinent.

We might use something like PERFORM as an acronym or format used to cover the main points of the counseling session: P-purpose of the counseling, E-excellence (what has the Soldier excelled at over that preceding period), R-requires change for the better (allows us to address mediocrity, for example we can talk about their 220 APFT score, while technically acceptable, we can develop a plan to raise it by addressing better life style behavior such as smoking and nutrition), F-failure (no one likes to be patronized, if a Soldier failed a task or challenge, let's talk about it), O-opportunities, (What schools, events, field problems, etc.. are coming up with chances to excel), R-relations with others (we need to address real concerns and explain those concerns from a mature perspective), M-maturity (talk about tasks that lead a Soldier to grow such as self-development through structured, guided or personal means, asking such questions as, "what is next for the Soldier"). When you review your notes, ensure you cover the eligibility of the Soldier for promotion, and how competent you view them in their current position. A final check should be to ask yourself if you are building upon or breaking down the Soldier's resilience (would you be motivated by the counseling if it was given to you). If yes, then you are ready to counsel.

In conclusion, we must break our bad habits of conducting last minute counseling that takes place over the hood of a vehicle, the checklist mentality that checks the block for counseling and the lengthy counseling form that details a litany of what took place over the past month. If we want to prevent suicide we must build resilience, one counseling at a time, one Soldier at a time and one day at a time. This is accomplished by following the simple and basic fundamental leader actions that are detailed in countless leadership manuals and doctrine originating from the very beginning of our Army. First line leaders must remain engaged, platoon leadership must enforce and role model leadership, Company/Troop/Battery leadership must emphasize its importance by ensuring time is scheduled for it, and Battalion/Squadron leadership must set and enforce the policy and standard. We can and must do it together. Building resilience and effectively communicating across our formation will help to develop a positive command climate, one built on trust and one that will ultimately eliminate suicide from our ranks.

CSM Mark H. Oldroyd
USAG Fort Drum, NY

Closing Thoughts

I would like to close this work by personally thanking each of the contributors who took the time to share their knowledge, insight, and experience. As professionals, each of these Leaders has demonstrated the essence of being a steward of our profession by helping to further develop our military expertise and professional body of knowledge. I would also like to thank the Combat Studies Institute for their efforts in turning this idea into a reality.

                    Joe B. Parson Jr.
                    CSM, US Army
                    Combined Arms Center,
                      Leader Development
                    and Education

The pessimist complains about the wind. The optimist expects the wind to change. The leader adjusts the sails.

-John Maxwell

www.ingramcontent.com/pod-product-compliance
Lightning Source LLC
Chambersburg PA
CBHW052047230426
43671CB00011B/1824